D0128247

Black and White in Photoshop CS3 and Photoshop Lightroom

Create stunning monochromatic images in Photoshop CS3, Photoshop Lightroom, and beyond

Leslie Alsheimer with Bryan O'Neil Hughes

ELSEVIER

AMSTERDAM • BOSTON • HEIDELBERG • LONDON • NEW YORK • OXFORD
PARIS • SAN DIEGO • SAN FRANCISCO • SINGAPORE • SYDNEY • TOKYO
Focal Press is an imprint of Elsevier

Focal Press

Focal Press is an imprint of Elsevier
Linacre House, Jordan Hill, Oxford OX2 8DP, UK
30 Corporate Drive, Suite 400, Burlington, MA 01803, USA

First published 2007

British Library Cataloguing in Publication Data
Alsheimer, Leslie
  Black and white in Photoshop CS3 and Photoshop Lightroom :
  create stunning monochromatic images in Photoshop CS3,
  Photoshop Lightroom, and beyond
  1. Adobe Photoshop 2. Adobe Photoshop lightroom
  3. Photography – Digital techniques 4. Black-and-white
  photography
  I. Title II. Hughes, Bryan O'Neil
  006.6'86

Library of Congress Control Number: 2007932105

ISBN: 978-0-240-52084-1

Typeset by Charon Tec Ltd (A Macmillan Company), Chennai, India
www.charontec.com

For information on all Focal Press publications
visit our website at www.focalpress.com

Printed and bound in Canada

07 08 09 10 11   11 10 9 8 7 6 5 4 3 2 1

Black and White in Photoshop CS3 and Photoshop Lightroom

CONTENTS

ACKNOWLEDGEMENTS

I would like to express my greatest and most heartfelt gratitude to the people in my life who went out of their way to give me the support and encouragement to finish this project: the entire Alsheimer family, especially my mom, my co-author Bryan and his fiancée Alex, and dear friends Cece Kurtzweg, Randall Gann, Amos Hockmeyer, Michael Clark, Jamie Baldonado, all the folks at Focal Press, and Desert Elements Design; Molly McDow Duncan and Cheryl Eisenhard.

Leslie Alsheimer

I'd like to thank everyone who appears in the credits of any Adobe application discussed in this text, each and every person touches the applications in some way. More specifically, I'd like to dedicate all of my own efforts in this book to Alex, my fiancée – whose support and dependable good nature always empowers me to fulfill my lofty goals and obligations.

Bryan O'Neil Hughes

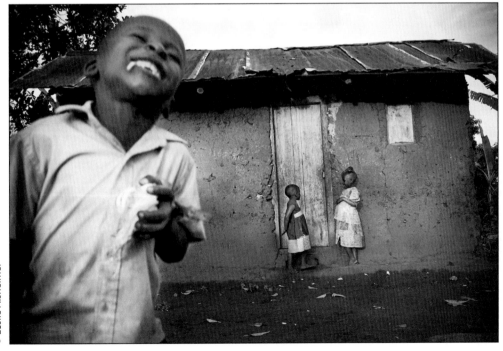

© Leslie Alsheimer

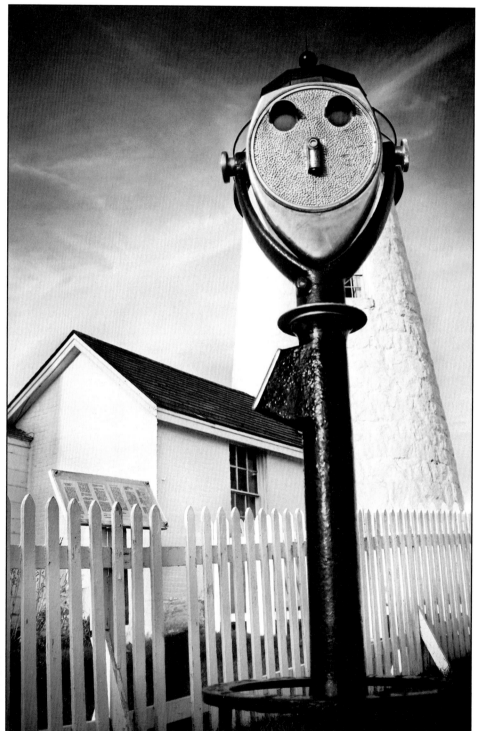

HOW TO USE THIS TEXT

Thank you for choosing Black and White in Photoshop CS3 and Photoshop Lightroom. From the highest quality capture to practical workflow practices, black and white conversion methodologies, non-destructive digital darkroom image processing, creative adjustments, to the latest printing techniques; this book is a fully integrated color managed workflow designed for the black and white photographer. Utilizing the power of both Photoshop CS3 and Lightroom, we have attempted to make this text both informative and fun by technically filtering the technology as much as possible with the creative user in mind. Software and digital imaging techniques can present a seemingly overwhelming amount of information to take on through text books alone, especially if the subject matter is not our full-time job. Most text books focused on digital photography and Photoshop, have historically taken either an extremely technical or all-encompassing approach to the subject matter. As creative users ourselves with extensive experience as workshop educators in the field, our approach with this text is to address the material more like a workshop, condensing and directing content specifically toward practical photographic application of the materials for the black and white enthusiast.

When teaching many of our workshops, we ask our students two questions: first, how many text books have they purchased on Photoshop? Second, how many of those text books have actually been read? The overwhelming majority own an average of three to four texts, most of which have never been extensively read. For the average user, professional or hobbyist, the interest in digital technology is practical. Most users know photography already and enjoy making images. How to apply this new technology to existing knowledge and skills tend to be the question of the day.

In this text, we go to great lengths to present concepts as simply as possible. We use metaphor extensively and sometimes even a few silly made up terms to describe more complex topics in order to help make the material more accessible and easier to understand. Most importantly, however, we have also weeded through the vast amount of information available in this digital domain, and eliminated a great deal of it in order to assist practitioners in gaining more practical and digestible information specific to black and white processes utilizing Photoshop CS3 and Lightroom. After all, any book that is too complex, too technical or too overwhelming to actually read cannot be very helpful in the learning process.

License to Drive

Learning about digital technology and new methodologies is similar to the process of learning to drive a car. Knowing about the rules of the road, signaling a turn, how to parallel park and when to stop for the school bus is enough to get a new driver out on the road with a license to drive. The rest of a driver's education is acquired on the road experientially over time, potentially hitting a few curbs and bumpers in the process. Learning how to change a tire, the engine oil or how to jumpstart a dead battery however, are not license requirements, and whether or not one chooses to learn these skills is optional. Although there is an enormous amount of complex mechanical information buried under the hood of an automobile that can be extremely useful on the road, a driver can still get to many exciting places with just a license (and maybe an AAA card). The process of learning digital technology is very similar in that much of the more complex information on how and why things work can stay under the hood for the more technically curious and adept to explore when and if they choose.

We hope this text will help you learn to drive the technology first, bringing you to fun places where you can play with your images, make mistakes, run into a few curbs, keep you from crashing off the road and leave the engine to the mechanics until you are ready for more complex technical information. There are many technical books on the market today written by qualified experts. We do not intend to try and reinvent the wheel, nor replicate information found commonly in other texts. Rather, we hope to provide a practical and integrated color managed workflow – specific to black and white processes – that will help you understand what you need to know to get you in the digital darkroom and playing, having fun, being creative and making images as quickly as possible. To that end, we present you with the latest information on Photoshop CS3 and Lightroom, pruned, refined, and simplified to increase your imaging enjoyment and productivity at the same time. Hopefully that is what it is all about anyway!

Happy image making and best wishes in all your photographic endeavors!

With every good wish,
Leslie Alsheimer & Bryan O'Neil Hughes

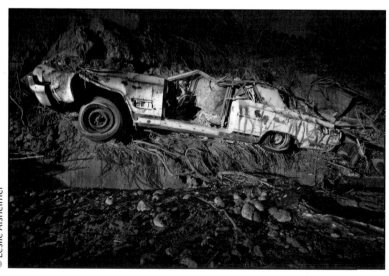

© Leslie Alsheimer

SALUTATIONS

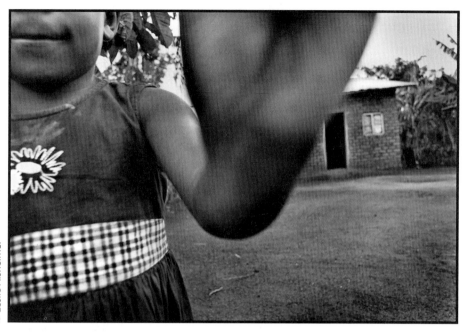

© Leslie Alsheimer

While the digital landscape has become less complex with the latest software releases, we also recognize that we are standing on the shoulders of giants. We salute the Photoshop gurus and divas who navigated the complexities of the digital world before us, who were not only willing, but enthusiastic and passionate enough to pass on their wisdom, knowledge and expertise. Because of their perseverance and dedication, the technology is where it is today. Hats off to all those folks for laying the foundation and paving the way for the rest of us!

Special acknowledgement and appreciation must also go out personally to all of my many mentors who challenged my vision and ignited the passion for the digital world that carried me into my career as a professional photographer and educator. To Julieanne Kost, Katrine Eisman, as the pioneering women of the industry, and my high school photography teacher Karen Jenks each of whom inspired me with great impetus and will forever be my industry heroines and role models!

To Jonathan Singer, Norman Mauskoph, Thatcher Cook, Stephen Johnson, Andrew Rodney, Mac Holbert, Jeff Schewe, George DeWolfe, Maggie Taylor, John Paul Caponigro, Jack Davis, Jerry Courvosier, Michael "Nick" Nichols, Dan Burkholder, David Alan Harvey, Sam Abell, Tom Gaukel, Josh Withers, Genevieve Russell, David Lyman, Reid Callanan, Martha Callanan, the staff and everyone at the Maine Photographic Workshops, and the Santa Fe Workshops.

Leslie Alsheimer

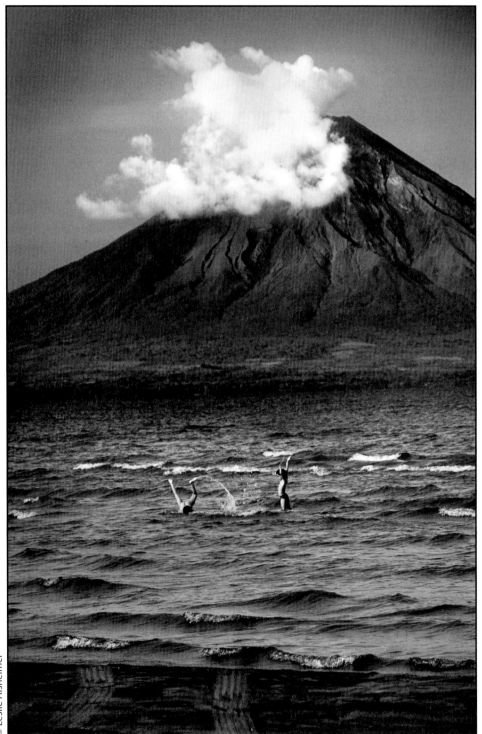

SEEING IN BLACK AND WHITE

I recall when shooting film that there was a mental shift necessary when I swapped from, Velvia to TMAX; shooting in Black and White required a different state of mind. Though much has changed in the never-out-of film, instant gratification world of digital, a change of mind is as important as ever.

In color you can have similar tonal values, but completely different colors, and so the two side by side can still create a dramatic image. The same colors in a black and white image simply blend together and appear drab. To look back again to those distant days of film use; many times I would find myself before a brilliant, colorful sunset, only to realize that I was loaded with black and white film. As a young rookie, I would snap away, insisting that something so beautiful would surely be so with or without the accurate reproduction of color; while a white sun, white clouds and a dark red (almost black) sky helped with the wrong film, my images were never the same.

There are several techniques that can help make compelling images in black and white; many of which lend themselves uniquely to a monochromatic image. What follows are but a few ways to visualize and look for clues to create more impact in your black and white images:

1. *Look for contrast*. Strong tonal differences in a color image can be both busy and confusing; in a monochromatic image, they can pull the eye and define the tone of the shot. Contrast is everything in a stunning black and white shot; and though you can digitally manipulate it after the fact, looking for it ahead of time helps greatly.
2. *Look for shapes*. Bold shapes, curves, edges and details become almost abstract in a black and white image; the same shapes can easily be lost in the splashy rainbow of a like color photo.
3. *Look for texture*. Whether it is wood grain, sand, skin or hair, texture is just yet another thing that seems to "look better in black and white". Combine a macro lens with good, strong texture and see how much better that color image looks in black and white!
4. *Look for lines*. Lines can break and bisect an image, true, but they can also direct the eye. In a black and white image with strong contrast, lines are so powerful that they can be the sole subject matter.
5. *Look for shadows*. Deep, black shadows, thin, almost invisible, light shadows; the mirror of a subject in a gray mask is always appealing.
6. *Look for patterns*. The same repetitive grain, stitch, row of hedges, sea of brick or set of waves can be noise for your eyes in a color image, and the same in black and white can become mesmerizing.

7. *Look for silhouettes*. A striking outline of a backlit object always appears interesting, and in a black and white image it can be anything from surreal to sinister.

One last tip: I often find that black and white can rescue images otherwise beyond repair – it can help fix ruddy complexions, awkward color balance, high noise imagery and just plain uninteresting shots. Whether you see in black and white before or after the shot, you will soon find that some shots just lend themselves to the bold, classic tones of the masters.

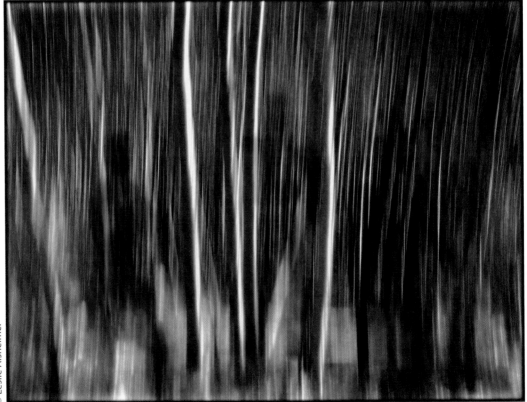

© Leslie Alsheimer

MISTAKES CAN BE MAGIC

Knowing which images to keep is an extremely important part of the workflow process. One of the biggest discussions in almost all of my workshops is about deleting images in camera, as I adamantly advocate a "no delete" policy. I think we often make images ahead of ourselves, and the possibility for realizing the artistic value of those images only exists over time. I adopted

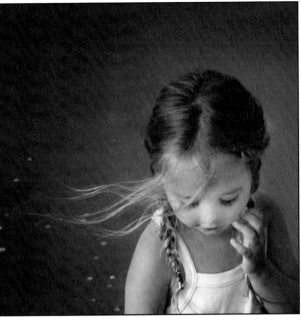

© Leslie Alsheimer

this policy after learning that one of Ansel Adams' most famous images, "Moonrise over Hernandez", was not actually printed until many years after the image was captured. The sky was extremely blown out in the negative, and if he had discarded the "mistake", he would have never been able to make such a profound and powerful print when his skill in the darkroom caught up with what he saw at the scene.

Sometimes we have a goal in mind when we begin to shoot, like a simple portrait for example, destined for a brochure or website. During the course of the shoot, perhaps the model lowers her eyes in gesture, or the camera was set on too slow of a shutter speed and the model moved swiftly, blurring the image. Often times, we are only able to see within the bounds of the immediate goal of the shoot, and our first impulse may be to delete that image, and any other "mistakes" that happen in the process. The anticipatory creative user, however, resisting the temptation to delete may later realize that those "mistakes" have value in a more artistic setting. Gesture, motion and time may all combine to produce an image that is more beautiful and more profound than you were able to see the instant after the shutter snapped. I continually browse through old images and every time I do, I am a different person with fresh eyes, able to see my images in a new and different light. I fortunately decided early on not to delete any images from my camera, and that turned out to be a wonderful gift to myself. Some of my greatest achievements began as what, at the time, I thought were mistakes. Frequently, I reference the words of Scott Adams who said, "Creativity is allowing yourself to make mistakes; art is knowing which ones to keep".

PHOTOSHOP CS3 AND LIGHTROOM: AN INTEGRATED COLOR MANAGED WORKFLOW

The Quick Reference Chart below maps out the key stages of the color managed workflow outlined in this text. Phase 1 highlights the methodologies for the highest quality digital capture. Phase 2 covers importing, editing and making global image adjustments in Lightroom. Phase 3 integrates the value of Bridge into the workflow for navigation and transference of images into Photoshop for digital darkroom processing. Phase 4 explores the multitude of adjustments that can be made in Photoshop through traditional and creative digital darkroom processing techniques. Phase 5 walks you through the fundamentals of a color managed printing process.

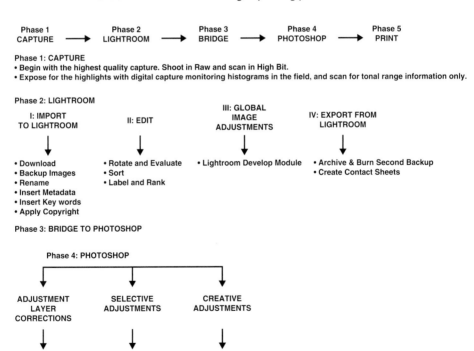

Phase 1   Phase 2   Phase 3   Phase 4   Phase 5
CAPTURE → LIGHTROOM → BRIDGE → PHOTOSHOP → PRINT

Phase 1: CAPTURE
• Begin with the highest quality capture. Shoot in Raw and scan in High Bit.
• Expose for the highlights with digital capture monitoring histograms in the field, and scan for tonal range information only.

Phase 2: LIGHTROOM

I: IMPORT TO LIGHTROOM	II: EDIT	III: GLOBAL IMAGE ADJUSTMENTS	IV: EXPORT FROM LIGHTROOM
• Download • Backup Images • Rename • Insert Metadata • Insert Key words • Apply Copyright	• Rotate and Evaluate • Sort • Label and Rank	• Lightroom Develop Module	• Archive & Burn Second Backup • Create Contact Sheets

Phase 3: BRIDGE TO PHOTOSHOP

Phase 4: PHOTOSHOP

ADJUSTMENT LAYER CORRECTIONS	SELECTIVE ADJUSTMENTS	CREATIVE ADJUSTMENTS
• Black & White Conversions • Toning • Levels • Curves • Black & White Point Settings	• Dodge & Burn (lighten & darken) • Selections • Masking • Vignetting	• Neutral Density Filter • Correcting Exposure Problems • Adding Film Grain • Digital Infrared Noise Reduction • Hand Coloring • Compositing • Adobe Camera Raw

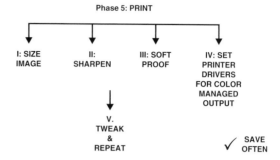

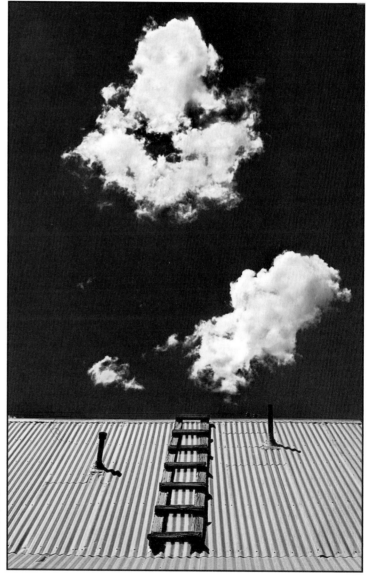

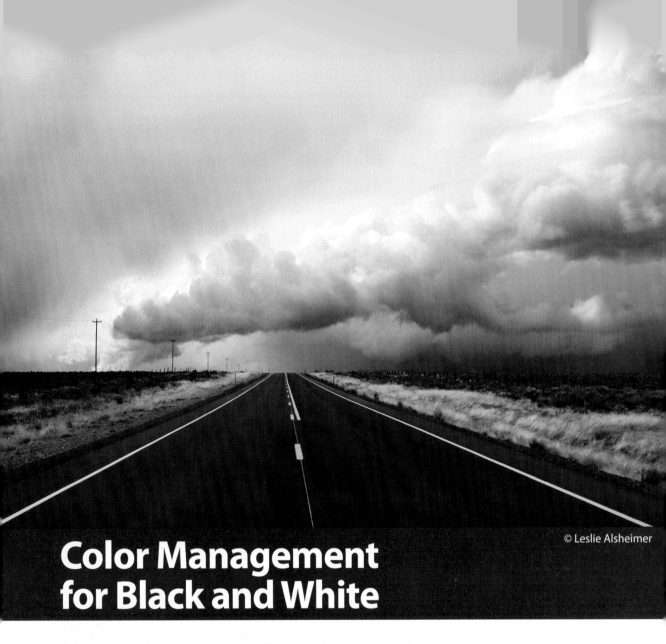

© Leslie Alsheimer

Color Management
for Black and White

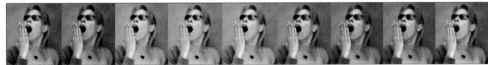

Pre-Workflow: Color Management Integration

**Color Management for Black and White, Really? Sounds like a
serious yawn fest!**

Color Management is an extremely complex topic and one that has
haunted digital photographers since its inception. Most students' eyes
glaze over when this topic comes up in my Workshops. "Extensive, confusing,

technical" and most of all "BORING" are the comments we hear in its wake. Color management was explained to me several times by several different Photoshop experts before it all integrated effectively into my workflow. As an honor student in my undergraduate studies, as well as my graduate work, I typically do not consider myself particularly stupid, but this color management stuff twisted my head into knots for quite some time – so much that I just decided to skip it for awhile. As an experiential learner, I love to jump into new things with both feet, and as a result, I often end up doing things the wrong way first. Although I did have more fun in the beginning of my digital learning process, I eventually learned the hard way that skipping over color management was definitely not the best choice. Color management is without a doubt an absolutely essential piece of the workflow process. Although not the most exciting topic, color management is the foundation upon which everything in the digital darkroom process is built. So whether you work in color or black and white, learning the basics up front will serve you well in the digital process.

Unfortunately for the creative user, color management really is quite complex. There are reasons why there are in-depth full-length texts devoted entirely to this topic alone. Fortunately, for most users, grasping the entire scope of all the technical information available is not an absolute necessity. For the purposes of this text, I have weeded through all of the technical jargon, and simplified the majority of the complexity into five easy steps. These five steps will not only get you in the ball park … but probably all the way to third base with color knowledge in your own personal digital darkroom. The last bit – from third base to the home plate – is the volumes of information within those full length texts that will either bore you to tears or tantalize your inner nerd beyond comprehension. So, for the sake of making this text user friendly, we hope to avoid boring you to tears, while leaving the rest to the technical gurus who have already extensively detailed all the finer nuances of this topic. Check out the Digital Dog a.k.a. Andrew Rodney's *Color Management for Photographers: Hands on Techniques for Photoshop Users* published by Focal Press for more in-depth information.

What does Color Management have to do with Black and White anyway?

It is true that color management for black and white purposes just does not seem quite right. Managing your system for color however, is actually the truest test for black and white accuracy. If you have a completely accurate color balanced system, you are in a position to produce more neutral black and white prints, make the best possible conversions, and assess contrast and tonality variations within an image. Understanding what all this is about can actually help you create far better prints than ever before!

The Essential Overview

Color Management defined
Color Management is basically the ability to consistently control the reproduction of color and tonality in the digital environment; or more

simply, making the print match the image you see on the monitor. A color management system attempts to maintain the "appearance" of consistent color as an image is transferred between different devices, that is; from the camera and/or scanner, to the monitor and across other monitors, through software and ultimately to an output device such as the printer. We like to stress the term "appearance" of consistent color in our definition because each of these devices (the camera, scanner, monitor and printer) has a uniquely different ability to reproduce and interpret color. We can therefore draw the analogy that each device tends to speak in its own "language" of color. The differences in how each individual device – over the hundreds of makes, models and manufacturers – interprets and "speaks" in color can actually be astounding. In order to resolve these differences, color management creates a system whereby the different devices can "talk" to one another in a common language of color.

Why Do We Need Color Management?

We want color consistency as the image travels through the workflow process across various devices, so we can ultimately make prints that have some resemblance to the image we evaluate and process on the monitor through our digital darkroom practices. For black and white, color consistency is ultimately crucial as the neutrality, brightness, tone, contrast and shadow detail are all functions of the color management system. It is, therefore, extremely important – whether we work in color or black and white – to be relatively certain that what we are looking at on the monitor has some level of numeric accuracy in concurrance with the actual image before we begin the digital darkroom editing process.

Why colors change

All devices such as cameras, scanners, monitors, printers, etc. have a different and fixed range of colors they are capable of reproducing, dictated by the laws of physics. A monitor cannot reproduce a more saturated red than the red produced by the monitor's red phosphor. A printer cannot reproduce a green more saturated than the printer's green ink. The range of colors a device can reproduce is called **color gamut**. It is probably easiest to think of gamut as the assortment of crayons a device is able to color or reproduce your image with. Remember the box of Crayolas? The box of 64 crayons with the sharpener

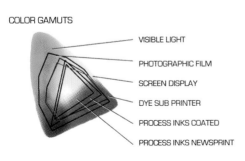

COLOR GAMUTS

VISIBLE LIGHT
PHOTOGRAPHIC FILM
SCREEN DISPLAY
DYE SUB PRINTER
PROCESS INKS COATED
PROCESS INKS NEWSPRINT

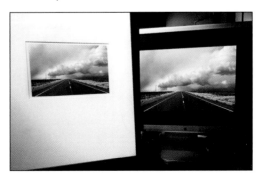

in the back had a larger gamut of color than the boxes of 8, 16 and 32. Burnt sienna, carnation pink and ocean teal provided a much greater gamut for the Crayola artist to work with. It is important to note however that no device can reproduce the full range of colors viewable to human eyes, and no two devices have the same color space/color gamut (or set of crayons to color with).

- The visual spectrum includes 16.7 million colors.
- The human eye can physically see only 12 million colors of those 16.7 million colors.
- The average 4 color press can reproduce only about 70,000 colors.

As an image moves from one device to another, image colors may change because each device interprets color differently. When a color cannot be produced on a device, it is considered to be outside the color gamut of that

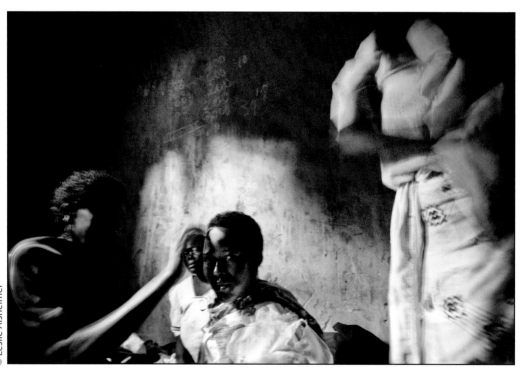

© Leslie Alsheimer

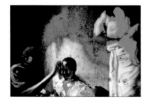

particular device, or, in other words, simply **out of gamut**. You can view out of gamut colors by turning this option on in Photoshop, or when softproofing the image before printing. The out of gamut colors, or colors not reproduceable by the ink and paper combination you have chosen for a print, will be displayed with gray as a default, however one can view them in other colors by changing this in the preferences. (See "Softproof", page 26 for more information.)

As this is truly an imperfect process, we are really learning to use its strengths to our greatest advantage while simultaneously navigating the weaknesses of the system. It is important to know that it is actually impossible for all the colors viewed on a monitor to be identically matched in a print from a desktop printer. There are many reasons for this. First, a printer operates in a CMYK (cyan, magenta, yellow, black) color space, and a monitor operates in a RGB (Red, Green, Blue) color space, each with entirely different color gamuts. (See "What is a Color Space?", page 8 for more information.) Also, some colors produced by printer inks cannot be displayed on a monitor, and some colors that can be displayed on a monitor cannot be reproduced using inks on paper. Paper surface types, such as glossy and matte also have varying abilities to reproduce color. Further, a monitor produces an image from an illuminated light source, while a print is viewed by reflected light. WHOA! Wait a minute …

View   Window   Help
    Proof Setup   ▶
    Proof Colors   ⌘Y
    Gamut Warning   ⇧⌘Y

If matching the print to the monitor is impossible … then creating a good print seems fairly hopeless

Actually this is precisely where the color management system fits in, and why it is so important. Since images come in from many different devices, color management helps you produce more consistent colors by creating **PROFILES** (or, translators) to correctly transform and resolve color discrepancy as an image travels from one space, or device, to another. This allows devices to speak to one another in the same language of color. Colors in the digital environment are described with a series of numeric values for each corresponding color, and neutral. For example middle gray can be described numerically in the RGB space as 128 Red, 128 Green, and 128 Blue; similarly a specific tone of red can be identified and matched by its numeric distribution between the red, green and blue values. Different numbers describe a different color.

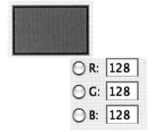

	R:	128
○	G:	128
○	B:	128

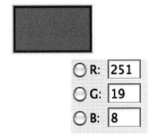

	R:	251
○	G:	19
○	B:	8

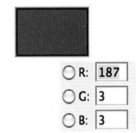

	R:	187
○	G:	3
○	B:	3

Profiles are embedded into the image data providing a definition of what these color numbers mean in terms of actual colors we can see, and consequently make translations from one device to another. In this translation, the differences in the color spaces of each device are reconciled as much as possible. Precision matches, however, are incredibly difficult because there are inherently different abilities and limitations to reproduce color with each device.

This color interpretation is just like how international policy and issues of world affairs are discussed in the United Nations among ambassadors who speak many different languages. Profiles are the digital equivalent to the translators that interpret the dialogue between ambassadors from one language to another. Therefore, it is extremely important to know how to set this profile information in your camera or scanner, create one for your monitor and use them effectively as the image transfers through the editing process to the output device (printer, paper and ink sets). If the digital devices that you work with are not tagging your document with profiles, the numbers for color become ambiguous to the devices, and maintaining consistent color in your workflow will ultimately be quite difficult.

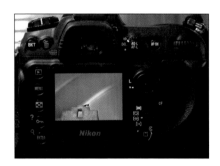 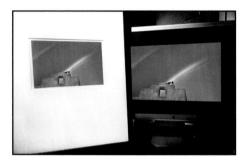

Managing color with profiles

1. *Camera Profile*: Digital cameras capture a wider range of colors than the human eye can see, and the camera's embedded profile determines the colors available to be processed.
2. *Monitor Profile*: Digital cameras also capture a wider range of colors than monitors can display, and the profile associated with the monitor determines what colors are actually displayed.
3. *Printer Profiles*: Digital cameras further capture a wider range of colors than most printers can print, and the profile associated with the printer determines which of the colors presented to it will be printed.

Outline: The Color Managed Workflow

The six basic components to managing color throughout the workflow process

Managing color as well as black and white processes – from film or digital capture to the final output print – is a challenge for even the most sophisticated user. However, before image editing begins there are some relatively painless steps one can take to standardize the process such as setting up your workspace environment to optimize color consistency, as well as system preferences and software tools to conform to a color managed workflow. These basic steps will aid in maintaining the appearance of consistent color as an image is reproduced on different devices – from capture to the print.

**Keep in mind that the nature of different devices makes, exact matches incredibly difficult.

I. Capture
• Set camera's color working space or embed scanner profiles

II. Workspace
• Control ambient lighting conditions and working environment

III. Monitor
• Calibrate your monitor for color accuracy and consistency over time

IV. Software
• Set Photoshop color management policies and color working spaces in accordance with capture and print output variables

V. Print Profiling and Printer Settings
• Set up the print driver with correct profiles for desired output

VI. Softproof, Evaluate, Tweak and Repeat
• View and evaluate the print under lighting conditions specific to the monitor calibration settings (6500 K for Adobe 1998 and D 50 for Color Match) and re-edit the image accordingly. (See Phase 5 "Print Profiling and Printer Settings", page 25 for more information.)

I. Set Up Color Working Spaces

In order to achieve the best possible color from your digital camera, especially the latest pro digital Single Lens Reflex (SLR) cameras, dealing with the concept of color working spaces, both those you choose in the camera and those you use for editing is a necessity. There are a few choices in the mix to evaluate, but choosing the best one for you will not really be that difficult. It actually is not all that crucial to learn everything there is to know about color spaces in the beginning. To keep matters simple, most users will want to work in **Adobe RGB**, as it serves as the industry standard today, until more sophisticated decisions become necessary. You will have to consult your camera manual, in order to establish this setting correctly for your specific camera make and model.

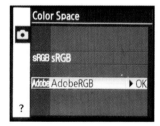

Camera Settings: Choose a Color Space
• **Adobe 1998**, also called **Adobe RGB**, is the current industry standard for most photographic purposes such as stock submissions.
• **ProPhoto RGB** is a larger space many professionals are turning to, but this choice brings in a few more advanced complications. Also this choice is not available for all cameras.
• **sRGB** is the smallest color space available and as such functions best for web work.

What is a Color Space?

Color spaces define specific boundaries of color within the visual spectrum. A color space is like the box in the crayon analogy: all the colors inside the box are represented in that color space; any colors that are not inside the box are not represented in the space. The colors inside the box are referred to as the color space's color gamut. Effective color management requires that a color profile be attached to every image or graphic to indicate its "native" color conditions – also known as the color space – under which the file was created. Adobe was actually one of the innovators in creating and implementing the concept of a color management system and introduced the idea of a "working" color space, with the ideal conditions for image reproduction and editing – not specific to any device. A device color space simply describes the range of colors, or gamut, that a camera can see, a printer can print or a monitor can display. Editing color spaces, on the other hand, such as Adobe RGB, sRGB, ProPhoto and Color Match RGB are device-independent. They also determine a color range, as their design allows you to edit images in a controlled, consistent manner.

The differences between the different RGB working spaces are predominantly defined by the color gamut of each space. However, as with many digital topics, there has been some recent debate over which color space is "best" for photographic purposes. The following definitions will outline some of the differences between the color working spaces and overview some of the reasons for the controversy.

sRGB is the smallest working space. It is ideal for web work as it was developed by HP and Microsoft, to approximates the color space of a typical computer monitor. It therefore serves as a "best guess" for how another person's monitor produces color, and as such has become the standard color space for displaying images on the Internet. The downside of capture in the sRGB space is that most cameras and output devices are capable of producing a much wider gamut, or a lot more colors, than sRGB space contains.

Adobe 1998 (or **Adobe RGB**) was designed by Adobe Systems, Inc. to encompass most of the colors that can be generated by using only RGB primary colors on a device like your monitor. The Adobe RGB working space has been widely adopted as the industry standard for the print world because it provides a relatively large and balanced color gamut that can be easily repurposed for reproduction on a variety of devices. Most users find that it contains a sufficient gamut for most output needs, while having only a slightly larger gamut than the monitor can display. Further, Adobe RGB improves upon sRGB's gamut significantly in cyan and green values. If your camera offers it, Adobe RGB is an excellent color space choice if your images are destined for the printed page, or both the printed page and the web.

ProPhoto RGB is the largest working space and contains even more colors than Adobe RGB. This space is competing for a position in the "which is best" debate, but is not available in all cameras.

Sensors on most high resolution digital cameras produced today are capable of capturing more colors than even the Adobe RGB color space allows. ProPhoto RGB is the only color space that can contain all of the colors digital cameras are capable of producing. At the moment, however, there are no monitors or printers even remotely capable of displaying or outputting the full array of colors ProPhoto RGB is capable of capturing, and therefore creates a large propensity for problems. At some point in the future, however, this may change. Many are starting to advocate for this space as a "better" space, as it gives you more freedom to grow into more colors as output devices get better.

Note:
Notice how Adobe RGB extends into richer cyans and greens than does sRGB.

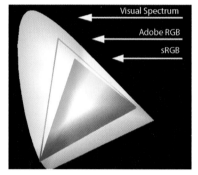

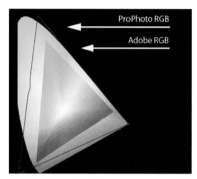

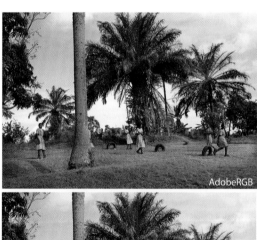

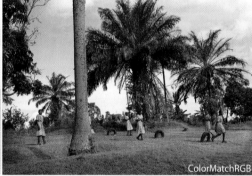

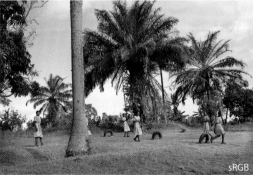

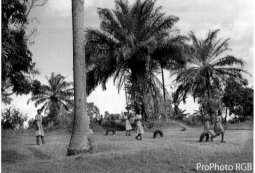

9

For a more in-depth discussion of color spaces and color management, check out Jeff Schewe and Bruce Fraser's white papers "A Color Managed Raw Workflow – From Camera to Final Print" published on Adobe's website.

ColorMatch RGB. This color space is not an available option on any camera as a capture space, but is an available choice in editing spaces. Its color space is wider than sRGB, but not as broad as Adobe RGB. As a mid-sized editing space, it can often help control over saturation problems with images captured in Adobe RGB, as well as produce better skin tones. Some fine art printers advocate using this editing space with Piezography black and white printing, coupled with monitor calibration settings at D-50. (See Chapter 6, "Printing", for more information.)

Hopefully, you can see that changing the color space definition of an image changes the appearance of the image altogether. The numbers that describe each pixel in the image are meaningless without a color space associated with those numbers. The color space defines what color is represented by a set of numbers describing an image pixel; it defines, in effect, what the color of the pixel actually looks like. Since achieving the best-looking color (and ultimately best tonality in black and white) is what we are after, selecting the right color space in the camera and in your viewing software is a fundamental step in the process.

Color Space Recommendations:

• *Grayscale Capture*: If your camera is capable of capturing in Grayscale, you will want to resist the temptation to choose this setting. Although it may be fast and easy, the results will be fast and easy as well. You get what you pay for, and image capture is no exception. The capabilities you gain with image quality as well as editing and conversion options are far superior with RGB capture and post production conversions.

• *Choose a Color Space best for you*: If your camera offers a choice of sRGB and Adobe RGB, choose Adobe RGB (if you are interested in learning more about ProPhoto RGB, read Bruce Fraser's *Real World Color Management*). There are some interesting and valid reasons for moving into ProPhoto RGB. One must, however, really understand the complexities of color space and the advantages and limitations well. The selection of a wider-than-sRGB color space does generally translate into an image with better color, and can be easily converted into smaller spaces. Going the other way, however, such as converting an image originally captured in sRGB to Adobe RGB does not bring with it the benefits of shooting in a broader color capture mode such as Adobe RGB.

• *Syncronize Capture Color Space with Editing Color Space*: When editing your images, make sure that you set the software to view them in the corresponding color space chosen for capture. For instance, if you capture an image in Adobe RGB, then you will want your image browser and image editor to display your images in Adobe RGB, so that the colors maintain consistency across the devices. (See "Set Up Color Working Spaces", page 7.)

• *Embed scanner profile:* While scanning, be sure to embed the scanner's profiles into the image files, so that Photoshop can make accurate conversions. (See Chapter 2, "Scanning Capture: An Overview", page 36.)

II. Workspace: Control Ambient Lighting Conditions and Working Environment

1. Control Ambient Lighting Conditions

When I first moved out of the darkroom, I was so excited about being in the light that I moved my computer right in front of the biggest window with the best view. Because I skipped my color management lessons, I had no idea why my prints were not quite right. When you are performing color and tonal adjustments to images on screen, it is essential that your digital darkroom lighting conditions be controlled properly. If your computer is set up in front of a big bay window with light pouring in, it would be a good time to invest in a dark shade to pull down during the day. Lots of ambient light hitting and bouncing off the monitor can make your images appear brighter. Also, overhead light and sunlight produce reflections and glare on the monitor which can influence our ability to achieve consistent results. It is a bad idea to be making decisions about your image based on varying lighting conditions throughout the day. It is important to turn off room lights and block out sunlight from the windows in order to keep your color and tonal evaluation results consistent day after day. A working environment with consistent ambient, or room light, eliminates uncertain color and tonal results in image evaluation.

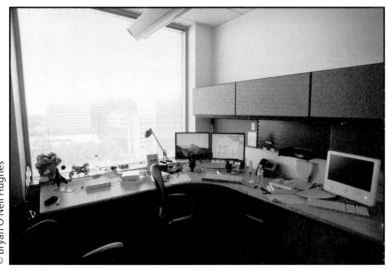

© Bryan O'Neil Hughes

Problematic workspace

11

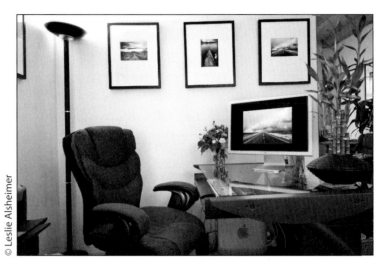

Controlled working space

2. Set Desktop to Solid Gray Medium

This component is for the Macintosh user only, as the PC sets up Photoshop on a gray screen regardless. For those of you who just love seeing your favorite image from your last surf trip to Mexico, or the happy snap of Christmas with the kids displayed while you work, this is going to hurt. Attempting to evaluate images on top of other images is not a very accurate way to evaluate color, nor the neutrality of grayscale images, as our eyes can play tricks on us based on the comparative differences. As illustrated with the color patches to the left, colors from surrounding sources can affect our color vision and influence decisions in the editing process in ways that we may not be aware of.

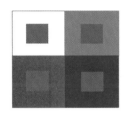

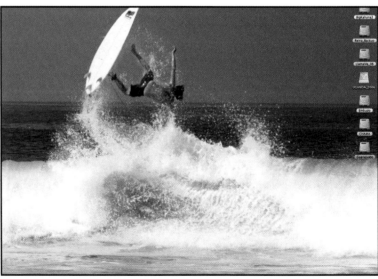

Problematic desktop

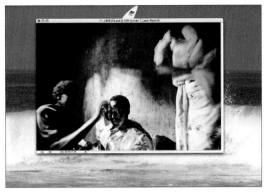
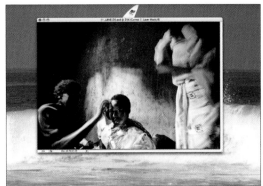

Not the best or most effective way to evaluate color or neutrality

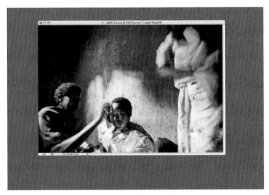
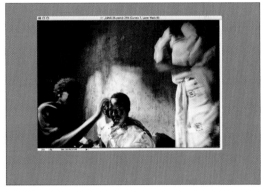

Best practice!!!

In order to control this phenomenon, it is best to set your desktop to a neutral gray.

1. Under the Apple Menu
Choose:
System Preferences

2. Click Show All

3. Click Desktop & Screen Saver

4. Select Solid Colors from the
Collection

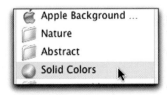

5. Choose Solid Gray Medium

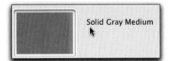

3. Set monitor resolution and color preference

Under Apple Menu > System Preferences > Displays, set colors to millions. This is also where you can adjust the resolution of the monitor. Depending on the size of your monitor, this number will be different. 1152×720, or 1440×900 are recommended.

Under the Display Preferences or Colorsync Preferences, you can also check to make sure the Display profile created from a calibration device is correctly chosen.

III. Monitor

Calibrate your monitor and change settings

Have you ever been to the home electronics store and noticed how every television set displays the same broadcasted information differently? While one set's display may look a little magenta compared to another with a lighter more cyan appearance, we would probably be most inclined to pick the one that looks the best and most pleasing to our eyes. Computer monitors are exactly the same in that each and every monitor right out of the box will display the same data differently. Monitors will age over time, and colors tend to shift with usage. Without several monitors in our home side by side how do we know if our monitor might be the slightly magenta one, or the lighter one with a more cyan cast? Although the side by side comparison for the most pleasing display may work fine for the television, it is important that what

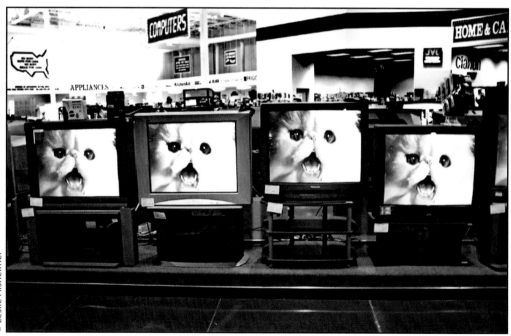

we see on our monitor be relatively accurate if we ultimately want our prints to match what we see on the monitor. If the monitor is not calibrated, or the calibration is inaccurate, we can end up making changes to data based on a false interpretation of the colors presented on the display, and ultimately maintaining consistent color results as the document crosses through different devices will be difficult at best.

In order to control the monitor output most accurately for color consistency, it needs to be calibrated. When you calibrate your monitor, a profile is created to adjust the behavior of the monitor so it conforms to known color specifications, and describes how the numeric color values in an image must be converted so that colors are displayed accurately on screen. Calibration neutralizes any color casts the monitor displays and adjusts its gamma (brightness of the midtones) to set black and white points for accurate color viewing. All monitors not only display color differently like the TV sets, they also vary their color output display over time as they age, just as a light bulb, or enlarger bulb will dim with use. Calibration, therefore, also keeps monitors operating in a stable way and returns the display to an accurate and known value.

How do I calibrate?

To calibrate and profile your monitor, you can use visual calibrators like Adobe Gamma as a starter; however, these are not highly recommended as they rely on the human eye and one's perception of color which is inherently inaccurate by nature. The best method is to use third-party software and measuring devices for more accurate results. There are many devices on the market today at many different price points. The devices are always packaged with their corresponding software as well as instructions on how to use them. Typically the software has a "wizard" or instructional feature to guide you through the process with ease.

The hardware calibration device affixes to the monitor and reads patches of color generated on screen by the software in order to create a profile that "fingerprints" the monitor. The software will typically prompt the user to

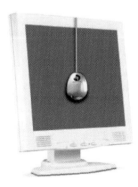
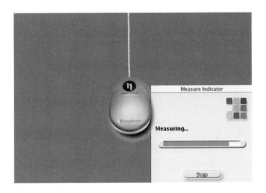

make a few adjustments in brightness and contrast during the process. The profile created then tells other applications (like Photoshop) how to convert or translate the color settings embedded from the capture device so that the image is displayed accurately on the monitor.

How often should I calibrate?

Just like you may want to change the oil in your vehicle every 3000 miles or wax and edge your skis to maximize their optimum performance periodically, a monitor needs the same kind of regular tune-ups and care to perform well over time.

- Monitors should be calibrated every 2–4 weeks depending on the amount of usage.
- For the most accurate results, be sure to let the monitor warm up for at least 30 minutes in order to stabilize before calibration is performed.
- Periodic calibration will help maintain consistent color display on the monitor over time.

Settings for calibration will vary depending on your output. If you are working in your own closed loop system – that is your own camera, printer and monitor – our best recommendation would be to work with daylight settings, 6500 K and Gamma 2.2 as a starting point for most users. This setting is usually best for working with Adobe 1998. If working with Piezography inks, results have often been more accurate using a D-50 or 5000 K calibration setting. You will need to experiment to find the best settings consistent with your workflow and output variables.

IV. Software

Set photoshop color management policies and color working spaces

The next step in our color management system is to set up the software color policies to interpret the color information correctly on your calibrated monitor! Just like the choices we have in setting the digital camera to a specific color capture space, we will want to set Photoshop policies to match the camera capture settings.

There are very few image browsers that offer control over the viewing color space. Instead, most software applications can only display the images in the color space of the operating system. In Windows XP, as well as most older versions of Windows, that would be sRGB (remember that is the smallest working space, which is not recommended for print reproduction work). Images captured in the Adobe RGB working space will appear on screen somewhat flat and desaturated when (incorrectly) viewed in sRGB.

Photoshop is, however, an incredibly color savvy software that offers the best environment in which we can view Adobe RGB images, ProPhoto RGB,

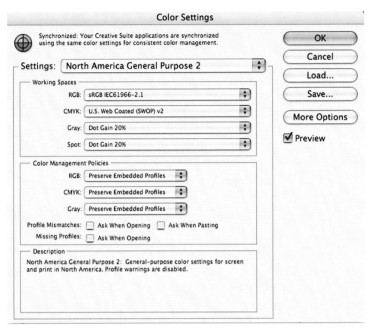

Photoshop default color working space and default color policies. Notice the RGB is set to sRGB

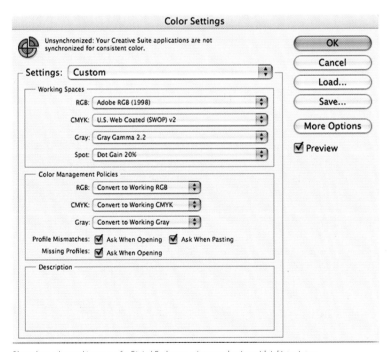

Photoshop color working space for Digital Darkroom print reproduction with inkjet printers

or images defined by any other color space. You can, with accurate color display for each space simultaneously view an sRGB image in a side by side comparison with an Adobe RGB image.

To specify color settings in Mac OS, choose Edit Menu > Color Settings and in Windows choose Photoshop Menu > Color Settings to bring up the color Settings Dialog Box in Photoshop. The dialogue box is the single most important place where color management information is gathered and controlled – one box, one convenient location. As incredibly color savvy as Photoshop is, however, it unfortunately ships out to users set with sRGB as the default working space, which is not the most ideal setting for print-oriented photographers. It is therefore necessary to make some changes in color setting policies before image editing begins.

Photoshop Color Management Policies and the Editing Color Working Space

Color Management Policies are simply a set of rules defining protocol for opening files into Photoshop with or without embedded profiles. The color working space specifies what colors (brightness and hues) will be available when working in Photoshop. Whichever color working space you choose to work in directly effects how many colors you will be able to see on your monitor and potentially reproduce in the print. The color space choices for image editing in Photoshop are Adobe RGB 1998, ProPhoto RGB, ColorMatch and sRGB. (See "Set Up Color Working Spaces", page 7 for definitions.)

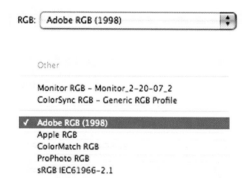

Working Gray Policies

Grayscale does have its own governing profiles independent of RGB or CMYK. However, it is important to note that the grayscale profiles do not contain any information about the papers nor the color of the inks, which are all factors in creating neutral values in producing a black and white prints with desktop printers. (See Phase 5 "Print Profiling and Printer Settings", page 25 for more information.)

The Gray working space determines how a grayscale image will look on your monitor. Within the grayscale working space, we have access to gamma settings, dot gain curves and the ColorSync Gray Working Space (Mac only) as well as the ability to customize the dot gain to specific requirements.

1. Gamma settings define the brightness of the midtone values on screen. The choices of gamma settings enable you to base the display quality equivalent to either a Macintosh (1.8) or PC (2.2) monitor, although there is evidence that all monitors have become 2.2 these days, whether it is Mac or PC.
    Gray Gamma 2.2 is probably the best for most users, but feel free to experiment. This setting anticipates the viewing conditions of a PC monitor (important for web graphics), and the darkening is roughly equivalent to a 25% dot gain setting.
2. The Dot Gain settings, choices of either 10%, 15%, 20% or 30%, depend on your printing conditions. The dot gain settings darken the on-screen image, effectively anticipating the effect of the ink dot gain (or spread) during on-press reproduction.
    (To set your own dot gain profile, choose "Custom" from the top of the pop-up.) Note that these values only lighten or darken the appearance of an image, while the actual output values are not affected.

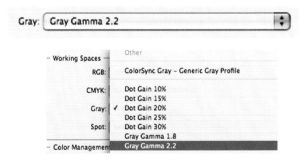

If you are outputting primarily to inkjet printers matching the Gray Working space to the RGB color space is a good move. Simply translated if you are working in Adobe RGB or sRGB, use Gamma 2.2. If you are working in ProPhoto RGB or Colormatch RGB, choose 1.8. This prevents any additional gamma adjustments as we switch back and forth between color and grayscale images.

If you work in a prepress environment, it is best to match the grayscale space to the dot gain of the black ink. North American Prepess 2 setting presets will create this match. Consult your service provider for customized settings in accordance with press specifications.

CMYK Working Space

Desktop inkjet printers from most of the major manufacturers (like Epson, HP and Canon) actually require RGB data rather than CMYK data to produce prints, even though these printers operate in a CMYK working space. What this means to the average user is that the choice you make for CMYK settings will have no influence in the actual image output (to an inkjet printer). Therefore, the CMYK settings are better left to the default US Web Coated (SWOP) v2 until you need to work with offset press. As press settings vary, you need to consult your service provider for best conversion settings according to the specifications of the printer and output variables.

CMYK working spaces are essentially printing processes characterized by various ink-and-paper combinations, dot gain settings and separation options such as ink limits. If you have a custom press profile, you would select it as

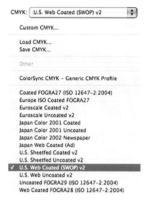

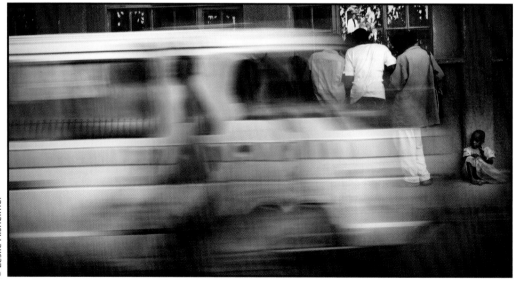

your CMYK working space. When you perform a mode change to or from CMYK, Photoshop will use the CMYK working-space profile for the conversion. Photoshop will also use the CMYK working-space profile when you open a CMYK image that lacks an embedded profile.

If you need to convert images to CMYK but do not have a custom press profile, and one is not available from your printer, select one of the profiles provided by Adobe, basing it on the type of printing process and paper that will be used, such as US Web Coated (SWOP) v2.

As with RGB working spaces, Photoshop provides the ability to create custom CMYK working-space profiles. This is useful if your print provider does not have a profile but can tell you what separation settings to use when converting your images to CMYK.

Spot Working Space

The Spot working space is somewhat similar to the grayscale space, but for spot colors. The options available are a series of five preset dot gain settings and the means for customizing the dot gain curve if desired. The Spot working space provides a setting for spot colors, such as Pantone colors, that may be used in the printing process. Similar to CMYK settings, spot settings are the most crucial when working with offset press and depend on ink and paper combinations to be determined. Leave this setting unchanged at the default until press specifications require otherwise.

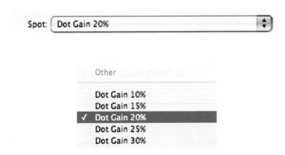

Color Management Policies

Color management policies therefore determine how to handle documents that do not match your chosen color working space. These policies provide guidelines for how Photoshop should proceed when a document is opened, color data is imported into an active document with color spaces that do not match the set policies. With specified predefined color management settings, Photoshop can proceed within the user defined color management workflow as standard protocol for all documents and color data that you open or import. These color management policies look for the color profile associated with a document or imported color data and compares the profile (or lack of profile) with the current editing working space settings in order to make default color management decisions for conversion and color display. If the profile is missing or does not match the working space, Photoshop displays a warning message that indicates the default action for the policy (as long as the alert option is selected in the color settings). For a newly created document, the color workflow usually operates behind the scenes; unless otherwise specified, the document uses the working space profile associated with its color mode for creating and editing colors.

In this text, we are going to set the color management policies to convert all incoming documents to the specified working space. This simply means the active radial button chosen will be to pre set Convert to the Working space. However, you will always be able to choose otherwise.

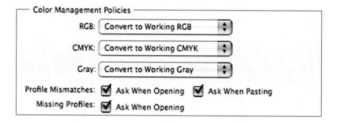

Profile mismatches

If you are presented with an "Embedded Profile Mismatch" dialog when you open an image, this means that the image was captured or created in a different working space than your chosen working-space policies. This warning dialogue is how you tell Photoshop to proceed with opening the document. Your choices are the following: (1) Use the embedded profile instead of the working space. (2) Convert to the working space and

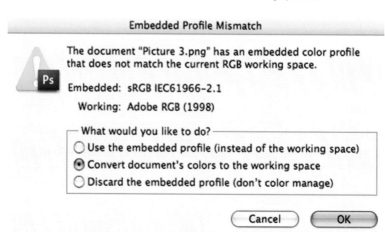

(3) Discard the embedded profile (do not color manage). In most instances, it is best to go ahead and convert everything over to your set working space in order to simplify and standardize your workflow, unless of course there is reason to keep the image in the space in which it was created.

It is still important to note however that, the optimum color space will not always be a match for what you set in the camera. With midtone heavy and/or overly saturated Adobe RGB images captured from the D1X and EOS-1D, for example, assigning the ColorMatch RGB color space often offers a more realistic and pleasing color translation with problem images.

Missing profile

This warning dialogue box is not a good one to receive. This means that the document file does not have any profiles or translators to convey information about the color of the image. Photoshop will have no idea where this file came from, nor how to translate its color information accurately and will have to just guess at color. Photoshop can do a pretty darn good job at guessing, but that is really like me giving a blank piece of 4×5 film to my students and asking them to shoot the image and process it in the chemical darkroom without knowing its ISO or film type. It would be fairly difficult for even a well-seasoned pro to render a good exposure and development time with virtually no information about the film. In this case the profile will need to be assigned. If you know that the image came from an sRGB space or any other for example, you would first assign sRGB, or the known space, and then convert to the working space. If the incoming source is unknown, assign the working RGB and move on from there.

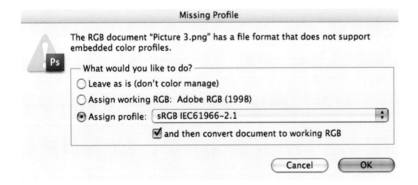

How to set: Photoshop color management policies

Setting up your Photoshop color management policies and preferences is absolutely essential before you begin working in Photoshop. Remember, these are the settings that specify the handling of color profiles associated with the RGB, CMYK and Grayscale color modes in every document. This means that the color management settings affect how images are displayed on screen, and how Photoshop operates color separations. These profiles are known as working spaces. Being aware of your color settings and image profiles will help you produce consistent color results for the most common on-screen and print output conditions.

Edit Menu > **Color Settings** You may choose a preset color management configuration from the settings menu or customize one of your own. Adobe sets the default workspace for web work, which is far too limiting for print output with high quality photographs. We are going to create custom settings for print output.

RGB > **Adobe RGB (1998)** is today's industry standard. This space is best for RGB print production work. You may want to research ProPhoto RGB for details on whether it might work for you.

Color Match > this space can be an excellent choice when working with offset press and converting to CMYK. It is also recommended for working with Piezography ink sets.

sRGB > is an excellent choice for images destined for the web.

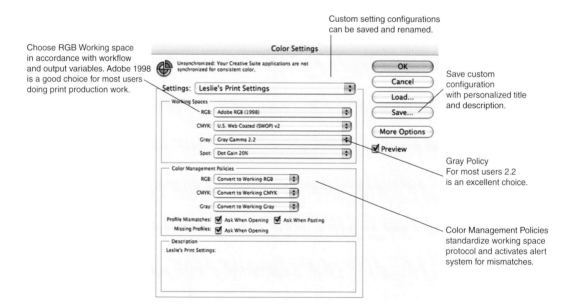

Custom setting configurations can be saved and renamed.

Choose RGB Working space in accordance with workflow and output variables. Adobe 1998 is a good choice for most users doing print production work.

Save custom configuration with personalized title and description.

Gray Policy For most users 2.2 is an excellent choice.

Color Management Policies standardize working space protocol and activates alert system for mismatches.

Save and Name

It is important to save your custom settings so that they can be reused and shared with other Adobe applications that use the same color management workflows, as well as with other users. The color management settings that you customize in the Color Settings dialog box are contained in a preferences file called Color Settings.

Comment

Enter your own description of the settings you just created for future reference.

V. Print Profiling and Printer Settings

Set up the print driver with correct profiles for output

Once a color space tagged image makes it from the camera (or scanner) and passes onto a calibrated monitor, and is edited through Photoshop and Lightroom, the next step is to pass the image out through the printer onto paper or other surfaces. This phase of the workflow requires a print profile. A print profile tells the printer how to translate and convert the colors from the monitor so that the image outputs correctly onto the paper. This translation is specified according to the type of printer, paper, surface and ink the image will be output onto. Every paper, however, will require a different profile because every paper, ink, printer combination has a different color gamut, or ability to reproduce colors. For instance, glossy papers have the ability to produce more saturated colors than matte surfaces. Most printers come with a number of common paper profiles installed with their drivers. These "canned" profiles are a great start in making the monitor to print color translation relatively well. At some point, however, you might want to invest in custom profiles, made specifically for your printer, paper and ink combinations. Custom profiles can be purchased online at an exceptional price from Santa Fe Camera's on-line store: www.santafecameracenter.com or call (866) 922-6372 for more information.

Because every paper, ink, printer combination requires a different profile, and the print settings in both the Photoshop and printer dialogue boxes are neither simple nor user friendly, many common mistakes inevitably happen. If the print driver options are not set correctly, using the correct profile, it will be difficult to even come close to replicating the image you see on your monitor to the output print. See Chapter 6, "Printing", for more in-depth step-by steps on print profiles and printer driver settings.

Important note:
Lightroom Users need to make sure that the Photoshop color management settings match the output color space in the Adobe Lightroom export settings. Images may have distinctly different colors than in Lightroom if the settings are not congruent.

Note:
The default location of the Color Settings file varies by operating system; use your operating system's Find command to locate this file.

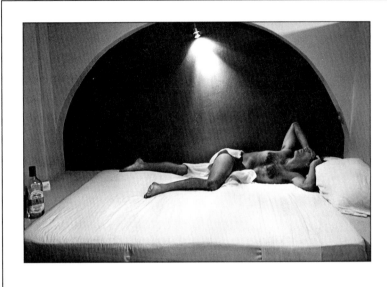

Glossy papers have a larger gamut than matte surfaces

Output and Media Considerations

Another significantly influential piece of the color reproduction puzzle involves the variable gamuts of chosen media surfaces. Glossy surface papers tend to have a much larger reproduction gamut than do matte and fine art surface papers. Larger gamuts allow for more saturated and richer color reproduction. It is often a difficult sacrifice for a photographer to lose color saturation in order to work with textured fine art papers. But if saturation is the look you are after, you may get the best results moving to glossy surface papers. Notice the difference in the color output reproduction gamut between Epson Matte and Semigloss papers.

Softproof, Evaluate, Tweak and Repeat

As we are limited by the boundaries of the laws of physics, the final component of both the print workflow and the color management system is the softproof, tweak and repeat system we apply in order to resolve the remaining differences in color and output consistency. The process of softproofing and tweaking is the final phase of practice that brings an image from the third base to the home plate in the otherwise nerdy tech speak world for achieving color accuracy within the system.

Softproof
This is a technique to simulate on your monitor what your image will look like when it is printed, before actually printing the image. This offers you a

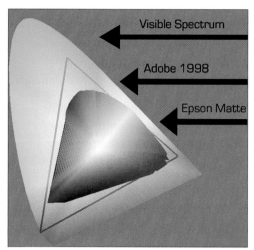

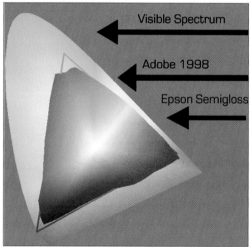

"reality check", or the ability to view the physical differences between what is displayed on the monitor, and how the image colors will translate on to the chosen paper, ink with the applied profile. Photoshop CS3 now incorporates softproofing into the print dialogue interface. Keep in mind however that the reliability of the softproof depends upon the quality of the monitor, as well as the monitor profiles, and the ambient lighting conditions of your work environment. Softproofing can also be simulated full screen under the View Menu > Show all Menu Items, View > Proof Setup > Custom. (See Chapter 6, "Printing", page 193 for more information.)

Evaluate
As various lighting sources have distinctive differences in color temperature, it is important to be sure to evaluate prints under the same lighting source as they are intended to be displayed. The kitchen fluorescent or office floor

lamp will have a distinctively different influence on color interpretation than daylight or a D-50 gallery flood light. Be sure to evaluate prints under the correct lighting source; try using a viewing booth in order to eliminate discrepancies and maintain more color evaluation accuracy.

Tweak – Making digital darkroom adjustments based on output results

This editing component is the heart and soul of color management and the print making process. Tweaking is truly the "art" of the fine art print. The process of tweaking occurs after you have followed all of the previous steps and suggestions in the color management workflow, and your print still does not match what you see on the monitor. Just as your first print in the traditional darkroom provided the visual feedback to drive any number of refined re-prints, the digital darkroom is no different. Tweaking is the process of making corrections again and again until you are satisfied with the results. This is the test print phase of the workflow. (See Chapter 6, "Printing", page 193 for more information.)

Now wake up! The rest will be much more fun I promise!

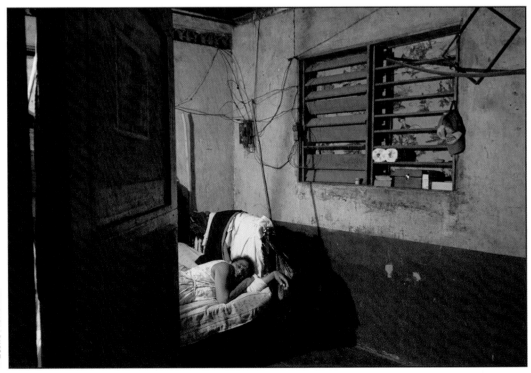

© Leslie Alsheimer

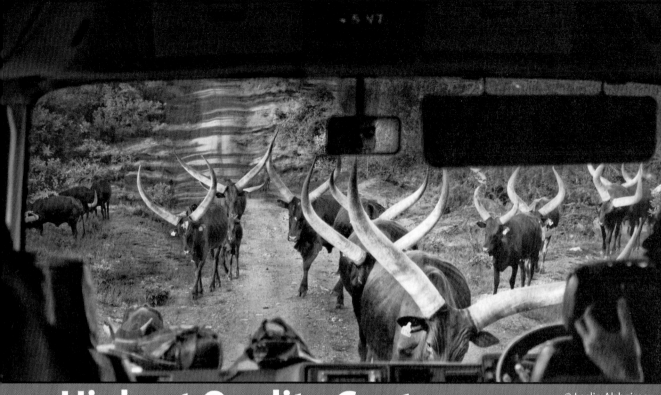

CHAPTER 2

© Leslie Alsheimer

Highest Quality Capture: Workflow Phase I

The best workflow practices begin with the highest quality images and a non-destructive editing philosophy. Ultimately, one of the greatest factors in determining the quality of the prints is the integrity of the originating pixels. Therefore, as the first phase of the digital workflow process, this chapter outlines the most important components of capture for acquiring the highest quality images possible.

I. Capture in Color

As outlined in the Color Management chapter previously, if your camera is capable of capturing in a Grayscale mode, you will want to resist the temptation to choose this setting. Although it may seem fast and easy, the results will be fast and easy as well. You get what you pay for, and image capture is no exception. For the highest quality capture, the capabilities you gain with image quality as well as editing and conversion options are far superior with RGB capture and post production conversions.

II. Digital Capture File Formats

1. JPEG vs. Raw Capture

Those of you with digital SLRs or high-end point-and-shoots have a choice when it comes to the file format that your camera writes: JPEG (the world and web standard for photographic imagery) and Raw (a proprietary, unprocessed, "negative" of your image file). As Raw files are exponentially larger than JPEG files, many users find they can "buy" 3–4 JPEGs for the cost of one Raw file, and thus never bother to explore the many advantages Raw capture has to offer. The Raw format does have significantly powerful advantages and those not (yet) shooting Raw should consider all of the following benefits.

Raw files are larger, but they are also uncompressed, high bit depth unaltered originals. This means many things as you bring them into your imaging application: first you have the best image fidelity that your camera can muster, the greatest amount of capture information, and the most control over image processing. Further, the Raw format maps to the image settings applied at capture, and every subsequent editing change applied in processing sits alongside the Raw file as an external reference component associated with each image file. Since changes and edits are not applied directly to the Raw image file, all Raw processing adjustments are completely non-destructive and infinitely editable.

Although programs like Adobe Camera Raw and Lightroom can now read JPEGs, the application of controls such as "temperature" and "exposure" are hacked into the JPEG file artificially.

While a Raw file contains the unprocessed and uncompressed image data captured by the digital camera sensor, images captured in JPEG format are compressed in the camera in order to make them smaller. This compression process, known as "lossy", is extremely destructive to image data. Cracks and artifacts can easily be seen in magnified viewing on screen. In addition, both JPEG and TIFF formats process the image data in camera, manipulating the image data by adding adjustments to all images unilaterally such as contrast and saturation. For this reason, JPEG files tend to look much better initially, but remove a great deal of control over image processing. JPEGs also freeze applied capture criteria and bake the settings into the pixels which unlike Raw cannot be undone. JPEGs can be extremely useful and beneficial if memory is essential, if the number of images you can capture on a card must be increased exponentially, general pre-processing speed outweighs custom image processing, or images are destined for the web.

Keep in mind however, that quality is significantly compromised in the exchange. Best practice therefore is to use JPEGs when resolution and image control are not as important, and use Raw for everything else!

DNG = Digital Negative Universal Raw format created by Adobe.

2. Digital Negative (or DNG) Format

Most camera manufacturers have created and maintain their own unique proprietary formats for Raw image files, differentiated by unique file extensions. For example, NEF defines a Nikon Raw file and CRW defines a Canon Raw File. As of CS3, Adobe Photoshop (via Camera Raw 4.0) and Photoshop Lightroom 1.0 support over 150 unique, proprietary Raw camera formats. The biggest issue for concern is that each and every camera model creates a different version of the Raw format. With the current, dizzying rate of change, cameras, computers, operating systems, etc., it would be foolish to assume that the camera companies that make each format would continue to support them once they become yesterday's news. The proprietary files that can be converted with manufacturer's solutions now are not likely to be supported years down the road and will certainly never be archival enough to last a lifetime. Furthermore, they presume that someone else that might want to read them will have the same camera and software!

For this reason, and with an eye toward the long-term future, Adobe proposed a universal, open (public SDK) format called DNG. The DNG format has the advantages of being future-proof (imagine, files written natively or converted to DNG would not require a plug-in update or new versions of specified software), publicly available, free of cost, and in classic Adobe style, it even compresses the footprint of the characteristically large Raw files (lossless, of course).

While several major companies such as Leica and Hasselblad have written to DNG natively, any file can be converted easily to DNG with any of the following methods:

• DNG drag and drop converter

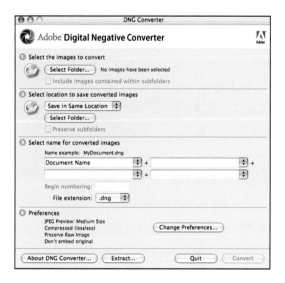

- Bridge CS3, via the new Photo Downloader

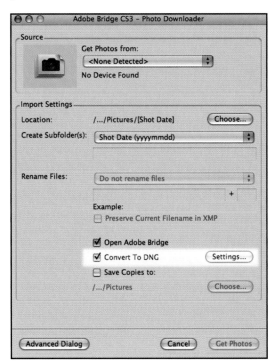

- Camera Raw

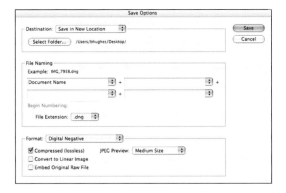

- Lightroom 1.0

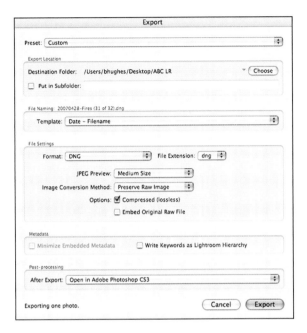

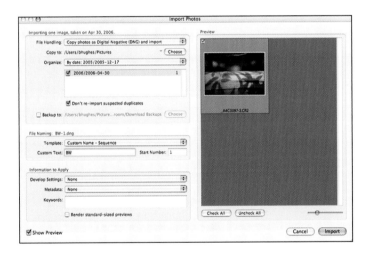

File formats: Quick reference

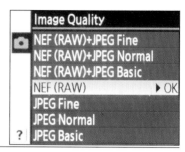

RAW:

Advantages:
- Highest image quality available
- High Bit data maximizes capture to include the greatest amount of image data possible
- Less destructive editing
- Image files are uncompressed and unprocessed. Image processing versatility far exceeds all other file types
- Faster capture rate than TIFF

Disadvantages:
- Large files
- Less images on card
- Requires Raw conversion process
- Storage

JPEG:

Advantages:
- Smaller files more images per card
- Best email format
- Pre-processed to look better initially
- Universally recognized file format that can be managed by almost every software type

Disadvantages:
- Image files are compressed to become smaller unwanted artifacts in images that reflect compression process
- 8-Bit capture, does not maximize data therefore less image information captured
- More destructive editing pre-processed for contrast and saturation

TIFF:

Advantages:
- High quality image files
- Uncompressed images
- No compression artifacts
- Highly functional file that can be managed by almost every software type
- No conversions necessary

Disadvantages:
- Largest file
- Less images on card
- Slower capture rate
- Storage

III. Bit Depth: The Advantage of High Bit Capture

Bit depth, also called pixel depth or color depth, measures how much color information is available to display or print each pixel in an image. Greater bit depth (more bits of information per pixel) means more available colors and more accurate color representation in the digital image.

For the technically curious, the explanation of bit depth requires some complicated math. For the less technically adept however, all you really need to know is that more bits are more better! Working in high-bit provides exponentially more information within the image file.

Fundamentally speaking, a pixel with a bit depth of 1 has two possible values: black and white, it can be 1 or 0, on or off.

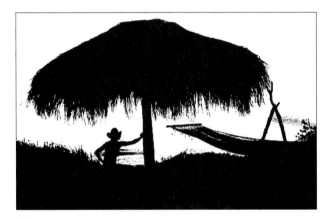

2 bit image

Digital files can be:

1. Low Bit: (8-Bit) = Most of the digital world operates with 8-bit images. This includes inkjet printers, most monitors and all JPEG files.
A pixel with a bit depth of $8 = 2^8$ has 256 possible values.
2. High Bit: (16, 24 or 48 Bit) = Only **Raw** capture, and High Bit Scanning can give you the advantage of high bit images.
A High bit image in contrast can have 65,536 (2^{24}) levels of information, which is significantly more than the 256 levels that an 8 bit image contains. The significantly greater amount of information available in the image file makes a dramatic difference when moving pixels and image data in the editing process.

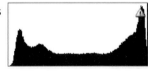

High Bit image with some editing contains more image data

Less destructive editing means less spikes and gaps in the histograms and smoother gradations cause less banding and posterization. (See "So what is a Histogram?", page 38 for more information.)

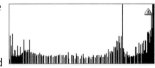

8-Bit image with same editing results in banding and posterization

IV. Scanning Capture: An Overview

1. How to Set Up for Optimal Scanning

While there are far too many scanners and software packages on the market to go in to any great detail with specific products, there are a few basic rules for guidance on how to achieve the highest quality black and white output with whatever hardware you prefer.

Note:
Many scanners have an optical resolution (true resolution) and an interpolated resolution where image data is resampled (or made up) to create larger files. Be sure to research your scanner specifications.

1. **Set the scan resolution** to the maximum optical resolution of the scanner in order to capture the highest quality image data for the largest possible output.
   4000 ppi is roughly equivalent to film grain.
   **If file size and storage is an issue, set the scanner resolution instead according to the number of megabytes necessary for the desired output size. (See "Resolution/Print Size", page 37, Reference Chart.)
2. **Set the scanning mode to high bit.** A high bit scan will give you exponentially more image data ... 65,536 as compared to 256 in an 8-bit image file which translates to less destructive editing. There are more points and more pixel information to effect change in a high bit file, therefore creating smoother gradations and less destructive editing.
3. **For black and white negatives set film type to positive.** Although I have not experimented with every scanner on the market, typically black and white negatives scan best if scanned as a positive (or at least tell the scanner it is) and invert the negative to a positive once its in Photoshop.
   Image > Adjustments > Invert
4. **Using the histograms,** set the highlight and shadow points ONLY. Use the scanner histogram tools to set the highlight and shadow input values to scan for the information in the image. Usually a flat scan is the most useful in Photoshop. (See "So what is a Histogram?", page 38 for more information.)
5. **Make correction in Photoshop.** Even the fanciest scanners and scanning software are not as sophisticated as Photoshop. Regardless of what you paid for your scanner, it is usually best to make adjustments to the image in Photoshop. Turn off all corrections in the scanning software whenever possible.
6. **Turn off sharpening.** This is essential! You will have much more sophisticated control over sharpening in Photoshop.
7. **Embed the scanners profile.** Photoshop needs to know where (or from what device) your image is coming from in order to make accurate color conversions. Embedding the scanners profile gives Photoshop crucial information in describing color. (See Chapter 1, "Color Management for Black and White", page 22 for more information).
8. **Scan grayscale images and negatives in RGB mode.**

2. Resolution/Print Size Reference Chart

Resolution and image size are interdependent, and combine together to generate a total file size. This can get particularly confusing in the scanning process – especially with 35 mm negatives – as their size dimensions are very small – requiring much higher scanning resolutions to produce high quality prints. Scanning for the total file size necessary for the desired output size is therefore the easiest way to translate resolution for scanning purposes.

If for example, you wish to make a 13 × 19 inch print from your inkjet printer at 240 PPI, choose a scanning resolution that creates a file size of 164.4 MB for a color or toned print, and 43 MB for grayscale.

File sizes refer to high-bit file size

Print Size in Inches	PPI @ 300 MB Size	PPI @ 240 MB Size	PPI @ 180 MB Size
5 × 7	18.04 MB	11.54 MB	8.66 MB
8 × 10	40.12 MB	26.4 MB	19.78 MB
13 × 19	127.4 MB	81.6 MB	61 MB
16 × 20	164.4 MB	105.6 MB	79.2 MB
24 × 36	445 MB	284.8 MB	213.6 MB

PPI 300 = Necessary for prepress and dye sublimation printers
PPI 240–300 = Perfect resolution for inkjet printers
PPI 180 = Lowest resolution recommendation for inkjet printers

Note: Grayscale images will only need to be 1/3 the size if not scanned in RGB.

V. Exposure Evaluation Tools: Utilizing Histograms in the Field for Optimal Exposures with the Greatest Dynamic Range

Digital technology brings with it one of the most exciting and compelling reasons for its use altogether, the instant feedback and gratification we get from immediately seeing the image on the LCD screen on the back of the camera. Although it is fun to see the image instantly, it is important not to evaluate exposure accuracy by the display image alone. How many times did you think you had great exposures in the field, and come home to realize that the shot was not exposed properly? Even if we find ourselves in the unlikely event in the field that we can actually see the display image without glare or reflections, it is still highly likely that the preview we see in the field will not be an accurate representation of how the image will look once you get it on your monitor.

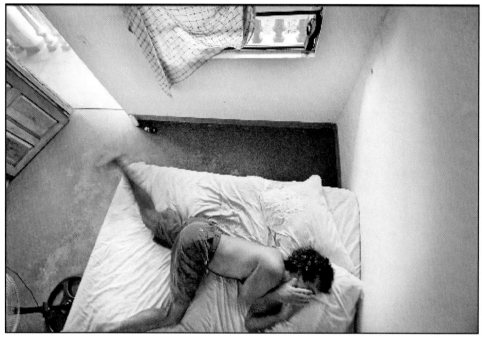

© Leslie Alsheimer

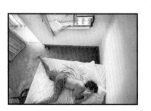

So if the LCD stinks for exposure evaluation is there another way to evaluate exposure in the field?

The histogram is, without a doubt, the greatest and most effective tool the digital photographer has for evaluating exposure and monitoring highlight and shadow information in the field; simultaneously however, it might also be the most mysterious and least understood. Utilizing the digital camera's histogram feature in the field can show you clearly and immediately whether your images are overexposed, underexposed or well exposed. And knowing how to read and evaluate them can guide you to make any necessary changes in exposure while still in the field. Therefore, taking the time to learn about histograms can help you not only gain mastery of the digital camera's image quality, but also improve your photography significantly.

Almost every digital camera on the market today – from the simplest point-and-shoot to the most advanced SLR – has the ability to display a histogram. In order to activate this feature, you will have to consult your camera manual to find out how to bring it up, as the method varies from camera to camera. The best approach for exposing digital capture is to keep your histogram active on the camera's rear LCD at all times, and make efforts not to evaluate too much about the image based on what you see on the image display.

So what is a Histogram?

A histogram is a simple bar chart that graphs the brightness values of individual pixels absorbed by the camera sensor within a digital image.

Basically, it displays where all of the brightness levels contained in the scene are found, from the darkest to the brightest. On a scale of 0–255, 0 representing pure black, and 255 representing pure white, the histogram maps out how many of the pixels within an image have each level of brightness or (luminosity) from black (0) to white (255). The portion of the histogram that is to the left of the chart shows the shadow information, or how much of your image is dark to black, while the part to the right shows the highlight information or the amount of the image that is light to white. The vertical height of the graph indicates the relative number of pixels that equate to each brightness level between white and black. Because each and every image is different, histograms are inherently unique for every image as well. The histogram, therefore, provides invaluable information to the photographer in its mapping of tonal values within an image, which effectively monitors, the dynamic range or range of input possible at the point of capture. Immediately one can see where shadow and highlight information begin and what sort of tonal range exists, and allows the photographer who knows how to read them the ability to make re-exposure decisions accordingly. Although this may not make sense yet, after we introduce a few more concepts, we can look at examples visually so that you can get more comfortable with this tool.

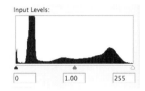

Before we look at examples however, we may need to clarify that there are two places we will be looking at histograms throughout this text. First, we will be using the histogram in camera to evaluate exposure in the field, and second, we will also use the histograms in Photoshop to evaluate the image data as we process images in the digital darkroom. Although the camera histogram is found in a different place than the software histograms, how they function and what they tell us is actually exactly the same. For demonstration purposes, I am using the software histograms as seen with the Photoshop CS3 Histogram Palette instead of the camera histogram, as the software histograms are easier to see, and they convey the same information as we would see if we were viewing them on the camera at the time of capture.

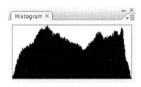

A camera histogram

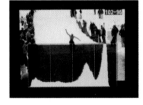

A software histogram

What is dynamic range?

Dynamic range is basically the range of input a device can capture. For example, the range of light under which the human eye can see extends from the brightest sunlight to the dimmest moonlight, and this range of extremes defines the dynamic range of the human eye. The range of human vision far exceeds that of most cameras and computer. Because the dynamic range of film and digital capture is more limited than the human eye can see, photographers must, therefore, be selective about what is important in a scene, and expose with this scale of limitations in mind.

Like transparency film, if a part of a digital image receives too much light or over exposure, that portion falls beyond that which the sensor (or film) can

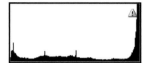

Lost highlight detail

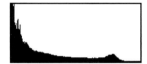

Lost shadow detail

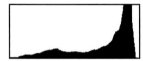

Preserved highlight and shadow information

record and the result is rendered as pure white. Once that portion records as pure white, the information is effectively "blown out" or no longer holds any image data, which translates photographically as no image detail in the highlighted areas of the image. The same is true if a part of the image receives too little light, and the capture data will fall beyond that which the sensor can record on the other end of the scale. The digital sensor will therefore under expose the corresponding image that information as pure black. A recognizable image is only recorded if the light hitting the film, or the digital sensor, falls within a range of about 5 F-stops. This is the approximate dynamic range of digital capture.

Exposing for digital capture is somewhat different than exposing for film, as digital cameras behave quite differently than film cameras do in the way they handle highlight and shadow information. With digital capture, extreme overexposure effectively saturates highlight information beyond recovery, and underexposure pushes shadow information and detail into noise, making quality rendering almost impossible. How sensors respond at the saturation limits at either end of the dynamic range limitations are also different from film, and how to deal with these characteristics are all embedded into the Raw conversion and subsequent post-processing procedures. Although digital cameras today have a much greater exposure latitude than most 35 mm films do, it is unfortunately still much easier to blow out the highlights on a digital sensor than it is with film. The digital camera's imaging sensor is very similar to color transparency film when it comes to its sensitivity to light. For this reason, the best exposure strategy with digital is to expose for the highlights, breaking the rules of the film day's lessons that taught us to expose for the shadows and print for the highlights.

Exposing for digital capture

Proper exposure with film or digital is difficult to define, as the best exposure for any given image will depend on the image itself and corresponding circumstances. There is really no such thing as a perfect exposure, as artistic preferences should drive exposure to vary depending on the tones of an image, and the resulting mood or impact the photographer creatively wishes to achieve. Predominantly, however, our general goal with exposure is to simply place the tonal values found in the scene most appropriately within the dynamic range of the camera's imaging sensor. "Most appropriately" means that the mid-tones found in the image fall roughly half way between the darkest and the brightest values, while taking into account the importance of shadow and highlight information within the image. If a subject is exposed too far into either extreme, the limitations of the sensor will become more obvious. If the values fall too close to 0 (absolute black), there will not be an image at all, or the image will appear very dark and noisy. If the values fall too close to 255 (absolute white), the pixels will appear oversaturated with no image information or detail. The best exposure strategy for digital capture, therefore, is to keep highlights from reaching the maximum output value of the sensor, except for specular highlights that do not detract from the image if they are blown out.

Once you have captured an image in the field, bring up the histogram on the back of the camera. The histogram data should indicate how the image data falls within the dynamic range of the camera at the time of exposure. Using that information, the photographer can evaluate what is important in the image, like highlight or shadow information and which takes precedence and re-expose the image based on creative interpretation of the data. You will have to consult your camera manual to find out how to turn this valuable camera feature on. Some cameras just have one histogram which is all three channels combined and averaged (Red, Green and Blue). Other more advanced cameras will show you the histogram for each color channel separately so that you can monitor each channel individually.

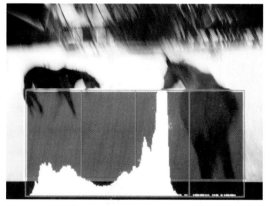

Histogram with all three channels combined and averaged (Red, Green and Blue)

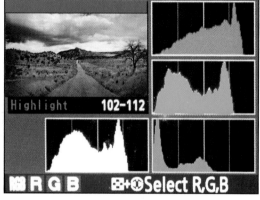

Histogram displaying each color channel separately so that you can monitor each channel individually

Reading and Interpreting Histogram Data

Clipping

Isolated lines or spikes or a pile at either edge of the data box is an indication of clipping or data loss within an image. Clipping indicates that improper exposure or image manipulation in the digital darkroom has caused some parts of the image to move beyond the maximum brightness level within the dynamic range of capture. Such a histogram shows that image data has been recorded as pure black or pure white without image detail, meaning that the image is becoming "blown out" as if it were over or underexposed.

Important Note:
Whether the exposure translates to a "good" or "bad" exposure actually depends on the image itself. If the corresponding image is of a black cat, the histogram data indicating clipped shadows would translate to a poor exposure because all detail in the shadows has been lost. However, if this same clipped shadow histogram represented an image that necessitated preservation of all highlight information, and where shadow detail was not as relevant, this same histogram would then indicate a good exposure for the corresponding image.

Clipped Shadows

The histogram below indicates clipped shadow information, or lost detail in the shadows of the image. Notice the slam of data on the left wall of the histogram, indicating that the data exceeds the dynamic range of the camera in the shadow values. Highlight information is preserved, as we can see the data clearly ends before the histogram wall on the right.

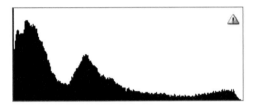

Clipped Highlights

The histogram below indicates clipped highlight information, or loss of detail in the highlight values. Notice the slam of data on the right side of the histogram. Shadow information is preserved, as we can see the data clearly ends before the histogram wall on the left side.

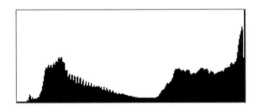

Whether this is "good" or "bad" exposure depends again on the corresponding image. If the histogram represented an image of a white flower, then this would be poor exposure because the detail in the highlights is lost. However, if this same histogram represented an image where highlight detail is not as important as preserving the shadow information, then this would indicate a good exposure for the corresponding image.

Clear as mud right? Do not worry if you are not seeing it all quite yet. Understanding histogram information and how to read and interpret the data for image capture requires looking at lots of images and their corresponding histograms in order to properly read and interpret the information they provide.

Clipped Highlights and Clipped Shadows

The following histogram indicates both clipped shadows and clipped highlights within the same image. The isolated spikes on the right and left indicate loss of both shadow and highlight detail.

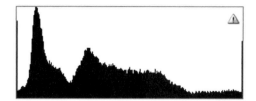

This would indicate a great exposure for a "blown out arty" fashion magazine shot, while simultaneously indicating a poor exposure for an image hoping to gain full tonal range in a print. In viewing a histogram such as this, evaluate whether highlight or shadow information should take precedence and re-expose for that information.

Preserved Shadow and Highlight Information

The histogram below would indicate an image exposed with full tonal range. Highlight and shadow information are preserved without clipping, as the data clearly ends before the walls of the histogram on either side.

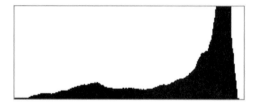

Contrast

The width of the data spread within a histogram reflects how much contrast the image contains. Narrow histograms indicate less contrast with a limited range of tones while wider histograms indicate greater contrast or a wider range of tones from light to dark.

High Contrast

The histogram below indicates high contrast within the corresponding image. Full tonal range is being utilized, without loss of detail in either shadow nor highlight information.

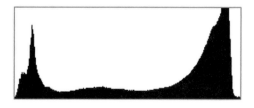

Note:
It is really important, however, not to get too overly obsessive about the histogram in a technical sense. The truth is a perfect histogram does not always equate to a good image and a bad histogram does not always dictate failure. Use the information to make creative decisions in the field, and experiment with how far you can push the extremes, and still create successful images.

Low Contrast

The following histogram indicates a low contrast image. The full tonal range is not being utilized. The corresponding image will therefore appear flat with little contrast, as the information is weighted heavily by mid-tone values. Good or bad? Answer: depends on the image.

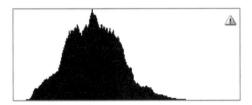

Histograms and images

Now that all those technical descriptions make perfect sense, let us look at some images to associate with the histograms and hopefully make better sense of it all. Because each and every image is different, histograms are inherently unique for every image as well. As the histogram maps the tonal values within an image, the instant the shutter is snapped you can immediately evaluate where shadow and highlight information begin, what sort of tonal range exists, and make important decisions in the field accordingly. Remember, there are no right or wrong histograms; as where data should fall will vary depending on the tones, content and the mood of an image. Here is how:

Example 1. Well Exposed for Corresponding Scene

One can determine and evaluate many things about an image capture in the field from the histogram data. The image below displays a "good" histogram for the corresponding scene in that both the shadows and the highlights are fully contained within the parameters of the histogram chart from right to left. There are no spikes at either end of the chart, and the data clearly ends before the edge of the histogram chart for both the highlight and shadow information. This image spreads the tonal scale with image data ranging from

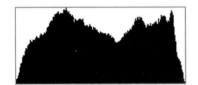

Well exposed for desired representation of the corresponding image

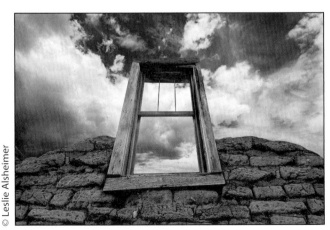

© Leslie Alsheimer

white to black and virtually every brightness value in between. All of the light and dark levels of the scene have fallen within the dynamic range recordable by the image sensor.

Example 2. Overexposed

If however, the image as seen on previous page is the scene you desire, but you see a histogram such as the one on the right. This histogram would indicate that the shot has been overexposed, and highlights are blown out, as the data slams into the right side of the chart. The scene of the window in the sky needs its highlights well exposed for detail in the clouds. Therefore, this histogram would indicate that exposure should be decreased via a faster shutter speed, narrower aperture, or lower ISO setting, and re-exposed, until the highlights (the data to the right) comes back into the chart, and is fully contained within the histogram chart, as seen in the previous histogram example on the previous page.

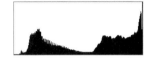

Overexposed image data for corresponding image on previous page

Example 3. Extreme Lighting Conditions

The image of the movie scene below is a difficult lighting situation. To expose to preserve both highlight and shadow information in such extreme lighting conditions would be impossible, as the brightness of light and the dim room light exceed the dynamic range of the cameras sensor. The corresponding

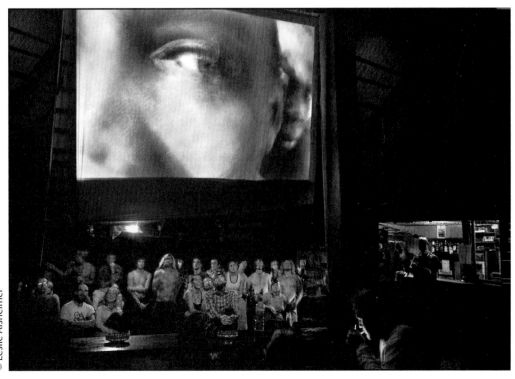

© Leslie Alsheimer

histogram displayed for this scene indicates loss of detail in both the highlight and the shadow information. There is enough detail in the overall scene however to make the image visually "work" despite extreme loss of detail at both ends of the scale. The histogram for this scene therefore actually indicates a relatively good exposure for these conditions and overall mood of the image.

Example 4. Extreme Lighting Conditions 2

This is another example of extreme lighting conditions exposed with lost information in both the highlights and shadows. Although another scene may fall apart with such a horrendous exposure, the mood and lighting effects in this scene make the exposure work well for the image overall.

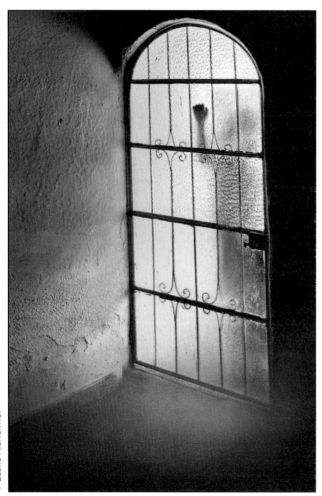

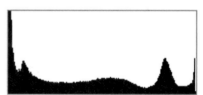

© Leslie Alsheimer

Example 5. Shadow Preference
Exposure for this barbershop scene requires some preferential treatment for the shadow information.

Notice the lost highlight detail indicated by the slam of information to the right of the histogram (Fig. 1). This lost information in the bright sky outside the shop and the florescent tube light over the mirror is not as critical as the detail inside the shop. An exposure weighting the shadow information in this case will ultimately produce a better overall print.

If the initial exposure for the same scene presented a histogram such as this see Fig. 2, the resulting image would be far too

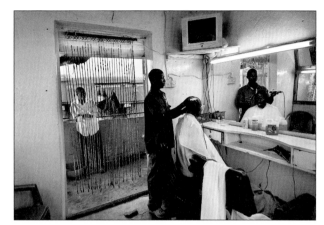

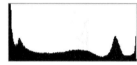

FIG 2

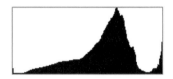

FIG 1

underexposed as pictured to the upper right with excessive loss in the shadow information.

Reading the histogram accurately in the field, directs us to readjust exposure and reshoot until we produce an exposure

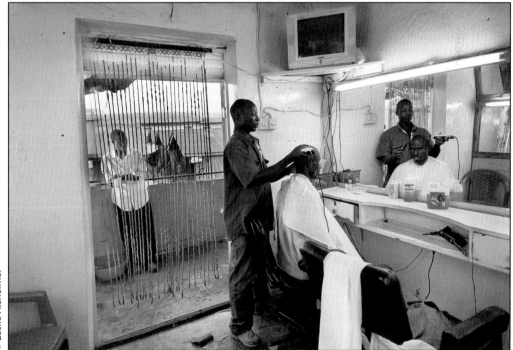

© Leslie Alsheimer

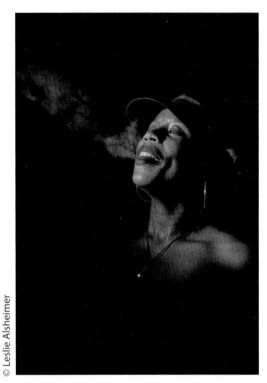

that maintains good shadow detail, such as the histogram illustrated in Fig. 1.

Example 6. Low Key Images Exposed with Highlight Preference

These two images images are both excellent examples of a low key image, whereby almost all of the data in the images falls within the darkest values of the data chart. Both images maintain a small amount of information towards the highlight values preserving the light and detail on the womens' faces. The corresponding histogram for both exposures indicate major loss in shadow information as illustrated by the slam of data to the left side of the histogram indicating much information falls to black. As no image detail extends beyond the right side of the scale, the

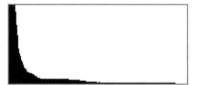

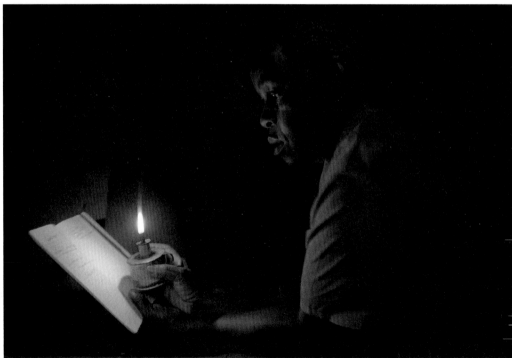

exposure captures all the important details contained in highlight information in this scene.

Example 7. High Key Image with Highlight Preference
The image of the white dress is an excellent example of a "high key" image, where almost every value of data is plotted toward the right side of the histogram. This histogram tells us many things about the exposure for this image. Most importantly, we can see immediately that highlight information has been preserved in the exposure, as the stack of data does not exceed the right side of the histogram chart. There is a long thin trace of information across the bottom to the left side, indicating that there are few pixels with darker brightness values. The information does not slam to the left, indicating that we have maintained the shadow detail (although there is very little) without clipping.

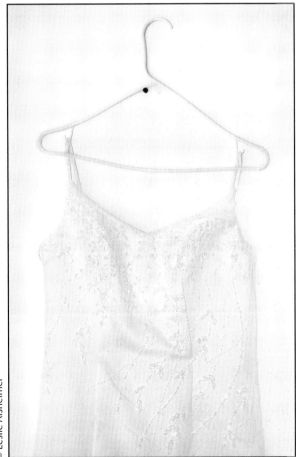

© Leslie Alsheimer

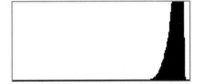

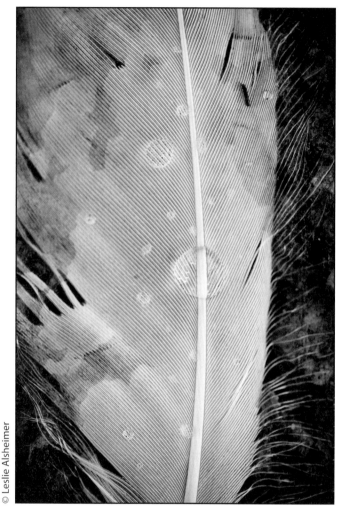

© Leslie Alsheimer

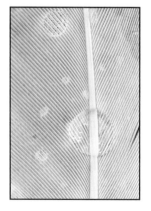

Exposed to preserve highlight detail.

Example 8. Preserved Highlight and Shadow Information
The feather image above illustrates a scene where the best exposure is achieved by maintaining both shadow and highlight information and detail.

Notice the histogram data above for preserved highlight detail. There is not a slam of information, as the data cleanly ends before either end of the chart. This image captures and preserves both highlight and shadow information.

In determining exposure for this image, it is best to keep the highlights close to the clipping point; the closer the highlights are to clipping, the less sensor noise will be visible in the image. Ideal exposure with a digital camera (capturing the greatest possible dynamic range with the lowest possible level of noise and other undesirable digital artifacts at a given ISO setting) is always to bring the Raw data as close as possible without reaching the clipping point for non-specular highlights.

Example 9. Over Exposed

If the same feather image on the previous page were overexposed, the corresponding histogram would indicate the blown out highlight information with a slam on the right edge of this histogram as pictured to the right. As the highlight information is more valuable in this feather image, it would be best to decrease exposure via a faster shutter speed, narrower aperture, or lower ISO setting, and re-expose.

In contrast, the exposure for the image below of the bird and woman has a histogram looking almost identical to the previous overexposed feather image however, this image was exposed for the subject, allowing much of

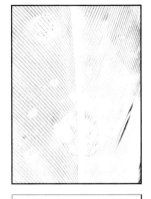

Overexposure

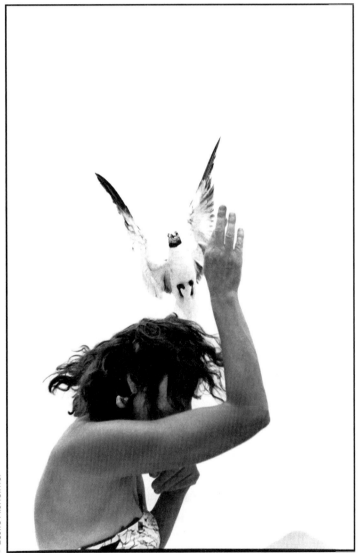

© Leslie Alsheimer

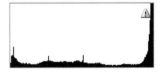

the background to fall off. The slam to the right indicates lost detail in the sky, suggesting that it is important to allow creative interpretation along with technical information to play a role in the elusive exposure decision-making process.

Example 10. Highlight Preference

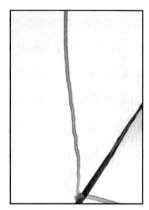

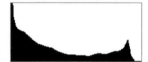

Preserved highlights

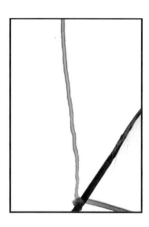

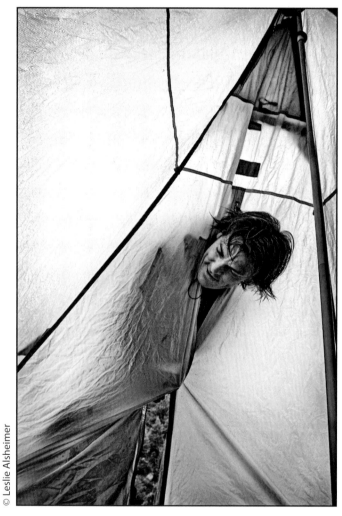

© Leslie Alsheimer

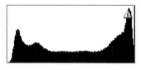

Over exposed highlights

This image and exposure histogram indicate preserved highlight information with some data loss in the shadow information. As the detail in the highlights would be my main concern with this image, I will watch the data on the right with more scrutiny.

If the image were not exposed to preserve the highlight information and over exposed, as the histogram to the left indicates, we would see a slam of information on the right side of the chart.

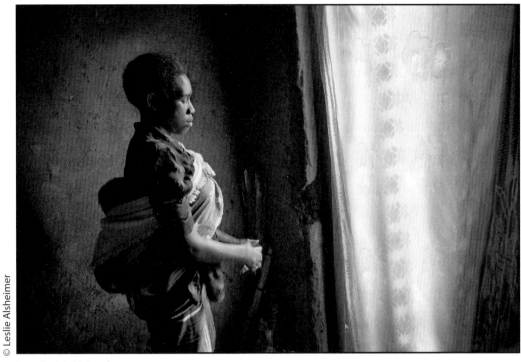

© Leslie Alsheimer

Exposed with highlight preference

Once again, if we notice a histogram indicating loss of highlight information with an image such as the tent or the woman by the window above, we would want to reshoot stopping down or speeding up the shutter speed to achieve an exposure that maintains highlight information.

Summary of histograms and exposure evaluation

Although it is important to learn to read histograms, it is also important not to get too overly obsessive about the histogram. The truth is that a good histogram still does not always equate to a good image and a bad histogram does not always dictate failure. Sometimes, loss of detail works, sometimes it does not. Knowing in the field when you have exposed well for the important information as creatively interpreted for a given scene, and when you need to reshoot is the most valuable advantage digital capture has to offer the photographer.

When shooting Raw, it is important to know that there is a difference between the clipping point indicated by the camera histogram and the clipping point of the corresponding Raw data. This disparity occurs because the camera histogram is created from the in-camera JPEG conversion of the original Raw data. In-camera JPEG conversions typically discard 1–2 stops of the sensor's dynamic range, (another reason to shoot Raw), which means that there is usually about a stop of extra leeway in the highlights information to play with in Raw capture data. The exposure intervals between the clip points indicated by the camera histogram and the actual Raw data, however, will vary from camera to camera.

Once you understand exactly what information the histogram can provide for you, determining the desired exposure in the field becomes relatively simple. For standard exposure techniques bias your exposures so that the histogram data is pushed up to the right side of the chart, while making sure that the highlights are not blown out. The ultimate indication of best exposure is the histogram coupled with artistic interpretation! Learn to read them and you can nail desired exposures in any situation! Depending on the subject reflectance and the camera meter's characteristics, the ideal exposure could actually be more than a stop below or above what the meter reads. We recommend using the camera meter as a guide to get initial exposure settings, and then fine-tune the camera exposure settings based on the histogram data.

VI. Exposure Evaluation: Monitor Highlights Utilizing the Blinking Highlight Indicator

Another very useful feature with digital capture is the camera's LCD blinking highlights display indicator which displays the blown out highlights within an image. This indicator illustrates blown out highlights by blinking the corresponding image components on the camera LCD image display

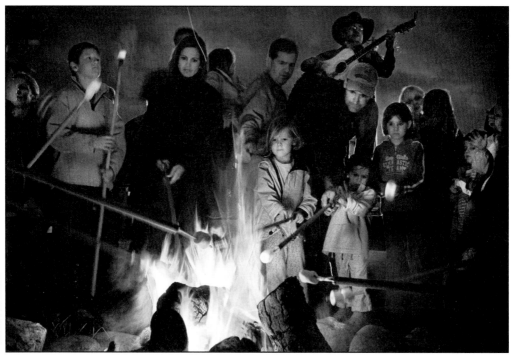

© Leslie Alsheimer

immediately after capture. Between the histograms and the blinking highlight indicator, we now have more information about our exposure than we ever had with film!

When activated in the camera menu, this indicator can be extremely valuable in displaying exactly where we are losing information in the highlights of the image when they do blow out with undesired exposure mistakes. Utilizing such important feedback, we can then make important decisions in the field about the importance of the lost highlight information in relationship to the shadow information and desired interpretation, and re-expose if necessary.

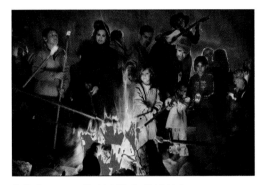

Red indicates areas of lost detail in the highlighted areas

VII. Histograms in the Digital Darkroom

Monitoring Image Detail with Image Adjustments for Highest Quality Editing Practice

Maintaining image detail throughout the editing process is absolutely integral for a high-quality print. Once you are sure that you have exposed for the highest quality capture in camera by evaluating histograms in the field, careful attention must be applied throughout the editing process ensuring your image adjustments are not desecrating the quality of the image data. Since we already know how to read a histogram, we can use the information they provide to monitor image data during each major adjustment and conversion in Photoshop. We can also determine whether image corrections have been too dramatic, possibly leading to clipping, loss of digital data including highlight and shadow detail, as well as posterization (see definitions below). As with any and all major editing within the digital darkroom, it is essential to monitor the histogram during each major adjustment and conversion. Once again, and it is worth repeating, always start with high bit capture for the highest quality especially if you know you are going to have a heavy hand in image editing. (See "JPEG vs. Raw Capture", page 30.)

VIII. Digital Darkroom Editing Dangers

Posterization a.k.a. Banding

Posterization is a tonal separation that occurs when an image has been edited or manipulated to extremes or if the bit depth of an image has been decreased so much that it has a visual impact on the image quality. Posterization is the loss of tones within an image which results in abrupt transitions between tones that appear as stripes or "banding" in areas which should have smooth gradations between tones. Typically extremely visible in skies, posterization

POSTERIZATION

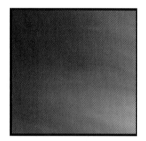

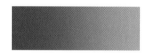

Posterization occurs when a drastic contrast or color correction is made

Posterization is the loss of tones which result in transitions that are abrubt

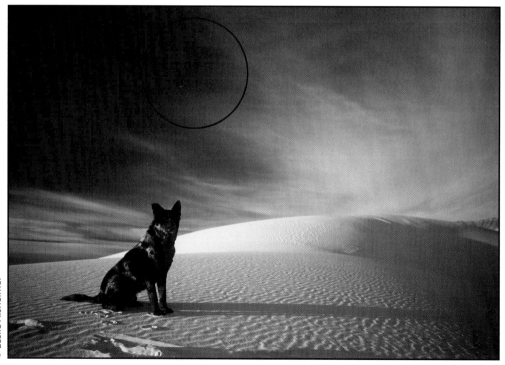

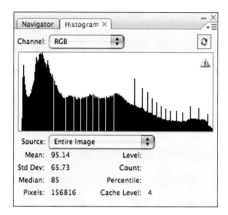

After an image is edited, it is natural to see some gaps and spikes. It will depend on the image and the amount if the loss of information will be discernable in the print.

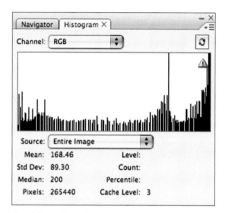

Yikes! A bit too far on the manipulation. Loss of digital information and posterization.

would cause the otherwise smooth transition in tonality from light to deeper shades of blue to print with various blue stripes as the tones deepened.

The term "posterization" is used because the effect looks similar to how the colors look in a mass-produced poster where the print process uses a limited number of color inks. This effect ranges from subtle to extreme, and whether this is discernible in the print depends on the level and location of the posterization within an image.

Any process which "stretches" the image data and histogram has the potential to cause posterization. Stretching can be caused by image editing techniques such as levels and curves in Photoshop, or even by converting an 8-bit image into Grayscale. The best way to avoid posterization is to work with high bit files, and monitor the histogram throughout the editing process, keeping image manipulation within quality controlled limits. Above are histogram examples in a side by side comparison that show results from common digital darkroom manipulation as compared to potentially problematic edited data.

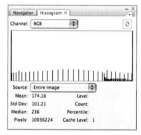

Posterization a.k.a. stair stepping or banding is an indication of extreme loss of many brightness and tonal values within an image.

Cache Warning

Inside the Histogram palette, a small triangle with an exclamation point inside appears as an indication that the histogram has not yet been accurately rendered by the software. The histogram is created from the image cache, which is a scaled down 8-bit version of the image file. Photoshop uses cached images in order to update the histogram dynamically as you make adjustments to the image. To create a more accurate Histogram, click on the exclamation symbol and Photoshop will refresh the histogram and display a fully rendered histogram.

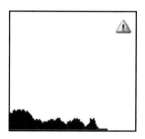

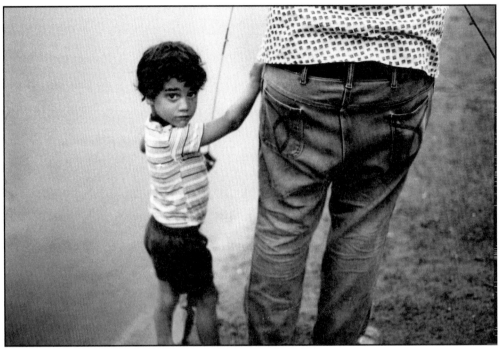

© Leslie Alsheimer

© Leslie Alsheimer

IX. Noise and Interference in Digital Capture

AKA grain in the film world

In order to optimize image data for the highest quality digital capture, monitoring and controlling the desired effects of noise produced is another important component of the capture workflow. Digital noise is created by randomly scattered pixels across a digital image. The effect is similar to the grain we traditionally see in film photography. Noise is usually most visible in images captured in very low light, and with slow shutter speeds or higher ISO sensitivity modes. It also appears in areas that are underexposed.

The images on the this page were captured in low light situations with 400 ISO film pushed to 800 and 1600. The grainy structure of the images illustrate a quality of film that often added to the mood and feel of a print.

The image of the boys running was digitally captured at 1/10 of a second with an ISO setting

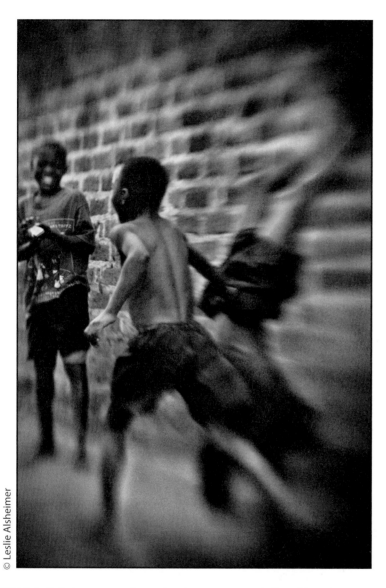

© Leslie Alsheimer

of 400. With digital capture, noise and grain appear very similar, although shadow areas tend to have a more blotchy look with digital noise. Noise in color images tends to have a more magenta-green look. (See image following page.)

The digital camera's sensor measures light for each pixel and creates a matrix of pixels that represent the image. The sensor itself carries a certain amount of noise inherently; however, in most lighting conditions, the light is significantly stronger than the inherent camera noise. In more extreme conditions where the light is low, or when a higher ISO setting is needed, the noise levels typically increase and produce more abrupt and jagged pixels with a christmas-colored pattern

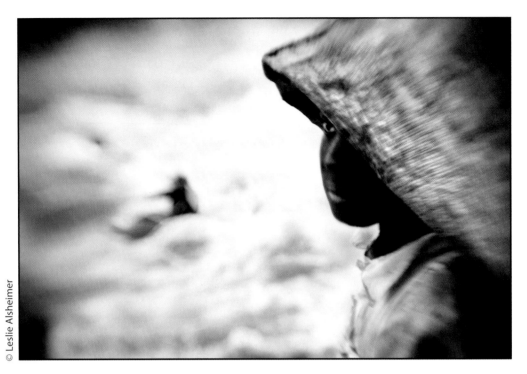

© Leslie Alsheimer

of red and green. This occurs because there is more noise data than light data available to the sensor.

Types of Noise:

Luminance Noise: This type of noise will make an image look grainy on screen, but will not necessarily have much of an impact when printed, unless it is incredibly severe. Luminance noise is much like the "snow" on your television after most stations stop broadcasting. The causes of luminance noise are typically due to static and other forms of interference and imperfections of the camera.

Blue Channel Noise or Chroma Noise: This type of noise will appear as blue and red dots in an image and is especially visible in images captured in low light with a high ISO setting. If there is not enough light for a proper exposure, the longer we allow the image sensor to collect the weaker light signals, the more background electrical noise it will collect. Similarly, when we use a higher ISO setting, we are also amplifying the signal we receive from the light photons. Unfortunately, as we amplify the signal, we also amplify the background electrical noise. The prevalence of noise is especially prominent at ISO ratings of 800 or higher. It is called "Blue Channel Noise" because more noise will appear in the blue channel of an image than in the other two channels. This type of noise is most like the grain structure of a high ISO-rated film.

Thermal Noise: Higher temperatures also have an affect of increasing blue channel noise. The hotter the sensor becomes, the more noise will appear. Heat can free electrons from the image sensor and contaminate the photoelectrons

60

present. These "thermal electrons" generate a form of noise called thermal noise. More noise can actually appear at the end of a shooting session than at the beginning as the sensor heats up the longer it is in use.

JPEG Artifacts: When an image is captured as a JPEG in camera, the JPEG format compresses the image to reduce its size so that you can get more images on your card. This compression, however, typically introduces a chunky pattern to the edges and flat aspects of an image. The higher the compression ratio, the greater the damage will be to the image. All the more reason to capture in Raw format!

Noise Controlling Factors:
Knowing how noise is produced can help you make important decisions in the field controlling some of the unwanted effects of digital noise.

- Low light capture.
- High ISO settings: The higher the ISO setting, the greater the noise produced. This is the exact equivalent to the differences between higher ISO films which produced increased grain.
- Underexposure can greatly increase noise. Watch your histograms in the field!
- Slow shutter speeds: When the shutter is kept open for a long time, more noise will be introduced to the image data.
- Sensor size and resolution: Larger digital camera sensors generally have less because each pixel can also be larger and each photosite can be a bit further away from its neighbor. This extra distance is often enough to prevent signal leakage from one photosite onto another whereby creating much less noise! Smaller sensors with a higher mega pixel count unfortunately also equate to more noise in the resulting image data.
- Physical size of the pixels on the sensor: Bigger pixels in general translate to less noise in resulting image data.
- Temperature of the sensor: Higher temperatures generate more noise on the sensor.
- In-camera processing of the signal: Camera manufacturer's processing software can effect the appearance of noise in an image.

While it is impossible to completely prevent digital noise from happening, there are a few options that allow you to decrease it significantly.

In low light scenes, ISO ratings and shutter speed are the two main variables to pay attention to. Increasing the ISO creates more internal noise, and slowing down the shutter allows for more noise to integrate onto the CCD. The amount of noise each action generates is different for each camera make and model. Experiment by setting your camera to manual mode and play with different shutter speed and ISO combinations to find which generates the least amount of noise for a given situation.

Some camera manufacturers include a built-in feature called "noise reduction" which generates and applies specific algorithms when a slow shutter speed and/or high ISO setting is used to reduce the amount of noise produced in the process. Although these algorithms cannot completely remove all noise altogether, substantial reduction can occur depending on the quality of the algorithm. The noise is typically removed by an interpolation method that creates a replacement pixel based on an evaluation of its neighboring pixels. This, however, typically produces a smoothing effect which comes at the expense of losing fine image detail.

For most photographers, digital noise can be significantly reduced by turning on your camera's noise reduction feature, optimizing the camera settings and removing noise with some simple noise reduction techniques. Be warned, however, many noise reduction techniques can have the effect of blurring or flattening the image. There is trade off between losing image detail and decreasing the effects of noise within an image. Keep in mind if you have ever shot a high ISO film, the grain often times offered the image a wonderful quality that many try to emulate digitally. Grain can be beautiful, and so too can noise if the image permits. (See "Reducing Noise with Photoshop CS3", page 172.)

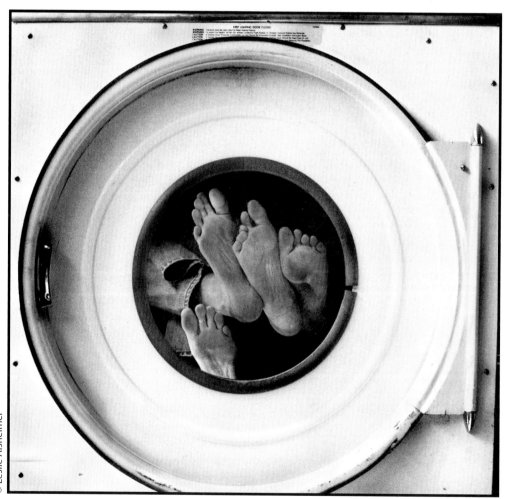

© Leslie Alsheimer

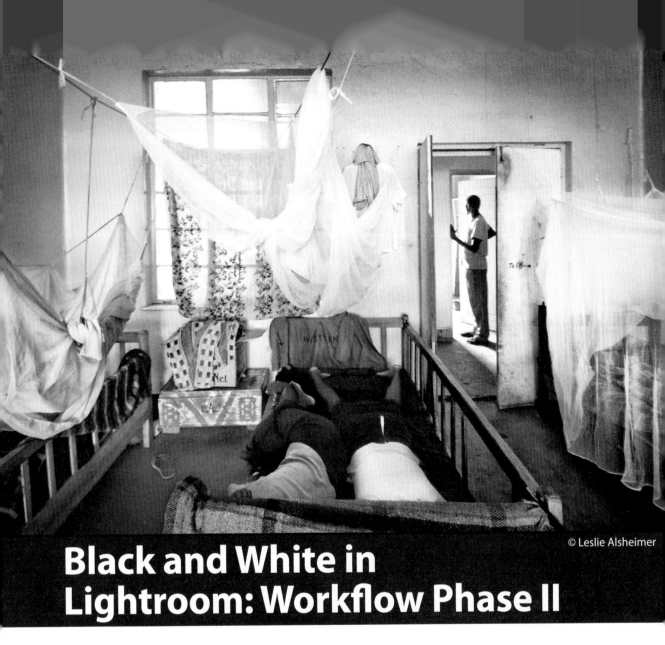

© Leslie Alsheimer

Black and White in Lightroom: Workflow Phase II

Integrating Workflow Practices

One of the most frequent requests I get from my beginner and advanced workshop students alike is for step-by-step tutorials detailing the digital workflow process – from capture to print – through Photoshop, Bridge and Lightroom. The disappointing truth for many of my students to learn is that with so many possible steps from start to finish, and so many different ways to handle images, there really is no single "right" way to manage workflow. There are as many different successful methodologies as there are industry experts and practioners to champion them. For the purposes of this text however, I have created an integrated hybrid workflow –

from capture to print – outlining a methodology I have found successful in practice. Follow these workflow guidelines as a roadmap, appropriate what works for you and discard what does not. Our hope is that once you jump in, you will find the confidence and creativity to experiment and play with techniques you never dreamed possible!

Workflow is dynamic: Go with the flow!

Workflow is not only user defined, but also an incredibly dynamic process. The images themselves should ultimately dictate the editing workflow and guide you in the process of image production. Images are uniquely created, and therefore every image will not require the exact same set of approaches and tools. As a kayak paddler, I have spent a great deal of time on rivers, and the concept of a dynamic workflow is much like the river experience. As rivers ebb and flow, there are rapids, eddies, rocks, holes and obstacles. There is a time to float, a time to eddy out, a time to paddle hard and a time to tuck and roll. One must first learn the skills of the river, and only through experience will one gain the wisdom to know when and how to use those skills in action – and still, even the experienced paddler will sometimes hit rocks. Similarly, workflow is an active process requiring learned skills to do what you want to do creatively, as well as the experience to know what skills to apply to image processing and when to use them. When paddling a river, the flow of

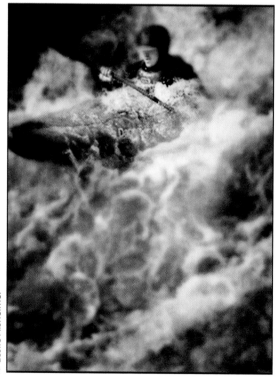

© Leslie Alsheimer

the water guides you just as the images themselves should guide you in the digital workflow process. Use this integrated workflow as a guide to get you started. Try new things, experiment with different methods, and save multiple versions of an image while you play and have fun. Remember the words of Scott Adams who said, "Creativity is allowing yourself to make mistakes; art is knowing which ones to keep." And, of course, go with the flow!

Lightroom Unleashed: The Editing Accelerator

Whether you are new to the digital domain or have significant experience, the release of Adobe Photoshop CS3 and Lightroom has truly revolutionized the digital workflow, making the process faster, more intuitive and user-friendly than ever before! As a powerful new accelerator for the editing process, Lightroom has already become an indispensable component of the integrated workflow and proves its value in the streamlined interface it offers to both the professional and recreational user. The interface in Lightroom lays out the global editing workflow structure in an intuitive and logical manner, allowing you to process and edit images in a non-destructive, straightforward manner with exceptional speed and control. Adobe Photoshop still plays a powerful role in the integrated system, especially for detail and selective adjustment editing once a file has been processed in Lightroom, Phase 4 of this Workflow. The addition of Lightroom to the workflow does not replace this powerful software tool; Lightroom simply adds speed and ease to the system.

History

The coupling of Camera Raw, and what was then known as the File Browser in Photoshop 7.0.1, provided the first hints of an abbreviated, subtractive workflow for photographers. As the proliferation of digital cameras grew at an amazing rate, more and more people were using a somewhat limited feature set in Photoshop to satisfy their basic photographic needs. It was soon apparent that a tailor-made, end-to-end workflow tool was just what professional digital photographers needed. In 2006, Adobe made a very unusual move and released just this tool, Lightroom, in the form of a free, downloadable public beta.

Throughout the course of multiple beta updates, the Lightroom team added more features, functionality and polish than anyone expected. By the time that Adobe Photoshop Lightroom 1.0 hit the shelves, it had, indeed, become a full-featured, workflow tool for photographers.

A Stepped Approach through Lightroom

Respecting that Lightroom is new to so many people, we want to take you through an easy, stepped approach from end to end, highlighting many notable features within the software interface. Although workflows do vary, our prescribed approach is easy to follow and remember, as it steps through the tools and controls in the same order that Lightroom presents them.

While you will perhaps notice that Camera Raw and Lightroom's Develop module share the same features (See Chapter 4, "Black and White in Adobe Camera Raw 4.0", page 127), there are many differences when it comes to how these settings are presented, applied to the image, shared with other images, retained and displayed. The feature parity that the two applications share is particularly convenient when it comes to consistency across platforms as with opening a previously adjusted Camera Raw file in Lightroom (or vice versa).

Module Overview

Library: For the import, conversion (Lightroom can render DNG files on the fly), flagging, sorting, ranking, key wording and organizing of thousands and thousands of files.

Develop: For the many facets of image adjustment, much like Camera Raw, Lightroom applies non-destructive edits to JPEGs, TIFFs, DNGs and proprietary Raw files.

Slideshow: For professional quality PDF presentations. This module offers controls for nearly every variable for a visual presentation including the incorporation of MP3 files with the slideshow.

Print: For easy, and yet very powerful, control of print output. Lightroom, true to its nature, presents printing in familiar terms and a friendly interface, while still delivering professional results.

Web: For the creation, customizability and even upload (Lightroom supports direct FTP) of imagery to the Web. Lightroom offers a dizzying array of Flash and HTML templates which can easily be custom tailored to the user's specific needs.

For the sake of this text, we address Lightroom in the modules most pertinent to black and white processes, the Library Module, Develop Module and on Printing from Lightroom.

Lightroom Library Module: Overview of View Modes

1. Grid View

The Grid View in the Library module serves as a basic image browser. Use this interface to navigate files and folders, create "Quick Collections", or image groupings, and sort images.

2. Loupe View

The Loupe View in the Library module displays a single large image in the preview window. A single click on the image will instantly zoom the preview window to 100%. You can also modify the enlargement factor with the zoom slider in the tool bar. The Loupe View is fabulous for quickly evaluating image sharpness. You can enter the Loupe View in both the Library Module and the Develop Module just by clicking on the image.

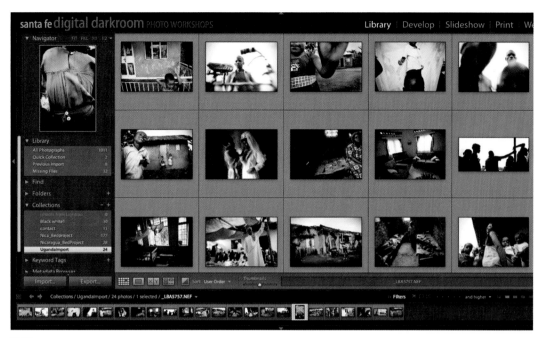

Grid View

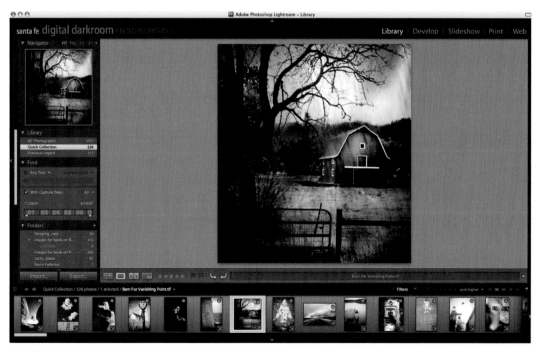

Loupe View

3. Survey View

The Survey View in the Library module allows you to compare any number of images side by side in the Library module. This is a great way to compare the overall composition of images shot in a series. First select the images you wish to survey and then click on the survey icon or go to View > Survey.

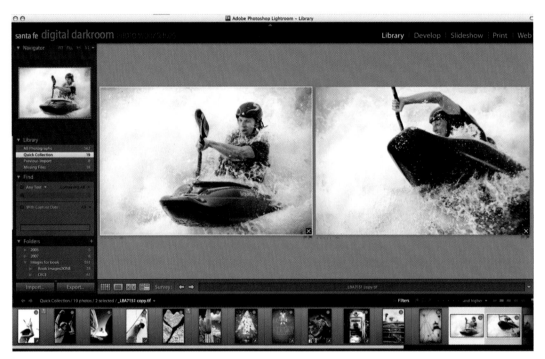

Survey View

4. Compare View

The Compare View allows you to quickly sort through a sequence of similar images to find the sharpest and best composition and rank the images accordingly. I usually move images into the Compare View after I have made an initial edit. The Compare View places one image as a selected image and the other as the candidate. You can zoom into both images simultaneously, to the exact same location or separate locations on each image. The lock feature icon will keep them together when locked and allow separate view zooms when unlocked.

You can use the arrow keys to scroll through the candidate images, the swap icon to exchange the candidate image with the select image, and the select icon to designate the candidate image as the select image. When you are finished comparing images, click the "Done" button to exit the Compare View.

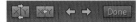

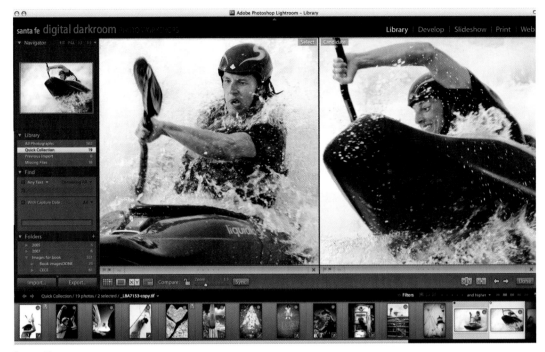

Compare View

I. Import: Includes Download, Backup, Rename, Keyword, and Copyright

There are many ways of downloading images to your computer. Lightroom innovations have streamlined the downloading process and integrated many practical features into one simple and amazing dialog box. The "Import Photos" box in Lightroom now allows us the benefit of file renaming, key wording, backing up, inserting copyright and metadata in a single dialog box interface.

Step 1: Launch Lightroom and Set Preference

Lightroom can automatically launch the "Import Photos" dialog when you attach your camera or plug in your card reader and insert a memory card. To enable this automatic feature, however, you need to set the preference for it in Lightroom. Open the preferences panel: Lightroom > Preferences. Then go to "File Management" and click the drop down menu next to "When a memory card is detected" to "Show Import Dialog". Since it is a good idea to rename camera file folders, you might also want to check the "Ignore camera generated folder names when naming folders" box as well.

69

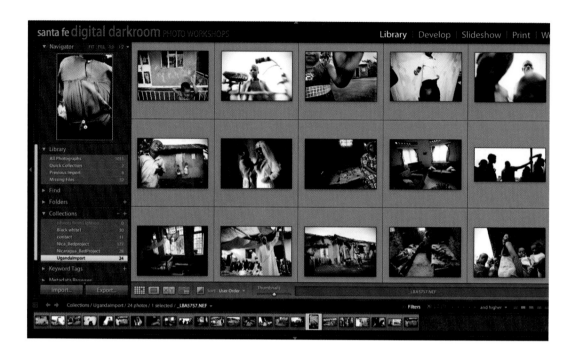

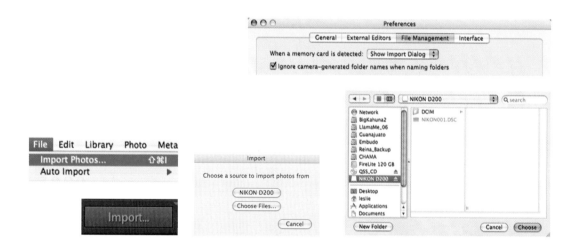

Step 2: Connect Digital Media

Place your media card into the card reader or attach your camera with its supplied cables. Lightroom will automatically recognize the input image data and launch the "Import Photos" window for you. If, for some reason, the import window does not appear, the "Import Photos" dialog box can also be accessed by choosing the File Menu > Import Photos, or by simply clicking the "Import" button at the lower left corner of the Lightroom interface, and choose either your card or device.

Step 3: File Handling
Next, the "Import Photos" dialog box will appear. It is always best to work top down within dialog boxes, so we will start with the first drop down menu at the top of the "Import Photos" box, "File Handling". This drop down offers a few choices to import your images into Lightroom. The first choice is to import images from their current location. This would be an excellent choice if you had already copied the image files onto the computer or an external drive. However, since we are starting from scratch and want to copy the image files to the hard drive first, I am going to bypass this choice. The next choices are to "copy or move the photos to a new location and import", or to "convert to DNG and import". As an advocate of the DNG methodology for Raw image storage, this workflow protocol highly recommends the "convert to DNG" option for import.

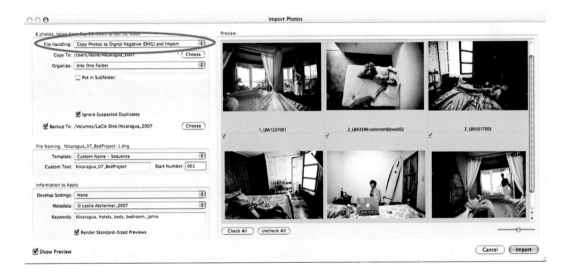

The name of the folder you choose will automatically be used as the import name in Lightroom. You can create a new folder in Lightroom with a specific name either before or after you import by clicking the plus icon next to the "Folders" list on the left interface panel in Lightroom.

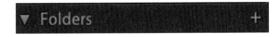

Step 4: Copy To
The next step, moving down the Import dialogue box interface, will be to choose the destination for the images to be copied. Navigate to your hard drive or external drive and create a new folder to copy the images into. It is good practice to create a logical naming system that works for you. I typically name by location first and by date secondary, as this is how I can best remember and retrieve my images. When finished, click "Choose".

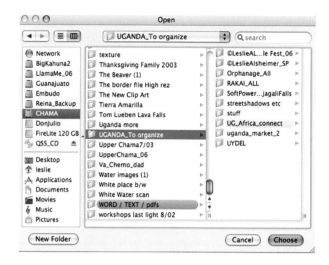

Step 5: Organize

Next, you will choose how you would like Lightroom to "Organize" the images. You can do so by date in several ways, by original folders or into one folder. If you have multiple sub-folders of images, you can choose exactly which images to import and which to exclude, or you can combine all the images into one single folder for the shoot. I usually choose to organize into one folder because I like to see all the images from a shoot in a single unified location.

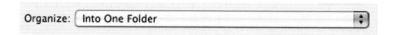

Step 6: Create Backup

Lightroom can also search for duplicate images during the import process, which can be helpful in keeping the cache from getting larger than it needs to be. However, I usually check to "Ignore Suspected Duplicates" just in case I may have different files with the same name. Next, check the "Backup To" check box and click "Choose" to navigate to an alternate storage device and create a folder for placement.

Backing up images onto multiple hard drives and/or CDs and DVDs is an absolutely essential practice within the workflow process. Best practice would be to always have the images in three locations at all times. Typically it is a good idea to have at least one copy in a different location than the rest, just in case of fire or other disaster. It really is not a matter of "if" a hard drive crash or other image disaster will happen to you, but more a question of "when" it will happen to you. Therefore, the best practice is to err on the side of caution and always be prepared.

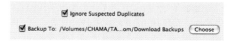

Step 7: File Naming

I do not know who can make sense of the camera automatic file numbering systems with digital capture images. With so many digital images over the years I cannot remember which image corresponds with which number, so I rename my images according to shooting location and date. Multiple files from a particular shoot can be renamed quickly and easily into a system that makes sense to you with the file naming feature in Lightroom. We can now rename all our files with one simple batch command as we import the images into Lightroom. Move down the Import Photos Box to the "File Naming" portion and click on the drop down menu next to "Template". There are many naming convention options to choose from here, I prefer "Custom Name – Sequence" and choose "Edit" so that I can type in specific information according to the shoot.

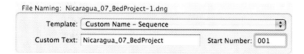

Create a name that you wish to give the files you are about to import. It is a good idea to use naming conventions that keep files universally compatible across operating systems; that is, try not to make the names too long, and use underscores – not spaces – to separate words.

Next I choose to insert a sequence number and I usually choose three digits to allow for lots of images in a single folder. My titling system includes the location and the date in non-numeric form so I do not end up with more of a number mess than I started with. Example: Custom text: Uganda07_SoftPower_001. Lightroom will show you an example of your choice at the top of the box so that you can make sure you are doing what you had intended.

Step 8: Information to Apply

Next choose a preset for developing the images as either Antique Grayscale, Cyanotype, Direct Positive, Grayscale conversion, Sepia Tone, Tone Curve, or Zero'd. I typically choose Zero'd to remove any additional data added to my Raw files. You may, however, find a reason for any number of the other choices at different times. Remember as Lightroom is non-destructive, anything you choose to do can easily be undone as no data is applied directly to your files!

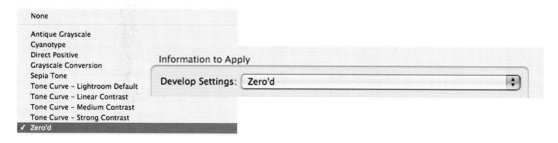

Continuing downwards in the dialog box, we come to the metadata and keywords insertion area. These fields work together and allow an amazing degree of control for customizing and inserting metadata during the import process.

Step 9: Embed Copyright Info with Metadata Template
Metadata is information embedded into the image file that describes the image in any number of ways. Digital cameras attach metadata that describe the camera make and model, the ISO, aperature, shutter speed and flash settings. Within the metadata panels, we can attach our own personalized information like copyright information and descriptions about the image location and subject matter for search engines to find.

Metadata:

Embedding your copyright information into the image files attaches your name and contact information to the image wherever the file travels. Last summer, I photographed some friends on a kayaking trip on the Rio Grande River in New Mexico. I emailed some of the images from the shoot to several friends sharing the memories of the trip. Those friends subsequently forwarded the images via email to other people, one of whom happened to be a magazine editor, and I was subsequently contacted to publish some of the images. If it were not for my copyright metadata tags embedded in the image files, that art director would not have been able to contact me.

In order to apply your copyright information to your image files, you will first need to create a template. Once you have created a template, it will live in this drop down menu for you to choose as a preset with a single click. The following steps will guide you in creating a personalized copyright template.

Click on the Metadata drop down menu and choose "New".

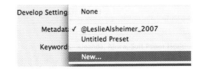

Move down the box and enter information into the fields that would be pertinent to all images you shoot. Make sure to enter a title in the "Preset Name" field so that you can access it again in the future.

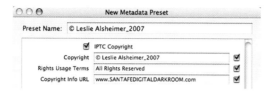

Step 10: Keywords

Keywords are text information that describes the important contents of an image. Embedded into the image files in the form of metadata, keywords are extremely helpful in identifying, sorting and finding images in library and database searches. Whether for stock submissions or just your own personal library, use keywords to start cataloging your image database. Move down to "Keywords" and type the words you wish to apply to all of the images for this import. These keywords will be added to every image so that it is best to keep them fairly general. Leave specific image information to selective image key wording in the library Keyword tags panel. I am importing images shot in Uganda while working with an NGO called Soft Power Health, so I have added the appropriate general keywords for that folder of images. I will later go in and add more specific keywords if needed. Once finished, click "Create", and select the preset name you just created in the Metadata drop down menu.

Step 11: "Render Standard-Sized Previews"

It is a good idea to check "Render Standard-Sized Previews" so that Lightroom can build the 1:1 previews of the images being imported. This is an important step in the import process for viewing and evaluating full image detail and sharpness, but unfortunately this process is also rather time consuming. The editing process will go much smoother and faster if you do allow the software enough time to build previews, but if you need to speed up the process and choose not to render previews, you can always render the previews in Lightroom later by going to the Library Module > Previews > Render Standard-Sized Previews.

Step 12: You are now ready to Import!

Lightroom will import the images, build the previews for your thumbnails, backup your files, rename them, apply your copyright and key wording to the metadata, in one incredibly smooth moving interface! Kick back and let it all happen for you!

II. Lightroom Editing

Step 1: Actual Editing: Sort, Rotate and Evaluate

Lightroom has created a streamlined interface that dictates workflow with a top down approach, whatever way you wish to structure the process within

Note:
You may want to burn another backup at this stage with all your Raw files to yet another device. At this point, I usually immediately stop and burn a DVD of the Raw files I just imported and backed up. This way I have multiple copies of the Raw files before I ever start the editing process.

your own workflow is ultimately up to you. I usually move from the Grid View to the Loupe View and move through my images with the full size preview to sort, edit and rank the images. Lightroom also provides a great deal of customizable attributes to the browser windows, allowing the user to edit panels in many ways. You can click the large arrows on the side of the interface to collapse the panels and provide more screen real estate for image evaluation. I usually leave the left panel open so that I can view the Navigator and see what part of the image I am looking at when I zoom into it. You can also compare any number of images side by side by selecting more than one image either in the Library mode or using the filmstrip and moving into Survey View. The following is an example of a customized window display.

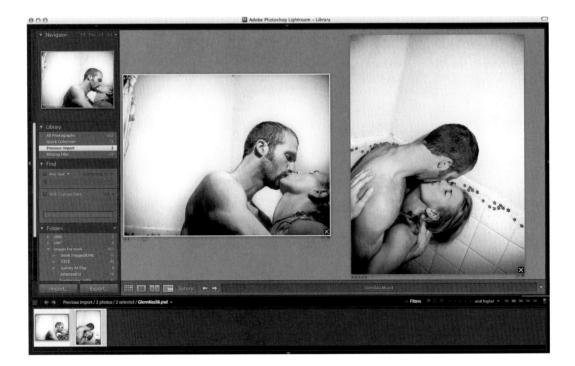

Use the right and left arrow keys to scroll through images quickly.

To rotate an image, use the rotate icons in the lower left below the image window.

Check the sharpness of each image quickly by clicking the mouse on the image preview, which will automatically zoom the image to a 1:1 preview. Click, hold and drag the mouse to scroll the image for detail views.

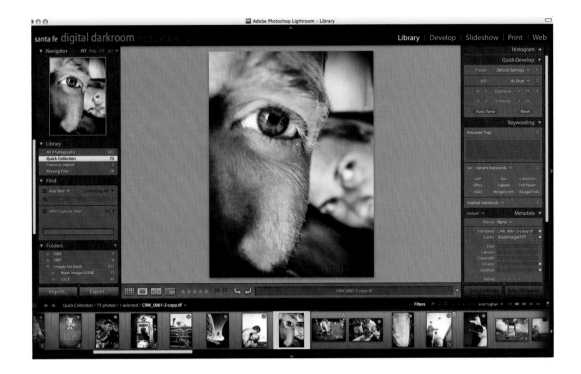

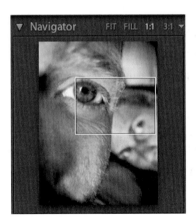

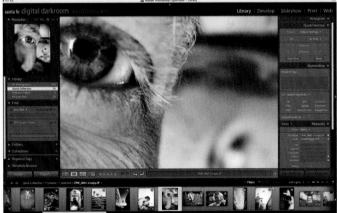

Step 2: Photo Menu: Label and Rank

Set ratings, color labels and flags to label and rank your images on the fly using the Photo Menu. Use the icons at the bottom of the interface, or tap the number keys from 1 to 5 to rank the images with the numbers assigned. Learning these and other keyboard shortcuts for these features will speed up your process exponentially! Flags and color labels can also be applied for categorizing, filtering and sorting images. I typically start my editing process by giving one star to each image that gives me even the slightest pause, and nothing to images I do not like. I usually make two or three passes and narrow the edit with two stars on the second pass, three on the third and so on.

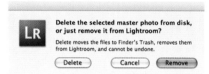

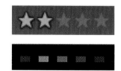

Step 3: Deleting Images

Hitting the "Delete" key on your keyboard will bring up Lightroom's safety dialog box, asking you whether you really want to delete the file or just remove it from Lightroom. This protects you from deleting files accidentally. Selecting "Delete" will move the files to your trash or recycle bin but will not actually delete them until you empty the trash, allowing you to retrieve the images if necessary.

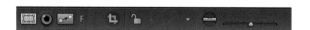

III. Global Image Adjustments: Lightroom Develop Module

Now that we are in Lightroom, let us get to work! Select an image for development and click into the Develop module. Of course not every image will require the same adjustments. The following will take you step-by-step through a streamlined workflow for the Develop Module, highlighting all of the features and specific tool functions.

Note:
As with all aspects of Adobe Camera Raw, crops are completely non-destructive and can be undone or modified simply by reselecting the Crop (C) tool

Step 1: Crop

1. Select the Crop Overlay (R) from Lightroom's tool bar beneath the image
2. Simply draw, drag or pull corner points to set crop guidelines
3. To straighten a skewed image, select the Straighten Tool (Shift+Command) and define a start and end point on a level axis
4. Now double click upon the image to apply the crop

Step 2: White Balance: LR_WhiteBalanceTool

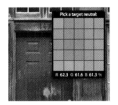

1. Select the White Balance Tool (I)
   The White Balance Tool is used to approximate the true color temperature of your image. To do so, click on a tone likely to be a true neutral
2. If your image needs further adjustment, either the Temperature slider or White Balance drop downs are good places to start

Step 3: Tone/Basic

1. By clicking on Lightroom's histogram arrows, we remind the application to show us regions of the highlights or shadows that will be clipped so that we can be certain to preserve all of our image's details. To do so, click each arrow icon at the far left and right of the histogram
2. Move the Exposure slider until Red overlays (clipped highlights) begins to appear

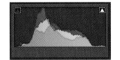

3. Now select the new Recovery slider, and move it to the right until the red portions disappear; in the case of my image, I chose to continue moving the slider to show even more highlight detail
4. Next move the Fill Light slider to the right, this will "dodge" the shadows. Continue adjusting until you have your desired effect. If the image does not have enough contrast, do not worry, we will get there next
5. We will now carefully move the "Black" slider to add true blacks back to the image; move the slider until the blue overlay is just barely visible (too much blue indicates clipped shadow regions)
5a. If you would like yet more contrast, the appropriately marked "Contrast" and "Brightness" sliders offer a good way to massage the details – remember to be mindful of the red and blue overlays

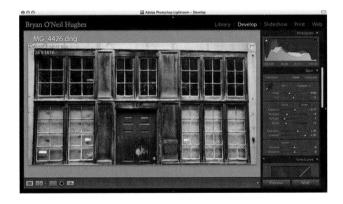

Step 4: Tone Curve

Everyone has heard of curves, the feature that is as intimidating as the cockpit of a jumbo jet, and promises to be just as powerful. Any Photoshop power user will tell you that magic is in curves; this gets troubling when you try to

Note:
Were you processing an image that you wanted to retain as color, you could then increase saturation, using the Vibrance (protects skin tones) and Saturation controls next.

put the gospel into practice. Something about trying to wrangle an s-shaped line to deliver a good exposure just does not seem intuitive.

Luckily, there is not a curves control more powerful or more intuitive than the one found in Lightroom. Let us look at the parts of the Parametric Curves control in Lightroom:

Histogram

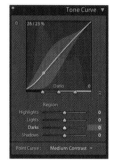

Behind the curve itself, Lightroom shows a large, clear histogram. Corresponding quadrants at the base of the Curve show which slider controls which region of the curve. As you mouse over the curve, the histogram shows which slider controls which region. Say, you wanted to only adjust the deepest, darkest black tones in an image with the Shadowslider, just pull the left most tab to the desired location – now Shadow maps only a small subset of the histogram.

Highlights: This control maps the quadrant from the brightest tones, adjusting this is a great way to pull down specular highlights in an image.

Lights: These are the areas that detail often hides, and that the bright side of contrast can often be found in.

Darks: Conversely, this is a region where light shadow detail is hiding or mid-contrast can be improved.

Shadows: This is the darkest portion of the image, and this slider can be used to have rich blacks or detailed shadows.

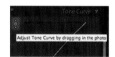

This is all fine and good, and like Camera Raw, it is an enormous step forward for Curves; Lightroom takes it somewhere completely unique, though. Note the tiny round button to the left of the Curve, the tooltip reads, "Adjust Tone Curve by dragging in the photo", and that is exactly what this does! With this button enabled, a user needs only to find the region on the image that they want to adjust, and simply mouse down upon it and drag upwards or downwards. This is by far the most powerful and intuitive way to make adjustments.

Step 5: Convert to Grayscale

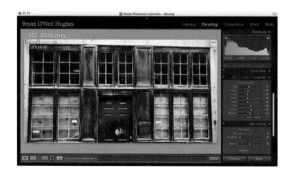

Like Camera Raw, "Grayscale" refers not to an image mode, but to the black and white conversion feature in Lightroom.

1. Within the HSL/Color/Grayscale palette, simply select "Grayscale".
1a. By design, this adjustment leverages the same "Auto" setting as Camera Raw. "Auto-Adjust" maps the color tones in the image to present the user with a nice, well contrasted conversion.
2. As with Camera Raw, each individual slider can control a given region of the monochromatic image. You may have noticed that familiar button from Curves; yes, you can interact directly with your black and white adjustment by first pressing this button!

In my case, I found that further darkening the building's door (Red) and further lightening the plywood in the windows (Yellow) presented me with an even more stunning contrast.

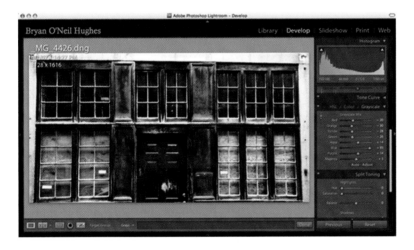

Step 6: Split Toning
Lightroom features a very easy and powerful ability to split tone, which is to apply two separate hues – one to the highlights and the other to the shadow regions.

1. Within the Split Toning palette, grab the Highlight Hue slider and pull slowly to the right.
2. Once you have decided upon a highlight tone, repeat step one with the Shadow tone.
3. Simply slide the Balance control back or forth to equalize the image to suit your taste.

Tip:
While moving the Hue slider, hold the Option key. This gives a preview of all hues at 100% saturation and saves a ton of time.

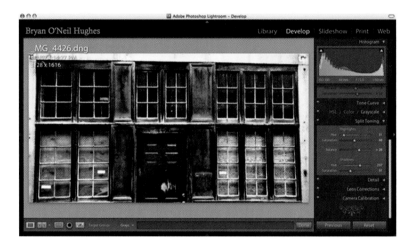

Step 7: Detail

All images benefit from some form of sharpening, or many, even this one shot at 100 ISO enjoys a bit of noise reduction. As with all of Lightroom, the controls are simple and very powerful. The best methods for user controlled sharpening are still in Photoshop; however Lightroom can be useful for speed and ease.

1. Before touching either slider, click with the (default) hand tool to zoom in to 100%.
2. Within the Detail palette, under "Sharpening", move the amount slider to the right until you see the results you like.
3. Now do the same with the "Noise Reduction" slider.

*Remember for both controls that these are only settings and can be adjusted at any time for printing, exporting or previewing.

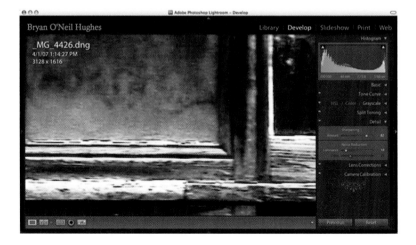

Step 8: Lens Correction

Vignetting is a way to dodge or burn just the corners of an image, doing so correctly brings the center of the image into even more prominent focus.

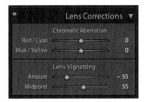

1. Within the Lens Corrections palette, under "Lens Vignetting", move the amount slider to the left (watch out for shadow clipping).
2. To control the range of the vignette, move the midpoint slider.

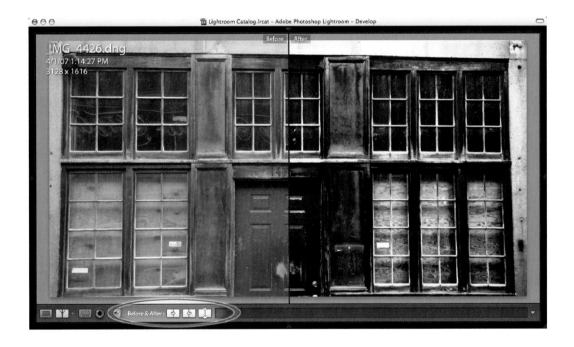

Step 9: Before and After

Lightroom offers a variety of ways to see "before" images beside, above or split with "after" images. You can see by our example how far we've come in a few short steps.

1. Toggle the Before and After button to get different views.
2. Click upon the Loupe View icon to revert to full screen.

Step 10: Presets

Detailed adjustments, such as the one we just did, take time, but in Lightroom all of that work can quickly and easily be saved as a preset. Presets can later be applied upon import, shared with individual images or even spread across hundreds.

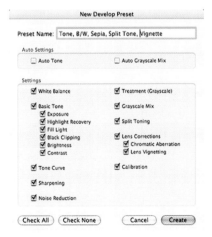

1. To add all that we have just done as a preset, simply disclose the preset menu on the left side of the Develop module.
2. Now, click upon the "+" icon to add the Preset.

Step 11: Photoshop

Lightroom is extremely powerful, and we have rendered a very nice split toned image in a relatively short amount of time. This particular image needs a perspective crop though, and I can only do that in Photoshop.

1. Either navigate to Photo (Menu)/Edit in Adobe Photoshop CS3, or use Command+E.
2. You are prompted with a variety of choices; let's go with "Edit a copy with Lightroom adjustments".

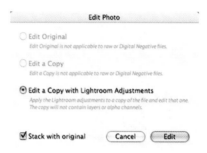

Photoshop will create a full resolution, 16-Bit copy, launch Photoshop and open the file; any changes applied and saved within Photoshop will be linked to the reference in Lightroom. In this case, a quick perspective crop is quickly updated in Lightroom upon completion and save.

Lastly, pressing "L" once shows us our finished product in a semi lights-out mode. Ta-da! Image development and processing can be done extensively and uniquely one image at a time or for incredibly fast batch processing Lightroom allows you to apply all the same adjustments to multiple images at once. You must first develop one image entirely the way you like it, and then select any number of images you wish to process with the same adjustments and click the SYNC icon at the bottom of the Develop module. A dialogue box will appear allowing you to choose which of the previous adjustments to sync. Uncheck the adjustments you feel should not be applied.

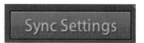

IV. Export: Archive, Contact

1. Export DNG and Burn another backup

After all the image processing, file naming, key wording, copyright embedding, sorting, ranking and global adjusting has been applied to your satisfaction, the best practice would be to burn another backup onto disk. Lightroom offers the option of burning large JPEGs to disk with one quick and easy step (great for registering copyright of your images). Since the Raw files are your "digital negatives" containing the highest quality versions of information, the best practice will always be to do everything you can to save them. I first export all the images as DNG files with all my latest editing and adjustments to a separate folder as "selects" for backup and burn that file to DVD.

Step 1: In Lightroom, click the big export button at the bottom left panel of the interface window, or go to the File Menu > Export. The Export dialog box will appear. As always, the top down approach is the most logical and effective way to address dialog boxes within both Photoshop and Lightroom.

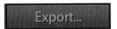

Step 2: Start with the "Preset" drop down menu. Here you can create your own templates catered to your specific output goals, or use one of the Lightroom templates. You can create as many different presets as you have destination output goals for your images. Lightroom already includes presets for exporting for email purposes, as well as burning JPEGs to disk. We choose the ready-made template for converting to DNG. WAY COOL. Choose Export to DNG.

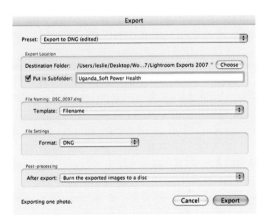

Step 3: Choose a destination folder. For organizational purposes, I have a permanent Lightroom export folder on my hard drive marked with the year. For each export, I check the "Put in Subfolder" box and title according to the shoot.

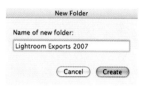

Step 4: "Template". I choose file name as that keeps the current file names attached to the images. You may want to create a custom name here to differentiate between the Raw files and the processed DNGs. Either approach is good workflow practice.

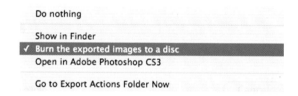

Step 5: Format: choose DNG.

Step 6: After export: choose Burn the exported images to disk.

Step 7: Click Export.
The CD drive of your computer will magically open and a dialog box will appear prompting you to insert a blank disk. Insert a blank disk and burn!

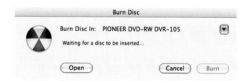

2. Print a Contact Sheet

At this point in the workflow, you may want to print contact sheets of the images from the shoot and store them in a file that can give you a visual reference to the images, what they are called, and where they live. Move to

the Print Module and choose one of the easy templates 4×5, 5×8, or 4×4.
(See Chapter 6, "Printing", page 204 for more details.)

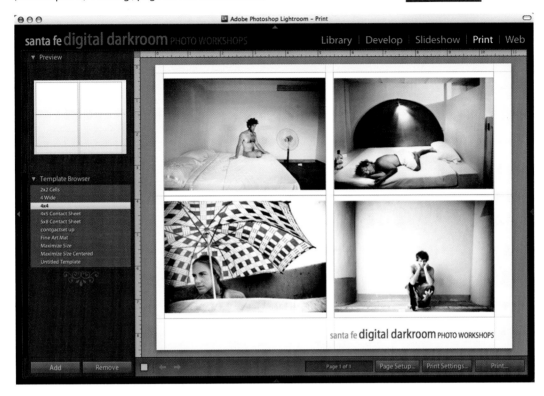

Once you have processed your images with all the global adjustments
necessary, and safely archived your images in at least three locations, you will
want to work with some choice images for the selective adjustment phase of
the workflow. Photoshop is the next step for applying sharpening techniques
for your desired output, selective editing and prepping images for print.

Special Note: Lightroom Color Management

Lightroom is extremely color savvy, and up until the point of Export, Lightroom
has done all the color management behind the scenes. Lightroom works with
all images in the ProPhoto RGB color working space and combines that space
with a special tone curve developed from the sRGB working space. Remember,
ProPhoto RGB is the largest working space, allowing for the greatest amount
of color possible; however, it is also so large that neither monitors nor printers
can reproduce all of the color within it as of yet. The added tone curve allows
Lightroom to create a realistic working space for image editing. The export
process is where color management, and your decisions about how you wish
to handle color, will come into play with your Photoshop color management
policies. (See Chapter 1, "Color Management for Black and White", page 23 for
details in setting up Photoshop to manage color properly.)

3. Bridge to Photoshop

Once you have processed your images with all the global adjustments necessary in Lightroom, and safely archived your images in at least three locations, you will want to work more extensively with some choice images for the selective adjustment phase of the workflow. Photoshop is the next step for selective editing, applying sharpening techniques for your desired output, and prepping images for print, and Adobe Bridge is the best way to get you there.

There are two options at this point to move images from Lightroom through Bridge to Photoshop. First, you can return to Lightroom and move through the export process again, with each individual file you wish to export to Photoshop selected. You can do this either one at a time as you are ready for them, or in a group with as many images as you can take on at once. Use the shift key to select multiple images at once. Or, the second option is to access the DNG files just exported for the burned backup through Adobe Bridge to launch them into Photoshop. I prefer the latter. The following steps outline how to use Bridge between Lightroom and Photoshop.

Step 1: Launch Bridge: It should still have an integral role in the workflow process as your primary image navigational tool, that is, use it for locating images visually and for launching them into Photoshop.

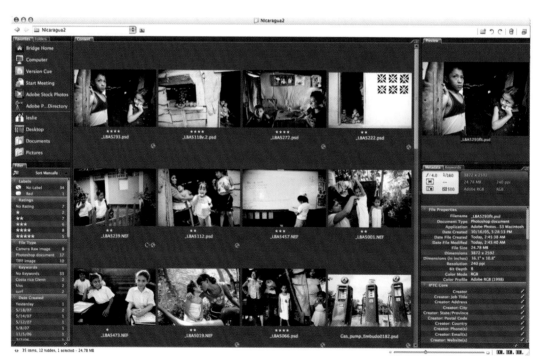

1 – Default thumbnail View

Navigate to and open the folder you created with the DNG files for burning is Step V. Export: Archive, Contact, and select an image you wish to work with more extensively in the editing process.

Step 2: Double click the chosen image to launch the Adobe Raw Converter (ACR). If you wish to make more global edits to the image, you can do them here in ACR. (See "Black and White in Adobe Camera Raw 4.0", Chapter 4 for extensive processing techniques.)

Bridge Overview

Adobe Bridge (introduced in Photoshop CS2) is a powerful file browser and navigational tool. Bridge synchronizes the entire Adobe Creative Suite in a stand-alone application. It allows you to see larger thumbnails of files with a greater number of options than any other navigational software to date. We could take an entire chapter demonstrating just how great Bridge is. For the specific focus of this text, however, the following is an overview of some of its great new features.

1. **Launch Bridge:** From Photoshop choose File menu > Browse, or Opt + Cmd + O. Or click on the handy icon in the options bar. As Bridge launches, Photoshop will disappear into the background, but nothing will be lost!

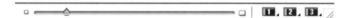

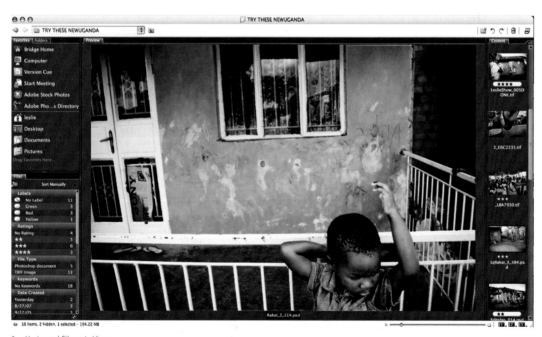

2 – Horizontal Filmstrip View

2. **View Controls:** Use the numbered quick icons in the lower right corner of the browser window to see different views of the thumbnails, and use the slider to change thumbnail size on the fly!

1 – Default thumbnail View

2 – Horizontal Filmstrip View

3 – Metadata Focus View

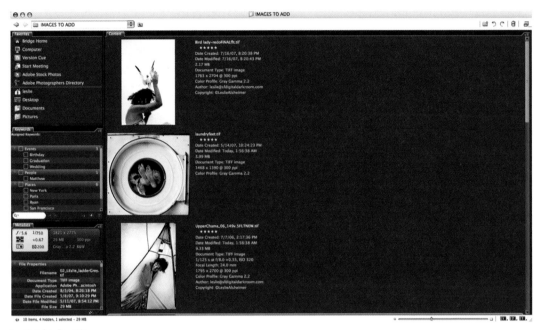

3 – Metadata Focus View

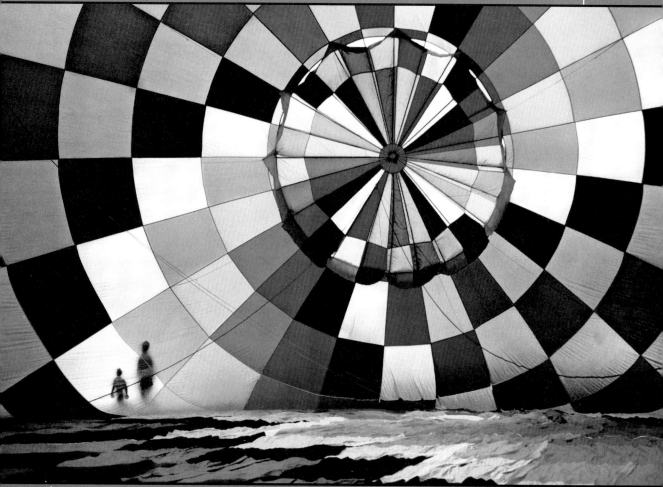

CHAPTER 4

Black and White in Photoshop
© Leslie Alsheimer

The selective image adjustment process from this point on is based entirely on aesthetic judgment. There is unfortunately not a step-by-step formula applicable to all images. Content and creative preference must guide you through the rest of the workflow. This chapter will outline, more advanced black and white conversion options available in Photoshop as well as their founding theories and methodologies, followed by step-by-step techniques outlining each option. Experiment with the differences. Create several different versions before you move on to more advanced selective image editing and the printing workflow.

Photoshop

Black and White Conversion Methods

For many photographers, the ability to convert an image from color to black and white is one of the most powerful and compelling advantages to working in the digital domain. Traditional film requires a photographer to choose color or black and white before capturing an image, or necessitates taking two images, which is not always possible. The ability to capture in color and make decisions after shooting about which images will be converted into monochrome – on a frame-by-frame basis – offers photographers enormous flexibility.

Converting an image to black and white can be a very simple process. However, when the visual impact of an image fails to transfer with those simple processes, the need for more complex conversion options increases. If the conversion method is not done most effectively, contrast and delicate gray tones can wash out, leaving an image looking muddy or lacking in adequate tonal range. Black and white conversion methods must honor the spectral relationships between colors, or the conversion can haphazardly dilute the overall aesthetic impact of an image.

The history of black and white conversion methods in the digital environment has continuously inspired great technical controversy. Every guru in the industry has an opinion supporting a particular conversion method. Unfortunately for the non-gurus (the rest of us), there are a substantial number of different conversion methods, and an even greater number of gurus to champion each method for any number of disparately convincing reasons. So how is a non-guru supposed to evaluate which guru's method to adopt? And further, why can't there be one best conversion method everyone can agree upon?

The answer to both questions is complicated. Although having just one "best conversion" method would greatly simplify the learning process, all images are not created alike, and, therefore, all conversion methods cannot apply unilaterally with the same impact. The reality is that most all conversion methods can effectively render reasonably pleasing results; the difference to the user in choosing the "best" conversion method depends on a number of factors including image content, exposure, contrast, tonality, luminance as well as time to invest in the conversion process, workflow and one's level of familiarity with the tools and software. If one needed to make quick conversions for an editor or newspaper for example, the "best" method may be the quickest and simplest one. If one had more time and the intention of creating a fine art portfolio print, the choice may be a more complex method. Just as each type of black and white film carried unique and distinguishing aesthetics, any number of variable factors can affect why one might choose any particular conversion method. Remember, just as what is good for the goose is not always good for the gander, your own "best" conversion will be best for your own unique set of reasons.

An analogy – for those who have spent time in the traditional wet darkroom – might be that every black and white negative could not be printed using the exact same exposure time, lens aperture, grade paper and/or contrast filter, and produce the optimal result each and every time. Each negative required a bit of testing to determine its unique best exposure and development technique including chemical dilution, agitation and temperature. Similarly to the digital domain, the reality in the chemical darkroom was that one could produce a beautiful print using any number of dilutions, exposure combinations and temperatures (within a certain range). Although the tools and the methods have changed significantly over the years, the methodology is really remarkably similar. Throughout this chapter, we try to keep reminding readers of the traditional darkroom and how to bring those principals back into the new technology. For those who have never experienced the traditional darkroom, my best alternative analogy would be cooking. Many recipes for green chili stew (a local New Mexico favorite of mine) can make a great meal, but the best recipe probably involves a few adaptations of one's own to suit preferences and taste.

The advantages and possibilities in the conversion process become more fun and dynamic as we explore the various options and tools at our disposal. The more of these techniques you have in your repertoire, the more adept you will become at optimizing your images with the most effective grayscale conversions. Notice in the images (below) each conversion method offers a slightly different result. With some images, this difference will be subtle and with others the differences can be mind blowing.

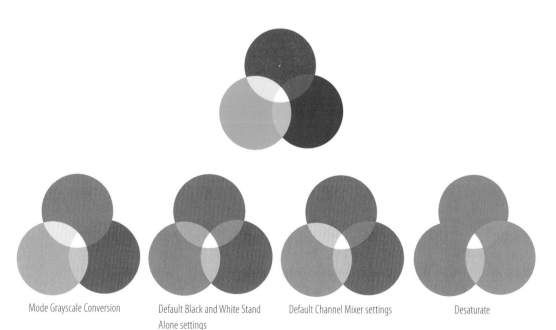

Mode Grayscale Conversion   Default Black and White Stand   Default Channel Mixer settings   Desaturate
                              Alone settings

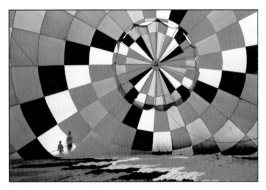

Desaturate

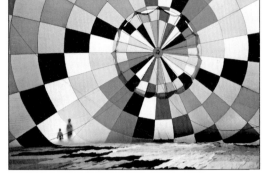

Mode > Grayscale

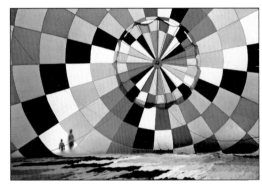

Channel Mixer

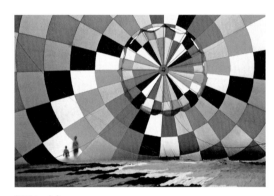

B/W stand alone

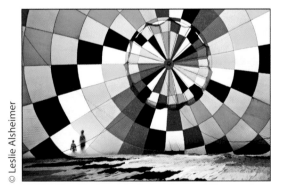

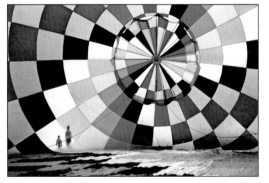

Advanced number 11

The Methods

Grayscale Mode Change

This method is by far the easiest, fastest and most straightforward approach to converting color to black and white. It creates a nicely balanced conversion with distinct separation in tonal values and serves as a great method for reducing file size, if necessary. Although this approach may be fast and easy, it does not, however, always produce the best results possible.

1. First open an image you wish to convert to black and white.
2. Choose from the Image Menu > Mode > Grayscale.
3. A dialog box may appear asking whether to "discard color information?"
4. Click "Discard".

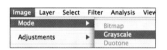 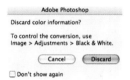

Photoshop will throw away the RGB (Red, Green, Blue) or CMYK (cyan, magenta, yellow, black) color channel information, creating a much smaller file and convert the image colors into black, white and 256 values of gray tones. Photoshop determines the tonalities each color will render with a pre-calculated formula (algorithm) in order to create the resulting grayscale image. This method of conversion attempts to simulate the look and feel of Kodak Plus-X film. While this method is exceptionally fast and easy to use, the photographer loses color information that cannot be recreated, as well as control and input in the conversion process. The results are usually relatively pleasing for many images, but rarely produce the optimal image the fine art photographer will be looking for. One can, of course, greatly improve the conversion by adjusting tone, contrast, as well as shadows and highlight information with adjustment layers and digital darkroom editing.

Advantages:
1. Fast
2. Moderately effective
3. Creates smaller files

Disadvantages:
1. Loss of control
2. Moderately effective
3. Discards color channels
4. Discards image data
5. Limits post-processing, filtration, gamut, etc.

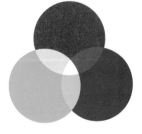 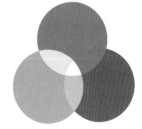

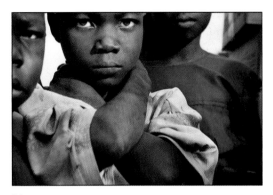

Color

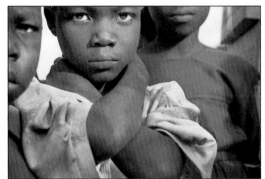

Grayscale

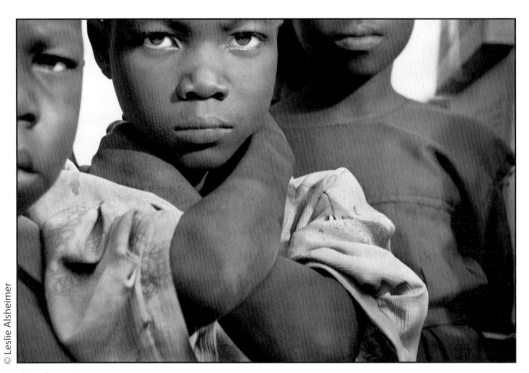

© Leslie Alsheimer

Advanced conversion

While this grayscale mode change method works fairly well and not much different from the advanced methods for the image above, notice the differences between conversion methods with the image on the following page.

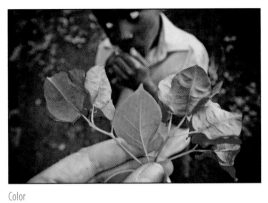

Color

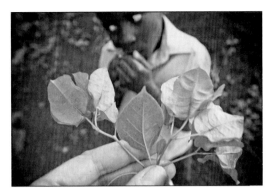

Grayscale

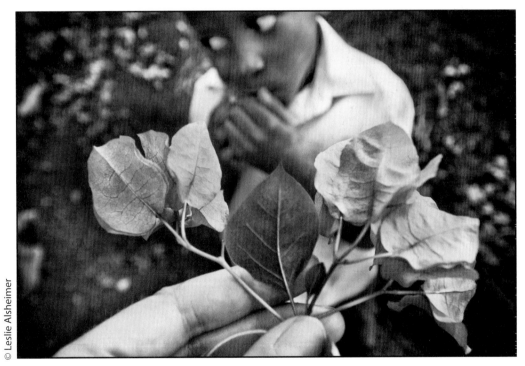

© Leslie Alsheimer

Advanced conversion

Desaturate

The second fast and easy option for going from color to monochrome is desaturation. While desaturation results in an image that appears to be grayscale, it is actually not. Desaturating removes the color from each of the RGB channels by equalizing the color pixel information to equivalent values. As this method does not actually discard the color information, the resulting image remains in the RGB color space. This method can be created as an adjustment layer, introducing many additional advantages for the creative user. As with any adjustment layer, it is non-destructive and offers the many cool features adjustment layers have to offer such as variable opacity and masking. This technique, though more advantageous, still tends to produce an image that needs more work. It will be fairly limited in range of gray detail and does not produce deep blacks. You will find that each conversion method will frequently produce noticeably different results, and sometimes very little.

There is more than one way to desaturate an image in Photoshop, believe it or not.

1. Choose Image Menu > Adjustments > Desaturate

2. Choose Image Menu > Adjustments > Hue Saturation

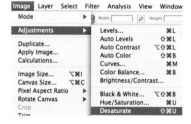
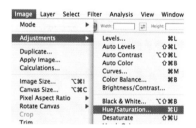

3. Layer Menu > New Adjustment Layer > Hue Saturation, or use the Adjustment Layers palette icon and choose Hue Saturation

All these access methods will get you to the same dialog box. The difference between them is that number 3 allows you the flexibility of an adjustment layer. We recommend you follow a non-destructive workflow and choose an adjustment layer whenever possible!

3a. Open the Hue/Saturation dialog box and slide the Saturation slider all the way to the left.

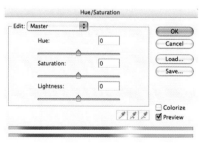
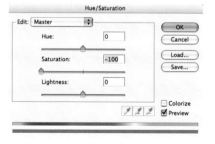

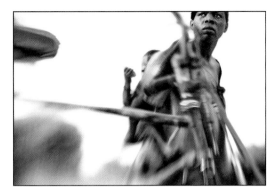

Color

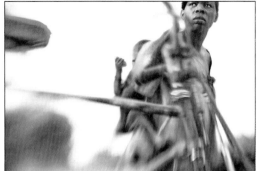

Desaturated

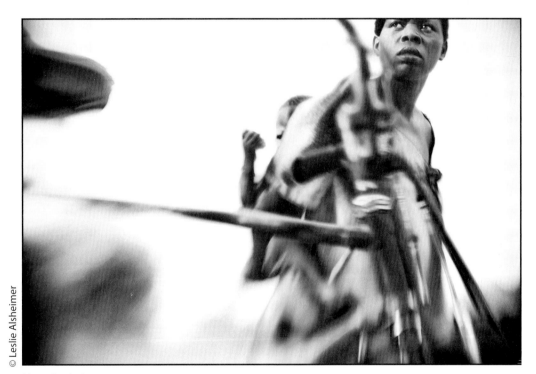

© Leslie Alsheimer

Advanced methods

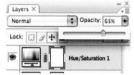

With an adjustment layer you can play with layer opacity and masking for fun and creative effects. Try the fabulous "Ben Holland Technique" of removing all colors but one.

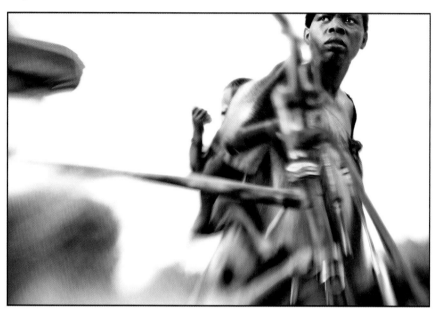

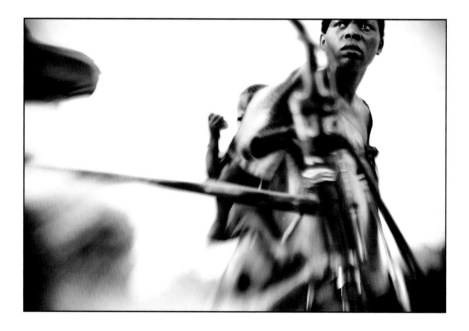

Advantages:
1. **1.** Fast and easy
2. **2.** Moderately effective
3. **3.** Adds all benefits of adjustment layers (i.e. variable opacity, and masking capabilities)
4. **4.** Non-destructive
5. **5.** Maintains RGB color mode and all color information

Disadvantages:
1. **1.** Loss of control
2. **2.** Moderately effective
3. **3.** Limited range in gray detail
4. **4.** Does not produce deep blacks

Lab Color Mode

Another simple and relatively quick conversion method is to convert the image to Lab Color mode and use the Lightness channel for the conversion. You will need to delete the two channels that contain the color information, labeled as "a" and "b". As you delete the first color channel, however, the others will automatically become renamed in the process. The Lightness channel should remain fairly obvious, as the other remaining channel will appear quite dark.

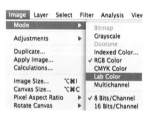

1. **1.** Choose Image > Mode > Lab Color
2. **2.** Open the Channels Palette
3. **3.** Drag the "a" & "b" Channels to the adjustment layer trash can

(Lightness Channel will automatically rename to Alpha 1).

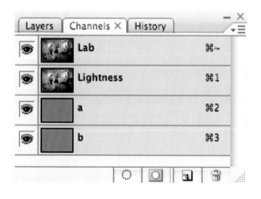

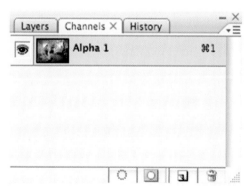

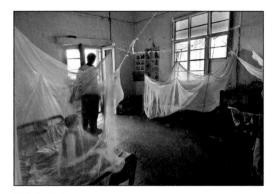

Original color image

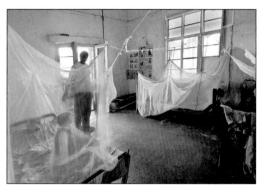

Lab conversion

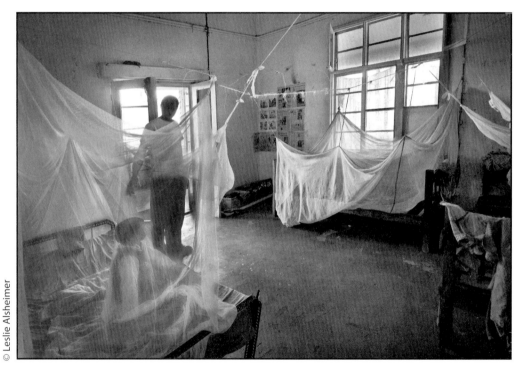

© Leslie Alsheimer

Advanced methods

Advantages:
1. Fast
2. Conversions are fairly pleasing for the speed
3. Creates smaller files
4. More control

Disadvantages:
1. Some loss of control
2. Moderately effective
3. Discards color channels
4. Discards image data

Color Filters and Black and White Images

The methods of conversion available today range from simple one step conversions to more complex multistep processes. Unless time and simplicity are of the utmost importance, converting a digital color image into black and white typically requires going beyond simply desaturating the colors or converting to grayscale. As we increase the complexity of the conversion method, we generally gain more control and variation over what is available with the more straightforward methods. Understanding the foundations and principles behind the more complex techniques as well as the advantages they provide will serve you well in putting these methods into practice.

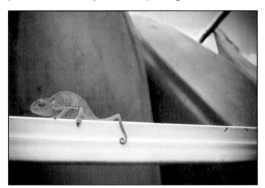

FIG 1

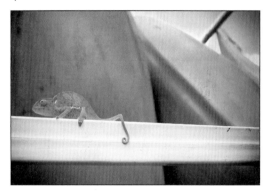

FIG 2   Simple conversion

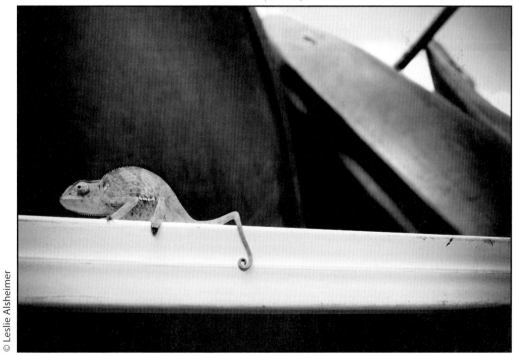

© Leslie Alsheimer

FIG 3   More complex conversion

First, however, let us look at an image with two striking contrasting colors like green and orange (see chameleon below). Sometimes the conversion method causes the contrasting colors to become a similar shade of middle gray, and the contrast and visual impact becomes lost in the translation.

It is possible, however, to use conversion methods that can map specific colors separately from one another and translate the differences into contrasting tones of gray. Notice the green color of the chameleon next to the orange color of the kayak in the image background. The pizzazz of the original color image maintains its integrity in the more complex black and white conversion, and that image now holds the some of same impact in black and white as it did in color.

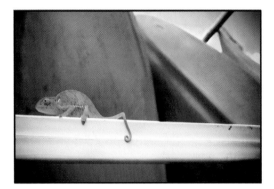

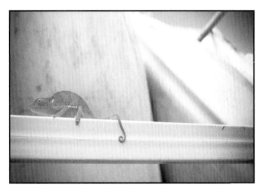

Red Filter

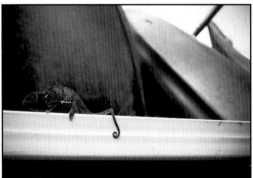

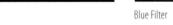

Green Filter

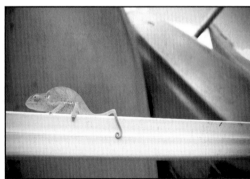

Blue Filter

Background: Color Filters for Black and White Film

Since photography began in black and white, it is impossible to truly understand any of its newer forms without at least a passing knowledge of its beginning. Traditional black and white photographers have always needed to be attentive to the type and distribution of color within their images. Just as with color photography, black and white photography can use the spectral relationships between colors and tonality to make a subject stand out.

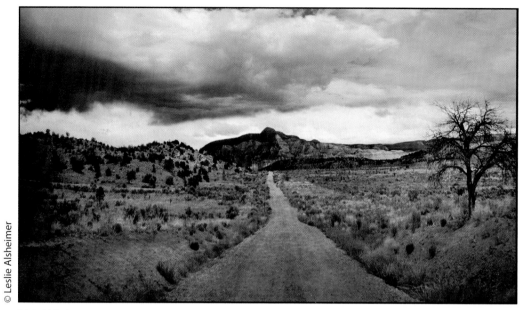

© Leslie Alsheimer

Original Color Image

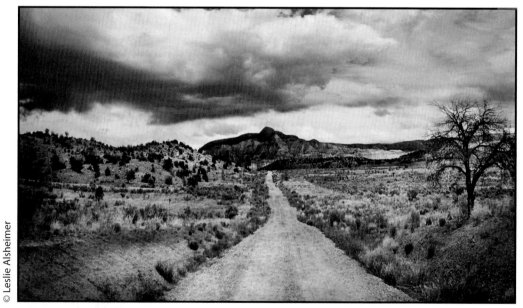

© Leslie Alsheimer

Mixed Filters

In order to maximize this principle, black and white photographers traditionally used color filters to manipulate how the spectral relationship between colors was translated into black and white. Colored filters such as blue, red, yellow and orange were used to selectively affect the gradient and

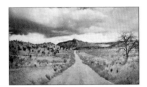

Red Filter

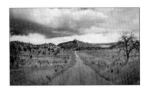

Green Filter

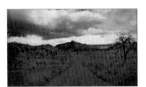

Blue Filter

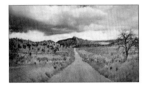

Orange Filter

contrast in the tonality of colors as they recorded onto film. By allowing colors that are similar to their own color to pass through and expose onto the film, while simultaneously blocking colors that are of opposite wavelengths to the filter color, colors were effectively lightened and darkened as they recorded on the film. Therefore, a strong red filter will lighten reds and darken blues, a green filter will lighten greens and darken reds, etc. For example, landscape photographers often use orange and red filters to cancel blue and green, making skies dark and foliage rich in tone. Careful selection of these color filters allows the photographer to decide which colors in the image will produce the brightest or darkest tones.

How Color Filters in Black and White Made Color Film

Even when photography was only black and white, visionaries were already laying the foundations to move photography into color. In the 1860s, less than 30 years after the introduction of Daguerreotype, the method of using color filters with black and white film was utilized by James Clerk Maxwell, who experimented with a three image projection process to create a color image from black and white film. He presumed that a color image could be created by exposing three monochrome images of the same subject, exposing each using a different color filter before the lens. Each of the red, blue and green filtered exposures was then projected using three lanterns, each equipped with the corresponding colored filter. The red and green filter together created a yellow image, and all the three colors together created a white image. The final image, although far from perfect, included all of the original colors in the subject. This experimentation laid the foundation for not only color photography but also the Technicolor process used well into the 21st century to create movies in color.

Well so what, you might be thinking: how does this help me with black and white conversions? Actually, understanding this concept and its development is the foundation for the concept of color channels in Photoshop, and the subsequent features software now provides for black and white conversions. If you can wrap your head around this concept, you will be very close to grasping the fundamental essence of the advantages digital photography has to offer the black and white photographer.

Channels

Just like James Clerk Maxwell's experiment in the 1860s created color, so too does a digital camera. However, instead of three separate images, we now have separate channels within the same image file composited together to create the full color spectrum of an image. Separated, they are the individual color "plates" that make up the image's color. A color image typically contains four color channels: a "Red channel", "Green channel" and "Blue channel", creating the "RGB" composite, and a fourth channel composite of all three. This composite channel allows you to view any one of the individual colors independently, or any combination of all three. There are five color channels

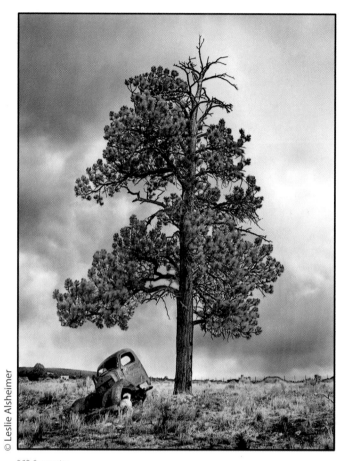

© Leslie Alsheimer

RGB Composite

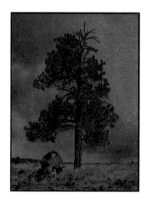

Red Channel

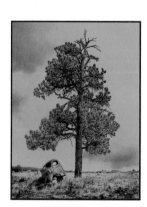

Green Channel

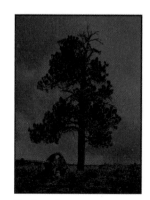

Blue Channel

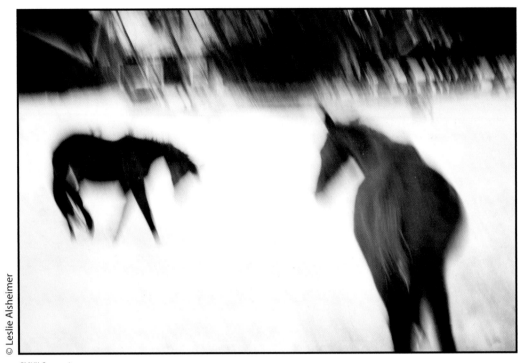

© Leslie Alsheimer

CMYK Composite

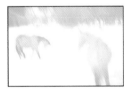

Cyan Channel

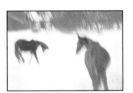

Magenta Channel

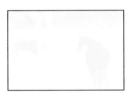

Yellow Channel

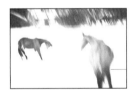

Black Channel

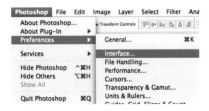

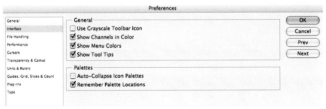

within a CMYK image (cyan, magenta, yellow, black and the combo of all four). These channels store all the color information for each individual pixel within an image and are generated automatically by Photoshop.

In addition to the standard four channels RGB or five channels CMYK, Photoshop will also support images with up to 20 more channels. These additional channels are called Alpha Channels, where selections created in Photoshop are stored and edited within a working document. The following example illustrates an alpha channel storing a selection of the horses.

Note:
Generally, under default program settings, Photoshop is set up to reveal channels in grayscale. This can be changed in Photoshop CS3 Preferences > Interface > Show Channels in Color

Digital RGB Capture is actually Grayscale First!

This may be surprising, but digital camera's do not actually capture in color at all. Camera imaging sensors have the capacity to capture luminance values or brightness alone, not color. All digital images, therefore, are fundamentally grayscale at the time of capture and then converted to color. How this works is a little complex, but basically, colored filters cover each photosite on the digital camera's imaging sensor. These filters capture the brightness of the light that passes through them. With the filters in place, each pixel can record only the brightness of the light that matches its filter and passes through it, while other colors are blocked.

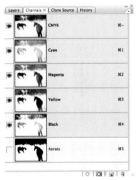

The grayscale in digital terms is a series of 256 increasingly darker tones ranging from pure white to pure black. 0 represents pure white,

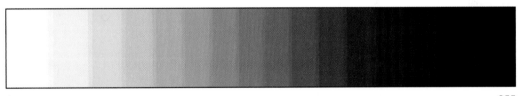

0   255

255 represents pure black and the other 254 brightness values being varying shades of gray that increasingly darken from pure white to pure black.

How the digital camera creates a color image from this brightness scale recorded on the sensor is much like Maxwell's 1860 experiment as well. Since daylight is made up of red, green and blue light, placing red, green and blue filters over individual pixels on the image sensor can create color images just as they did for Maxwell in 1860. For example, a pixel with a green filter knows only the brightness of the green light that strikes it. A process called "interpolation" then determines the actual color of a pixel, which uses the colors of neighboring pixels to calculate the two colors that the pixel did not record directly. By combining these two interpolated colors with the directly measured colors, the full color of the pixel can be calculated and then recorded. Interestingly, the human eye is more sensitive to green than it is to red or blue, so most digital camera sensors have twice as many green filters as red or blue filters to accommodate this preference.

Channel Mixer

Utilizing these founding color principles, the channel mixer puts theory into action. With the same effect color filters produced, you can dynamically interact with the translation of the spectral relationships between colors in the conversion process by mixing the individual channels within a document. The channel mixer tool allows you to control how much each of the three color channels (red, green and blue) contribute to the final grayscale brightness. This method, therefore, has the ability to act as a digital set of black and white filters, all in a single interface allowing you the flexibility and power of having the whole color filter pack in post production.

The channel mixer has been traditionally and undoubtedly one of the most powerful black and white conversion methods; however, it may take some time to master since there are many parameters which require simultaneous adjustment.

There are many ways to mix the channels in this process, and the "right" mix will vary on a per image basis. Photoshop CS3 provides a few great presets to start with, but it is important to play with the mix until you find a pleasing effect.

Color to Black and White with the Channel Mixer

Open
Open an image that is in RGB color mode.

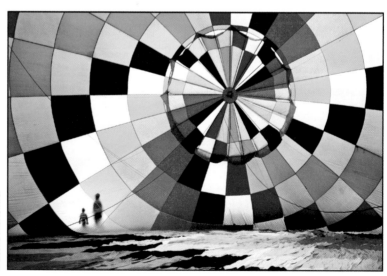

© Leslie Alsheimer

Analyze the Channels
(Note this step is for viewing purposes only)

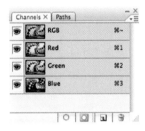

Open your channels palette and click on the individual channels by clicking on the **WORDS** "Red", "Green" and "Blue". These different views will provide a guide for how to customize the black and white conversion.

You will choose which channels offer you the most detail and tonality on an image by image basis. The red channel typically contains most of the detail in the image. The blue channel typically contains the luminosity, skin tones and contrast and frequently the most noise.

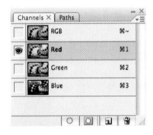

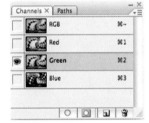

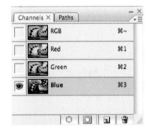

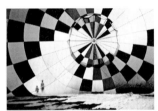

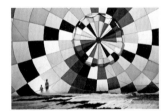

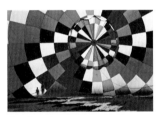

Red Channel

Green Channel

Blue Channel

Select the channel with the most detail to be the dominant channel for the channel mixer. For this image, the Green Channel was selected.
Be sure you **click back on the RGB letters at the top of the channels palette to return the image to color before moving to the next step.

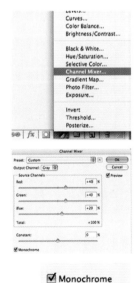

Channel Mixer: The Method
Choose Channel Mixer from the layers palette by clicking on the adjustment layer icon at the bottom of the layers palette. Or you can choose Layer > New Adjustment Layer > Channel Mixer and click OK.

Check Monochrome
Check the box next to the word "Monochrome" in the lower left hand side of the Channel Mixer box. The image will immediately turn to grayscale.

The initial mixture predetermined by default in Photoshop CS3 opens with Red 40%, Green 40% and Blue 20%. These better default values are actually another cool new feature in CS3, as CS2 used to just map to 100% red. Photoshop lessens the amount assigned to the blue channel because the blue channel typically holds more noise than the other two channels of red and green.

☑ Monochrome

111

Note:
Curiously, the image will not return to Color if the Monochrome button is unchecked. To Reset, hold down the Option key and the cancel button will turn to reset.

Note:
Be careful of the blue channel as it typically holds more noise than the other two channels of red or green. Unless the goal is to create a grainy looking image or some exaggerated effect, it is best to steer clear of using too much blue channel in the mixture.

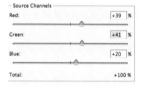

The advanced user may wish to monitor the Histogram palette in this process. (See "Highest Quality Capture", page 29 for more information.)

Make Custom Changes
Adjust the Red, Green and Blue sliders to add and subtract amounts or percentages of each channel to produce an image to your liking. The choices made are purely aesthetic. The user has complete control of how each channel will be represented in the final image outcome.

For an even more pronounced effect, some colors can even have negative percentages.

It is advised that the percentage totals should not exceed 100%, when all three channels are added, in order to maintain the density or overall brightness of the image, although creative interpretation should always take precedence over numbers. Experimenting with different color settings will enable you to find the combinations that your prefer. Be mindful though, if the number totals do equate to over 100% there is a risk of losing highlight information. Notice how cool Photoshop CS3 is to provide us with a calculation total feature at the bottom of the channel sliders! So fabulous not to have to do all that math on the fly!

Other cool new Channel Mixer features in CS3 include: the ability to save, load and share settings and presets.

Click OK when finished.

Play!
There are as many interpretations of how an image can be conveyed as there are number combinations within the tool. Create several different interpretations and decide which one you prefer the best!

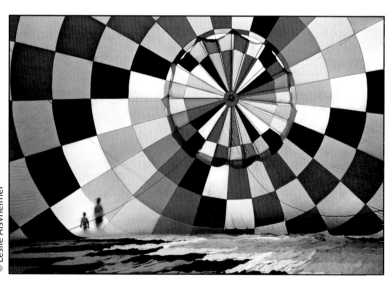

© Leslie Alsvheimer

Digital Like Film

For some digital photographers, the ultimate goal is to make black and white digital images that look as if they were captured on film. The gritty quality that came from pushed Kodak Tri-X film sometimes seems aesthetically so far removed from the crisp digital files we see with today's high resolution cameras. There is a unique elegance in film's simple grain and mysterious qualities. For the film photographer, certain specialized looks have always been achieved by choices in chemistry, paper and technique coupled with the type of film or emulsion chosen. The varying differences in the consistency of light sensitivity in emulsions typically give each type of film its unique aesthetic. With many films being taken off the market today, it is still incredibly useful to keep those traditional names and what they meant to the film photographer alive, and use them as points of reference. For the black and white photographer, whether traditional or digital, using black and white effectively is about choosing a "look" that matches your image and intention.

Film stocks replicated from Channel Mixer!

Of course, you will still have to add noise and grain to achieve the "look" of some films.

Note:
A close approximation to the luminosity perceived by the human eye would be settings of red = 30%, green = 59% and blue = 11%. An approximation to the default grayscale mode change might be red = 60%, green = 30% and blue = 0%, and a mix of red = 34%, green = 33% and blue = 33% is approximate equivalent to desaturation.

In monochrome mode:

Film Type	Red values	Green values	Blue values
Agfa 200X	18	41	41
Agfapan 25	25	39	36
Agfapan 100	21	40	39
Agfapan 400	20	41	39
Ilford Delta 100	21	42	37
Ilford Delta 400	22	42	36
Ilford Delta 400 Pro & 3200	31	36	33
Ilford FP4	28	41	31
Ilford HP5	23	37	40
Ilford Pan F	3	36	31
Ilford SFX	36	31	33
Ilford XP2 Super	21	42	37
Kodak Tmax 100	24	37	39
Kodak Tmax 400	27	36	37
Kodak Tri-X	25	35	40

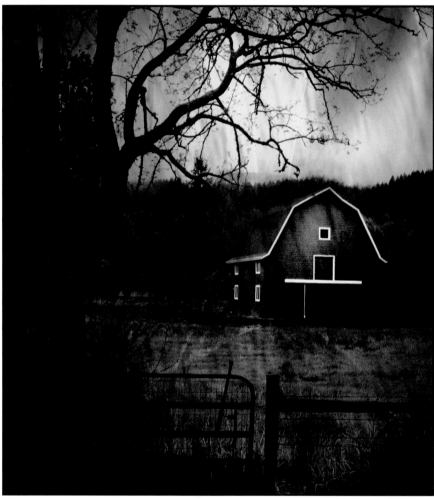

©Leslie Alsheimer

Before

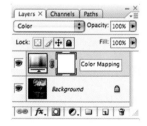

Hue Saturation Technique

This method, patented as "The Russell Brown Tonal Conversion Technique", lays the foundation for CS3's new Black and White stand-alone feature. This method uses two Hue/Saturation adjustment layers to make the initial conversion and creates a customized set of color mapping options at the same time! How does it work?

Step 1: Open an image you wish to convert, and click the adjustment layer icon at the bottom of the layers palette (looks like a little yin/yang) and choose Hue/Saturation. You can also go to the Layer Menu > New Adjustment Layer > Hue/Saturation. We are going to work with this layer later. So when the dialog box comes up, do not make any adjustments. Just click OK.

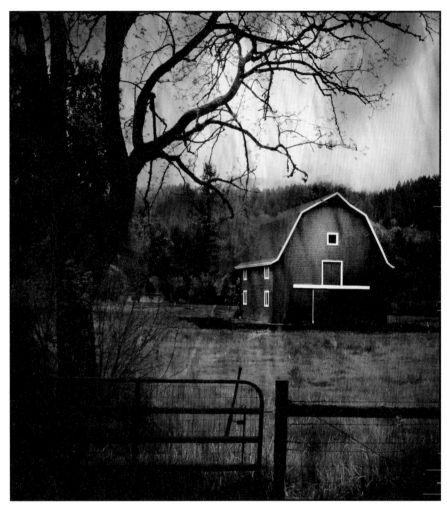

After

Step 2: Change the Blend mode of this new adjustment layer from Normal to Color. This option is one of 20 or so available blend modes from the drop down menu in the layers palette. This blend mode will allow us the ability to adjust the hue and saturation simultaneously. (If we think about this technique in photographic terms, this layer will act as our Filter layer ... or the Remapping color layer.)

Step 3: Make another Hue/Saturation adjustment layer by clicking on the adjustment layer icon at the bottom of the layers palette and choosing Hue/Saturation a second time. This time, however, we will pull the saturation slider all the way to the left, reducing the saturation to −100 (in photographic terms again, this will be the "film" layer, or simply "convert to gray").

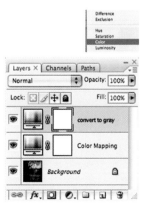

115

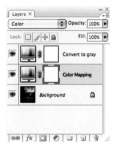

Step 4: Now we are ready to create the black and white conversion dynamically by playing with the individual color channels within the Hue/ Saturation dialog box's drop down menu. Here's how:

Step 5: Double click the adjustment layer thumbnail icon on the middle layer in the stack, which is the "filter" layer, or the first layer you created and set to color. This will reopen the Hue/Saturation dialog box. Adjust the Hue slider and notice how you are interactively changing the spectral relationships between the colors as they translate into black and white. Isn't that cool?

Step 6: You can also play with the Saturation slider and make further adjustments to give more emphasis to tonal values within the image.

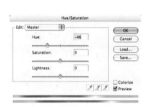

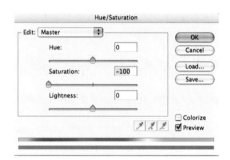

Extra Bonus Tip!
You can also expand the color range of the sliders by using the eyedroppers. If you have some red in the image and you wish to add yellow and green to that adjustment area, select the "Add" sample eye dropper tool and simply click on the colors you wish to add, such as blue and green. The tool will expand the range of colors and result in better blending values.

Hint:
It is always a good idea to name your layers! Double click on the letters in the layers palette that spell out Hue/Saturation and type in a name like "Color Mapping". This will help make it easy to remember what each layer does when you come back to the image later.

Step 7: This process actually gets better, believe it or not Check this out. If you go to the Edit Menu in the very same dialog box and click on the drop down menu, you can change the "Master" composite to isolate each color separately. Pull both the Hue and Saturation sliders for each color independently. Watch out for unwanted posterization effects as this can happen fairly easily if you are not paying attention.

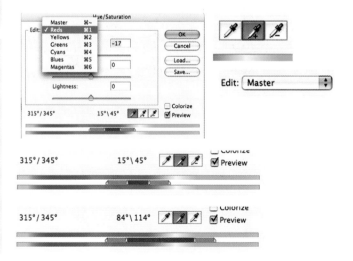

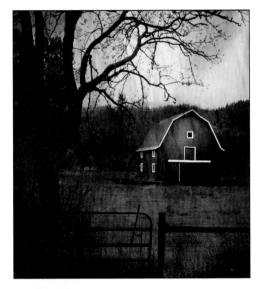
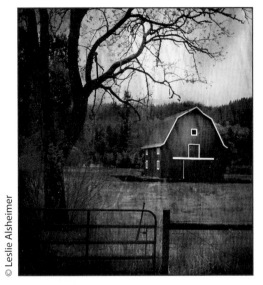
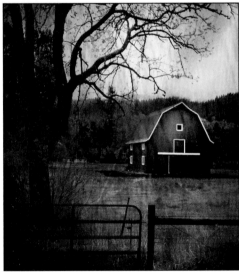
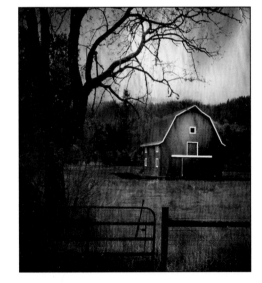

© Leslie Alsheimer

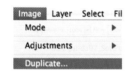

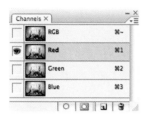

Turn Up the Volume! This One Goes to 11!

Coined by Nigel from the film "This is Spinal Tap", this pop culture phrase commonly refers to anything capable of being exploited to its utmost abilities, and to exceed them; the act of taking something to an extreme.

So this technique is #11: The ADVANCED Maximize Detail Combo Conversion Technique! To the MAX!

Once you have explored the fundamental conversion methods, you may be ready to delve deeper into the conversion process. If you have not noticed yet, converting to monochrome is most notably about reestablishing the spectral relationships between color and tone within an image. The advanced printer will know that image detail plays an integral role in successful black and white fine art print making. Be warned this fancy technique takes a fair bit of time, is not simple and can be incredibly confusing. It does, however, maximize your control over the conversion process, whereby allowing the user to selectively maximize detail and tonality in the conversion process. Althought there are a few variations on this technique, no other method quite matches its power, as this one really does go to 11!

Begin with an RGB image file processed for an optimal color rendition of the scene.

Step 1: Duplicate your image. Image Menu > Duplicate Open the channels palette and analyze the channels by clicking on each of the individual channels in the channels palette. Do this several times and make notes on the differences in how each channel translates the information and detail. (See "Channel Mixer", page 110 for more information on how to analyze the channels.) For this image, I noticed that there was more detail in the doorway (where the man is standing) in the blue channel, as well as in the top of the window. In the green channel, there was more information in the flowered curtains, the girl's feet on the bed, and the skirts they are wearing, as well as with the flip flop on the floor. The red channel holds more detail in the empty beds.

Step 2: Convert the Duplicate Image to LAB mode.

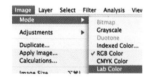

Step 3: Go to the Channels palette and click on the Lightness Channel. Select All > Edit Copy.

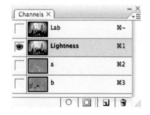

Step 4: Reactivate the original color image and create a new layer. Layer > New Layer, or click on the new layer icon.

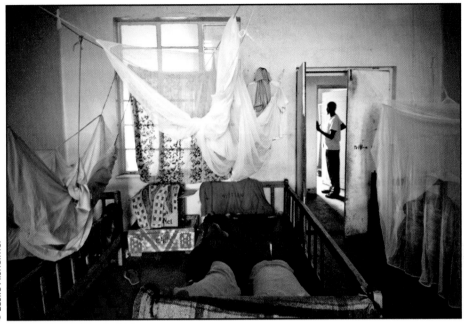

© Leslie Alsheimer

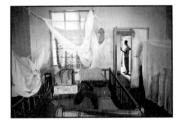

Blue Channel

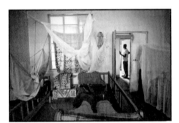

Green Channel

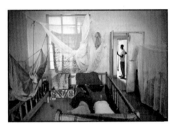

Red Channel

Step 5: Edit > Paste the Lightness channel into the new layer and Rename the layer "Lightness".

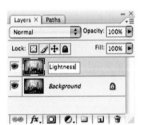

Step 6: Create three more empty layers and rename them "Red", "Green" and "Blue". You are going to copy and paste each of the Red, Green and Blue Channels into these layers.

Step 7: Turn the visibility off on the Lightness channel by clicking on the eyeball next to it in the layers palette. This will ensure that the Lightness Channel will not affect your channels. Copy and paste each channel into the appropriate new layers you have just created.

119

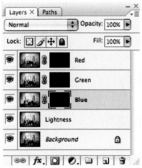

You can make excellent conversions by simply lowering the opacity of the different layers at this point. But who is stopping there? I said this one goes to 11!

Step 8: Add a "Hide All" layer mask to each of the Red, Green and Blue channels. Do this by holding the option key as you click the "Add Layer Mask" icon in the layers palette, or simply, use the Layer Menu > Add Layer Mask > Hide All.

Step 9: Use a paintbrush, set to the default colors of black and white at various opacities, and hide or reveal the different aspects in which you noted. I revealed the doorway on the blue channel, the curtains, feet and skirt on the green channel layer and the empty bed detail on the red channel layer.

Note:
You will need to retarget the Background layer and the corresponding channel each time you want to copy a channel.

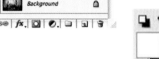

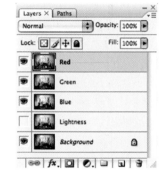

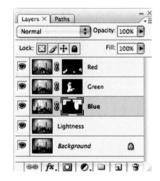

Try this technique with images shot in low light. The blue channel is great for bringing out lost shadow detail. But be careful, as it also holds the most noise!

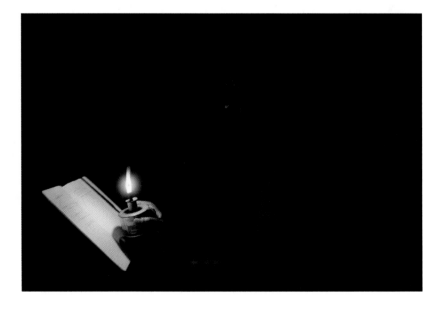

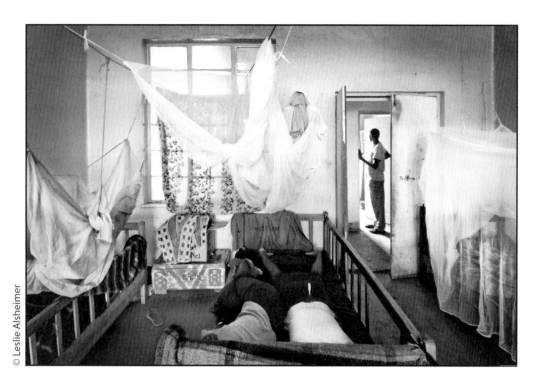

© Leslie Alsheimer

If you love this method, you may want to create a customized action in Photoshop that sets up the layers for you to make the process a bit faster. Visit the Santa Fe Digital Darkroom website for downloadable actions coming soon, www.santafedigitaldarkroom.com

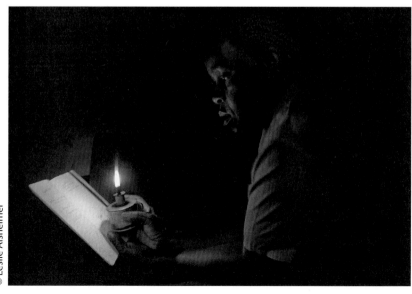

© Leslie Alsheimer

Black and White Standalone Feature

The new black and white feature in Photoshop CS3

Photoshop has always offered many ways to convert color images to black and white, each having its own unique advantages and quirks; let us be honest though, none have ever been particularly intuitive.

Photoshop CS3 offers a great deal for black and white photographers – changes to the power and usability of selective editing (and previewing via the new refine edge controls), a myriad of changes to camera raw, new controls for HDR conversions, new ways to adjust brightness/contrast, curves and the incredible advent of smart filters. Specific to black and white, CS3 improves greatly on the popular channel mixer method of converting to monochrome. In Photoshop CS3, the experience is simple, easier and faster.

For readers of this book, however, nothing is likely to be more exciting, useful, easy or powerful as the features and functionality found in the new stand-alone black and white feature in Photoshop CS3. When the Photoshop team looked at making a black and white feature, they surveyed the landscape, listened to user requests and threw in a bonus on image control compliments of the family's newest application, Adobe Photoshop Lightroom.

The feature exists as both a regular (pixel-based) image adjustment and as a new addition to a growing list of non-destructive adjustment layers.

Let us step through a common conversion:

1. In the interest of best practices, we will use an adjustment layer; do so either by navigating to Image Menu > Adjustments > Black & White, or by using the fly-out menu from the layers palette.
2. By default, Photoshop gives a nice set of fixed conversion numbers.
3. At this point, you can choose to use the "auto" button to map contrast amongst various tones. The effects of "auto" will vary from image to image, but in essence, Photoshop is adjusting sliders to give a well-contrasted adjustment.
4. For further control, each of the individual sliders can be moved to control the tonal value of that region.
5. The best control yet is the ability to interact directly with the document. In this new feature, you need only to click upon any region of the image and then move right or left to lighten or darken it! You will notice that whichever region you click upon maps to the appropriate slider in the black and white control. This is the only Photoshop feature to benefit from this workflow, and the success of Lightroom's implementation has proven how popular working directly with the image can be.

Note:
First, it is always a good idea to get a good, working exposure before applying any sort of black and white conversion. See Chapter 2: Capture in color for tips.

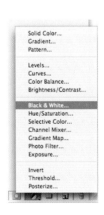

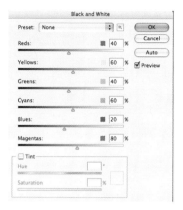

6. Now that you have spent a couple of minutes setting a nice conversion, let us save your hard work. Just to the left of the "OK" button is a preset options toggle, click it to "save settings". These "BLW" settings reside in the presets directory of the application folder; because they are small files and can easily be emailed or posted on the web for others to use.

7. The same preset button allows you to load other settings, or access one of the many presets that ship with CS3. Let us take a look at what they do.

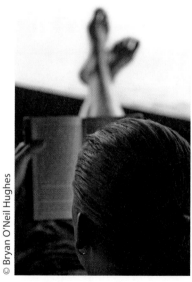

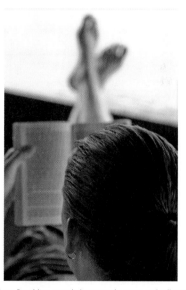

© Bryan O'Neil Hughes

Blue filter: By adding more lightness to the blue, cyan and magenta regions, this filter dramatically lightens sky and water while darkening leaves and foliage

Green filter: By adding more lightness to the green and yellow regions, this filter brightens foliage and leaves skies and other areas fairly neutral

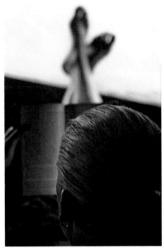

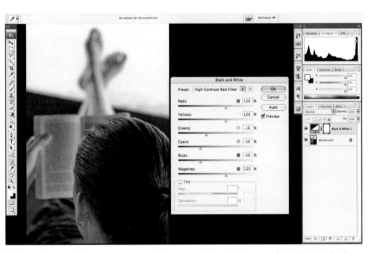

High contrast blue filter: A more extreme version of the blue filter, this magnifies the differences between the blue, cyan, magenta regions and others, creating a very high contrast image with a dark ground and light sky

High contrast red filter: Always popular in landscape photography because of its ability to make the sky dark and bold, while preserving the luminosity of shadows and foliage, the high contrast red filter boosts reds, yellows and magentas, while slightly darkening the others

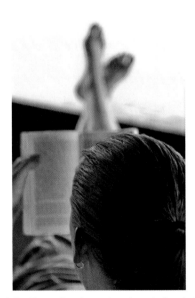

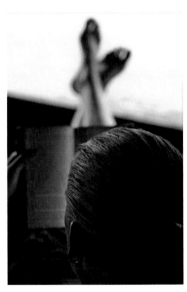

Infrared: This filter emulates the popular and surreal effect of using infrared film, that which measures reflective infrared light outside of normal measurement or perception. Infrared film shows greens and yellows in an ethereal glow

Maximum black: Just as it sounds, this filter darkens all sliders −50%

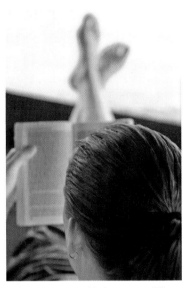

Maximum white: The opposite of the last mentioned filter, maximum white brightens all sliders to 150%

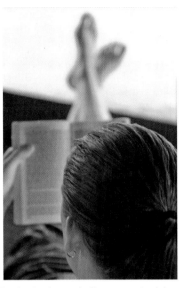

Neutral density: Another popular filter in conventional photography, this filter often exists in various degrees of lightening and darkening

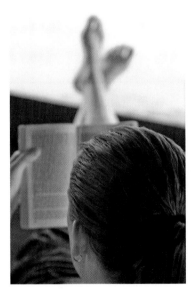

Red filter: The most used filter in black and white photography, the red filter adds contrast by darkening blues and brightening reds and yellows

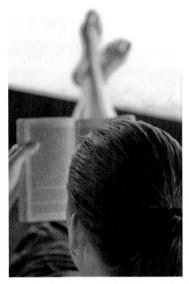

Yellow filter: The yellow filter is a slightly different take on adding contrast

Tinting

Tinting very often goes hand in hand with black and white conversion. A sepia or selenium tone can make a drab black and white image pop. Toning a monochromatic image gives it mood and personality. Unlike some of Photoshop's less discoverable other methods, tinting in the new black and white feature is as simple as pulling two sliders.

1. First check the "tint" checkbox.
2. Then slide the hue slider to the desired effect. Here are two popular ones:
   Sepia – hue 42 degrees saturation 20%
   Cyanotype – hue 200 degrees, saturation 10%
3. To further adjust your toning, pull the saturation slider in either direction.
4. You can also click upon the color picker to the tint control's right to select your own custom color.

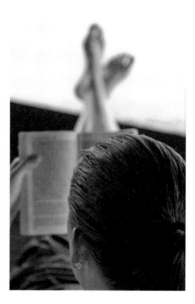

Sharing saved settings:
Remember that saved settings can also be shared with others, here is how:

1. Navigate to the Photoshop application folder/presets/black and white
2. Select the files that you want to share, copy (do not move) them to another location, and simply attach those to an email, post them to a Website or burn them to the media of your choice
2a. To load settings from another user, move their .BLW files to that same directory, or select "load" from the preset drop down and target the directory of your choice

In addition to the non-destructive benefits of using this new tool as an adjustment layer, you will recall that doing so gives you a host of blend modes. As with everywhere in Photoshop, experimentation is a great door to discovery, so do not stop with your conversion – consider what the many blending modes and selective edits can bring to your image.

Samples:

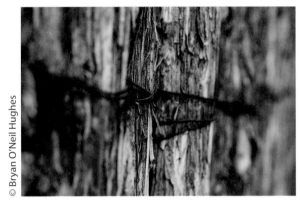

B&W stand-alone with on-image adjustments made

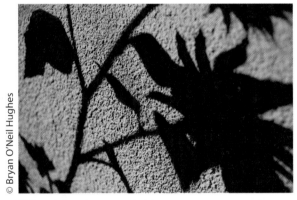

B&W stand-alone adjustments with tinting

Black and White in Adobe Camera Raw 4.0

A very brief background

The Adobe Camera Raw (or "ACR" for short) plug-in became available shortly after the release of Photoshop 7.0. What is now taken for granted as a self-loading portal into Photoshop, was at inception a very new, forward-thinking, powerful and flexible alternative to each individual camera company's proprietary methods for raw file conversion. From the initial version 1.0 of the plug-in, Adobe provided a quick, consistent and intuitive interface for photographers who preferred the high image quality and non-destructive nature of the raw format.

I don't think that anyone then knew how much ACR would catch on; but with an easy-to-learn stepped interface, terms familiar to photographers like "temperature", "exposure" and "white balance" coupled with a layout that was both familiar to legacy users and approachable by those new to the application – it really couldn't lose.

Why use Adobe Camera Raw?

The most powerful aspect of shooting in raw, and subsequently using ACR is not perhaps immediately obvious – it is entirely non-destructive. "Non-destructive" is a term that gets used a lot these days, but what does it mean? In the case of ACR, any adjustment applied in the plug-in, from tonal adjustments, to sharpening are all a system of settings associated with each file – each list of adjustments is simply a set of instructions to be applied to the original. For those converts from a film-based workflow, think of a raw file as your negative – pure, pristine, and unaltered.

Beyond giving the user an easy way to constantly make changes to a file, settings also have an incredibly powerful advantage – they can be shared! This means that when you give five or ten of your precious minutes to massaging the tonal adjustments in ACR, you can subsequently share any of those adjustments with other files with the mere seconds it takes to make a mouse click or two. So, reading between the above lines, this equates to a harmless system of adjustments that are entirely extensible – essentially, the preservational benefits of adjustment layers and the power of batch conversions without any requisite knowledge of either.

Why a plug-in?

ACR was lauded as brilliant when it came out, and raw shooters the world over welcomed it with open arms – after all, it supported nearly every major camera capable of shooting a raw format at that time. Unfortunately, getting ACR to work on the proprietary formats of so many cameras was only part of the problem. Change is inevitable, and change in digital photography, especially hardware, is constant! ACR thus needed to be flexible. Luckily, Photoshop has always been built upon an architecture which supports the extensibility of, literally thousands of plug-ins.

Plug-ins are basically applications within an application, they can range from the simplest of file readers (which, first and foremost ACR is) to the full-featured adjustment tools (which, as it happens ACR also is) and filters. Plug-ins constitute many of Photoshop's abilities to read, write and filter images and are developed by Adobe as well as a dizzying network of hundreds of third-party developers.

Advantages of shooting raw:
1. Flexibility
2. Extensibility
3. Preservation

4. Ease-of-use
5. Constant updates

Disadvantages of shooting raw:
1. Large files (raw files can be 3X the size of JPEGS!)
2. Limited hardware (only DSLRs and a small subset of pro-sumer point-and-shoots support the format)
3. Updates

Version 4.0, Adobe Camera Raw for everyone!

Photoshop CS3 ships with version 4.0 of ACR; a landmark update, the feature list reads like a magic marker though the above list of disadvantages. ACR can now read not only the omnipresent JPEG format, but the ever-popular TIFFs too! This means that any user of any camera or scanner now has access to all of the power and flexibility of ACR!

As if that weren't enough, ACR now has:

New tools (which leverage the like algorithms in Photoshop)

1. Red-Eye Reduction
2. Spot-Healing and Cloning

New Controls

1. "Recovery" (think of this as the "Highlight" control in Photoshop's Shadow/Highlight)
2. "Fill Light" (think of this as the "Shadow" portion of that same Shadow/Highlight feature)
3. "Vibrance" (a less heavy-handed saturation control mindful of skin tones)
4. "Parametric Tone Curve" (the powerful but daunting curves control, now hooked-up to intuitively marked sliders! – *don't worry, there's a standard point curve for you old-schoolers*)
5. "Convert to Grayscale" (yes, you read that right – ACR now has a black and white conversion feature! No more modifications of the calibration controls or extensive methods of desaturation, we now have a powerful and intuitive method of making gorgeous monochromatic images!)
6. "Split Toning" (it's now incredibly easy to make gorgeous multi-toned "black and white" images)

To those of you using the exciting new Adobe Photoshop Lightroom (see Chapter 3 for an in-depth look), you're probably thinking that all of the new features in ACR look very familiar – with good reason. Not only do Lightroom and ACR share the same underlying engine, but they were designed to read each other's files and settings with complete consistency.

Lastly, Adobe Camera Raw now has the smarts to update itself; when an updated version is detected, you no longer have to install the plug-in yourself – ACR and the Adobe Updater do it for you! Now you always have the latest features and support, and never have to hassle with figuring out where to put what. Enough already, let's get our hands dirty …

A stepped approach through ACR

This being a book primarily intended for black and white conversions, we presume a certain aptitude for adjusting the tonality and composition of an image; however, ACR being a relatively concise application, and one that's certain to be new to many of you, we want to take you through an easy, stepped approach from end to end.

Although workflows vary, ACR is constructed with an array of tools that are logically ordered; our prescribed approach is easy to remember, as it steps through the tools and controls in the same order that you find them presented to you.

Opening Files in ACR

One of the most common questions surrounding ACR is, "how do I get there?".

From Photoshop

Photoshop will automatically open raw files in ACR, however, if you'd like to use Adobe Camera Raw to open your JPEG files, you must first do the following:

1. From within Photoshop, navigate to Photoshop (Menu) > Preferences > File Handling
2. From within the preferences dialogue, check the box, "Prefer Adobe Camera Raw for JPEG Files"

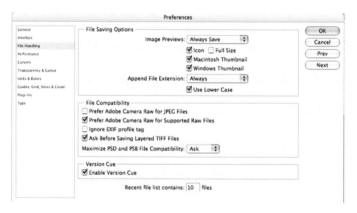

From Bridge CS3

Although Photoshop will automatically open raw files from Bridge in ACR, choosing to open JPEGs and TIFFs requires first:

1. From within Bridge CS3, navigate to Bridge (Menu) > Preferences
2. From within the preferences dialogue, check the box, "Prefer Adobe Camera Raw for JPEG and TIFF Files"

From the Operating System:
Apple OSX

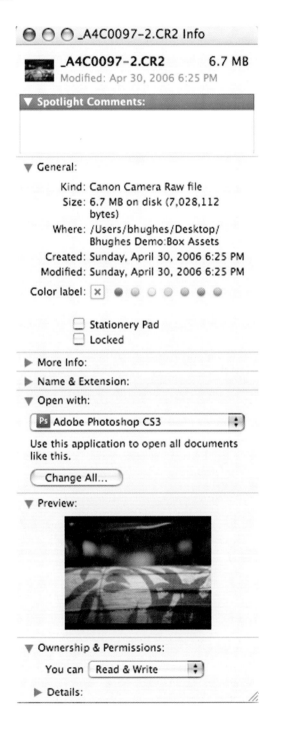

Tip:
To automatically straighten a crop, hold (Shift 1 Command) and draw a straight line for the crop tool to set guidelines from.

Now that we're in ACR, let's get to work!

Step 1: Crop: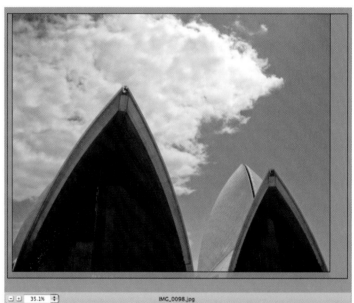

1. Select the Crop tool (C) from ACR's horizontal tool bar.
2. Simply draw, drag or pull corner points to set crop guidelines.
3. Now select any other tool (in this case the White Balance Tool) to apply the crop.

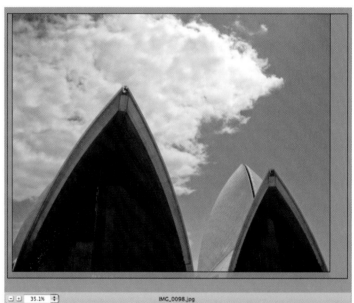

Note:
As with all aspects of Adobe Camera Raw, crops are completely non-destructive, and can be undone or modified simply by reselecting the Crop (C) tool.

© Bryan O'Neil Hughes

35.1%   IMG_0098.jpg

Tip:
Unbeknownst to many, you can also click on an area thought to be true black.

As Shot
Auto
Daylight
Cloudy
Shade
Tungsten
Fluorescent
Flash
✓ Custom

Step 2: White Balance:

1. Select the White Balance Tool (I).
2. The White Balance Tool is used to approximate the true color temperature of your image, to do so, click on a tone likely to be a true white.
2a. If your image needs further adjustment, either the Temperature slider or White Balance drop-downs are good places to start.

Step 3: Tone

1. First, let's remind ACR to show us regions of the highlights or shadows that will be clipped, so that we can be certain to preserve all of our image's details. To do so, click each arrow icon at the far left and right of the histogram.
2. Move the Exposure slider until Red overlays (clipped highlights) begins to appear.

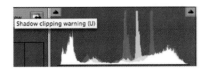

3. Now select the new Recovery slider, and move it to the right until the red, portions disappear; in the case of my image, I chose to continue moving the slider to show even more highlight detail.
4. Next move the Fill Light slider to the right, this will "dodge" the shadows. Continue adjusting until you have your desired effect. If the image doesn't have enough contrast, don't worry, we'll get there next.
5. We'll now carefully move the "Black" slider to add true blacks back to the image; move the slider until the blue overlay is just barely visible (too much blue indicates clipped shadow regions).
5a. If you'd like yet more contrast, the appropriately marked "Contrast" slider is a good way to massage the details – remember to be mindful of the blue overlays.

Step 4: Convert to Grayscale
There's reason for a bit of confusion here, isn't "Grayscale" an image mode in Photoshop? Yes, but it's also a way of describing a monochromatic image – think of this feature as it was intended, Black and White in ACR!

Unlike film, shooting digitally allows a photographer to shoot in both color AND black and white; in ACR, not only can you do that, but you can revert at any point because the conversion is only a set of instructions. If we like our conversion, those same settings can be shared with other files in the form of a preset with a single mouse click!

1. Within the HSL/Grayscale palette, simply check the box, "Convert to Grayscale".
1a. By design this adjustment leverages ACR's "Auto" setting, "Auto" maps the color tones in the image to present you the user with a nice, well contrasted conversion. If you compare this to selecting "Default", you'll see that the image looks much flatter otherwise.
2. With a mind towards what the colors WERE (remember, you can always toggle the "Preview" button in the upper right of ACR to see the image without adjustments), you can now move the sliders to lighten or darken any of the listed tone values.

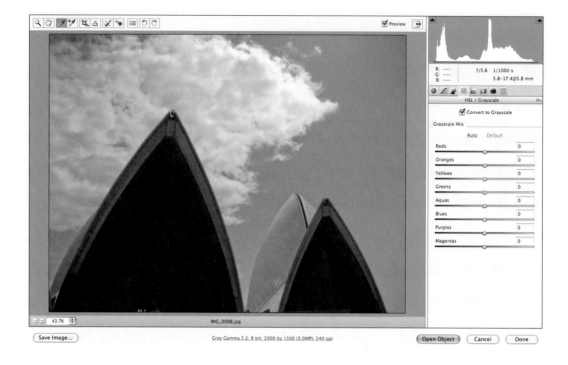

In my case, I found that further lightening the building's tones (Oranges and Yellows) and further darkening the sky (Blues) presented me with an even more appealing monochromatic contrast.

Step 5: Split Toning
One of ACR's easy and powerful features not found anywhere in Photoshop is the ability to split tone, which is to apply two separate hues – one to the highlights, and the other to the shadow regions.

Tip:
While moving the Hue slider, hold the Option key, this gives a preview of all hues at 100% saturation and saves a ton of time.

1. Within the Split Toning palette, grab the Highlight Hue slider and pull slowly to the right.
2. Once you've decided upon a highlight tone, repeat step one with the Shadow tone.
3. Simply slide the Balance control back or forth to equalize the image to suit your taste.

Step 6: Vignetting
My image is close to where I'd like it to be, I have a clean crop, nice contrast, a sepia-toned black and white conversion that snaps – it just needs one more

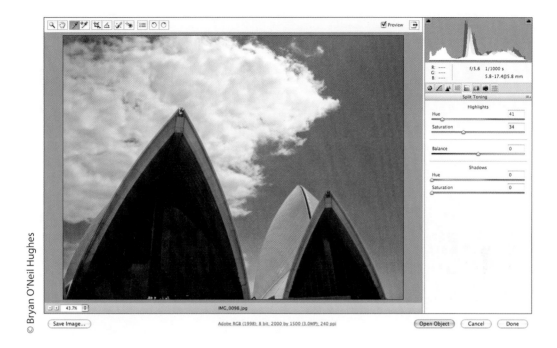

© Bryan O'Neil Hughes

thing. Vignetting is a way to dodge or burn just the corners of an image, doing so correctly brings the center of the image into even more prominent focus.

1. Within the Lens Corrections palette, under "Lens Vignetting", move the amount slider to the left (watch out for shadow clipping).
2. To control the range of the vignette, move the midpoint slider.

Step 7: Saving Preset
By saving our work as a preset, we can use it later to apply settings quickly to one or many images.

Step 8: Sharing Settings
Our settings can also be shared with others, to do so navigate to the appropriately named .xmp settings files in the user's Adobe/Camera Raw/Settings folder; these small files (sets of instructions) can be passed on to others via email, etc. and loaded into camera raw. To load files, simply select the Load Settings option from the preset flyout.

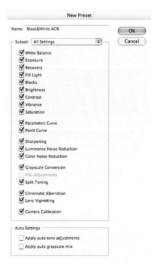

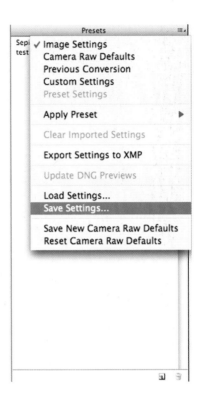

Note to Intel-based Mac users:
Legacy plug-ins (those from CS2 and before) can still run in Apple's translation environment, "Rosetta". To run those older plug-ins, you must run Photoshop itself in Rosetta; to do so press Command+I on the Photoshop CS3 application icon (in the Application folder) and select "Open using Rosetta".

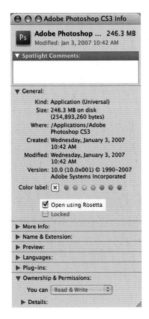

Black and White Beyond

A Selection of Photoshop Plug-ins

Thanks to the extensibility of its plug-in architecture, Photoshop has always had tremendous powers beyond the features that it ships with. In fact, many of the features that are included in Photoshop are actually plug-ins themselves; some are built by Adobe, others licensed from outside providers.

Plug-ins are in essence programs running within a program, and they can be anything from a reader of an obscure scientific file format to a 3D manipulation tool. As digital photography has exploded in the past years, a number of third-party plug-ins have been introduced to help in color correction, lens correction, noise removal, High Dynamic Range and – you guessed it – black and white conversion!

You may ask yourself, if I have black and white conversion abilities in Photoshop, Camera Raw and Lightroom, what more do I need? Well, as you are about to see, there are some very powerful features found in some of these add-on solutions. There are dozens of products out there, and sites (like Adobe's own http://www.adobe.com/products/plugins/photoshop/index.html) can help you find nearly all of them. For the sake of this book, we will focus on just a couple of the more current ones, offering abilities well beyond Photoshop's own.

Imagenomic's Real Grain

http://www.imagenomic.com/

As of the time of this writing, Real Grain runs natively on Intel-based Macs in CS3!

Far more than just additive grain, Real Grain offers film stock and grain simulation of dozens of film stocks (both black and white and color). For those of you looking to replicate the effects of, say, TMAX 3200, not only does this plug-in help match the grain, but also the tonal aspects of the film.

Like Camera Raw and Lightroom, Real Grain offers easy controls to add split toning and balance the end result. Other features of this plug-in are black and white conversions, tinting, the ability to split previews, and to have multiple "snapshot" previews in the case of the latter, each slider changes to represent the previewed effect.

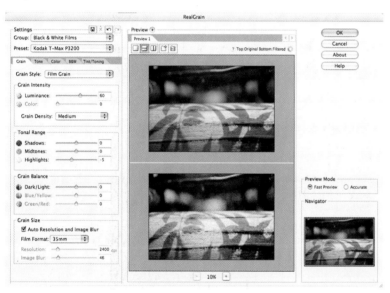

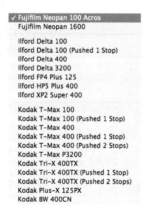

Fred Miranda's B&W Workflow Pro
http://www.fredmiranda.com/

Fred Miranda's solution also offers additive grain, film ISO emulation, black and white conversions, tonal effects and common black and white filters, all in an easy to navigate user interface. Most unique in B&W Workflow Pro is the innovative smart channel mixer; this is a channel mixer which automatically biases channel balance in real time – it is easy and powerful, and it produces great results.

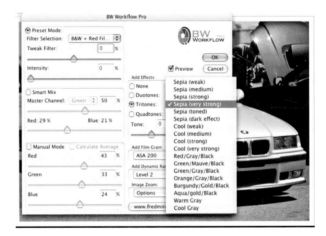

Imaging Factory's Convert to Black and White Pro
http://www.theimagingfactory.com/

In addition to a clean interface in its black and white converter and a series of strong controls for toning, Image Factory has some support for 32-Bit processing (aka High Dynamic Range), also unique to this group is the plug-ins ability to be scripted. Think of scripting as Actions gone wild; a user can define and call upon their own steps and procedures and vastly expand the speed and productivity of the plug-in.

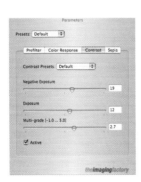

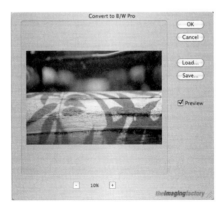

Power Retouche Studio's Black and White Pro
http://powerretouche.com/

As of the time of this writing, Power Retouche Black and White Pro runs natively on Intel-based Macs in CS3!

Like the others before it, Power Retouche Studio's Black and White Pro offers film stock emulation, easy and powerful conversions and photo filters; unique to this plug-in is a powerful contrast control and a way of applying strength and opacity, which is very evocative of the power found in adjustment layers. This plug-in has a clean enough interface that you often feel as if it must have come with Photoshop.

Power Retouche Studio's Toned Photos
http://powerretouche.com/

As of the time of this writing, Power Retouche Toned Photos runs natively on Intel-based Macs in CS3!

Power Retouche makes a separate plug-in just for toning, and it delivers on the expectations of a stand-alone. This plug-in has a wide array of presets and features the same strength and contrast controls found in Black and White Pro.

As mentioned before, there are hundreds of other plug-ins out there, and at least dozens which help when it comes to black and white conversions – what we have mentioned here are a few of our many favorites. Most plug-ins are available as limited trials, which is a great way to test what they might mean to your workflow.

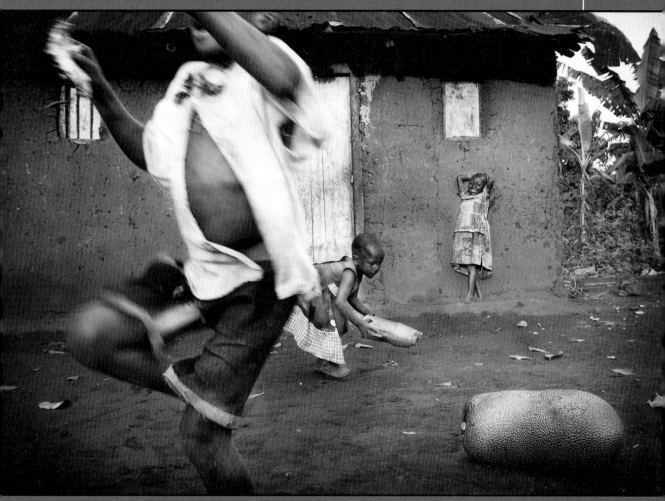

CHAPTER 5

Image Editing in Photoshop

© Leslie Alsheimer

Photoshop is far too extensive to cover any and all possible adjustments and creative tricks available for a given image. There are countless books on the market today outlining the array of tools and techniques Photoshop has to offer. For the purposes of this text, we have concentrated on some of the digital darkroom processes most pertinent and most useful for the black and white photographer.

1. Non-Destructive Editing: An Overview of Best Practices and New Features in CS3

The notion of "non-destructive editing" has received a tremendous amount of buzz in the last couple of years, but it has actually existed in Photoshop since version 3.0 in the form of layers! Today, we think of non-destructive editing as the system of settings that accompany a raw file, but that is just the latest example.

For a digital photographer, non-destructive editing in Photoshop means adjustment layers. Adjustment layers are virtual "sheets" placed over an image background that contain the entire content of an image adjustment. Because they keep the effects of the adjustment from being applied directly to the pixels in an image, they can be adjusted infinitely and without compromising the quality of the original. Specific to the needs of digital photographers, adjustment layers are truly the digital photographer's modern darkroom.

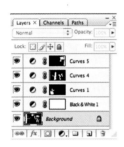

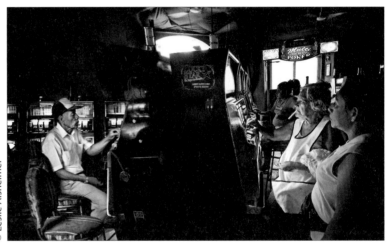

© Leslie Alsheimer

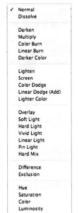

In addition to preserving the image's original detail, all layers also have the benefit of a myriad of blend modes.

Blend modes are an extremely powerful set of controls which dictate how layers "speak" to each other and to the image with which they interact. This chapter will illustrate some great techniques utilizing blend modes in the step-by-step tutorials.

Another unique attribute of Photoshop is its arsenal of selective editing tools. Selections, whether made by tools, masks, channels or subsets of layers, govern which portion of a given area Photoshop focuses its powers. When the power and flexibility of layers and selections meet, it becomes very obvious why Photoshop is the world standard for image adjustments.

Remember that only a few file formats preserve Photoshop's adjustment capabilities, they are:

– Photoshop (.PSD and .PSB)
– PDF (.PDF or PDP)
– TIFF
– DICOM

Non-destructive editing has made leaps and bounds in Photoshop for CS3; after years of wanting and waiting, we now have Smart Filters, which are essentially filter layers. As with other layers, filter layers multiply the dozens and dozens of existing filters exponentially with the extensive reach, depth and breadth of complex blending modes. Manipulations possible within Photoshop for many years now look fresh and new because of how they are able to non-destructively "speak" to the original image through blending, opacity and masking.

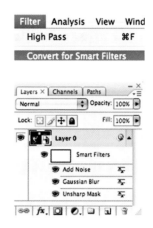

CS3 has added much for non-destructive workflows. Smart Objects introduced in CS2 are references linking a file with its original. As an example, were you to take a high resolution image and scale it down or crop it, the image would only be as good as its final incarnation; with the use of Smart Objects, the image, when later up-scaled, references its original, pristine state and thus continues to assure maximum fidelity.

CS3 made changes to Curves, Brightness/Contrast and the Channel Mixer, all benefiting black and white workflows; CS3 also introduced the exciting new stand-alone black and white control; all of these exist as adjustment layers in Photoshop CS3.

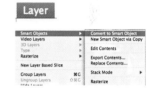

Lightroom 1.0 and Adobe Camera Raw 4.1 (which ships alongside Photoshop CS3 and CS3 Extended) now benefit from non-destructive support for both TIFFs and JPEGs that translate to a preservational workflow for everyone! From a cell phone image to a burst of space-saving files off a pro SLR, anyone can now enjoy the walk-up simplicity of these application's non-destructive workflows. In the case of these two applications, image integrity is preserved not through layers, but through a system of settings applied to the original image; these settings can either be baked into the file, or sit alongside the original in what's known as a "sidecar" file, which is a ride-along file full of .XMP metadata (a set of the adjustment instructions). Further, benefits of metadata driven adjustments are speed, intuitive controls (everything is non-destructive by nature) and sharing of effects; the one detriment is that Camera Raw and Lightroom are global editing tools, and adjustments are made to the entirety of an image – their big brother, Photoshop, is the home for selective edits.

A truly non-destructive workflow is about best practices and methodologies. Throughout this book, whenever applicable, we suggest methods which protect your valuable assets as best as possible. As stated, a non-destructive workflow is the only workflow with Lightroom and Camera Raw; here is a set of guidelines for keeping your files pristine in Photoshop.

1. Use the highest resolution and highest bit depth file (the original) as possible.
2. Use Smart Objects (that way anything done that threatens the original can always reference the first incarnation). When using filters, use Smart Filters.
3. Use adjustment layers whenever possible.
4. When saving, always save in a format that allows for full support of all of your data.

2. Using Adjustment Layers for a Non-Destructive Workflow

Adjustment layers allow you to make multiple edits to your image without degrading the original image data. This is one of the components of non-destructive practice. Using adjustment layers in Photoshop will give you more freedom and flexibility in your editing process, without sacrificing valuable image data.

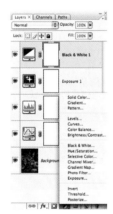

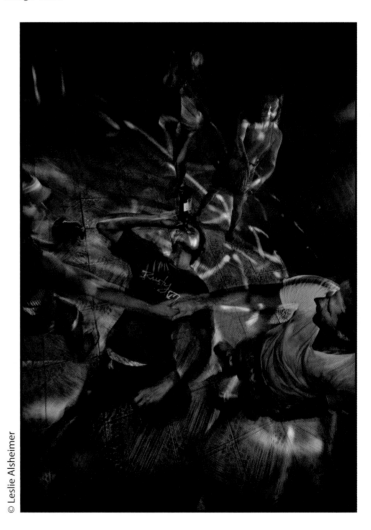

© Leslie Alsheimer

Creating Adjustment Layers

There are two ways to create adjustment layers. Go to the Layer Menu > New Adjustment Layer > and choose the adjustment you would like to perform, or in the layers palette, click on the adjustment layer icon and choose the adjustment layer from the drop-down menu.

Benefits of Adjustment Layers

1. *Non-destructive*

Applying image adjustments and edits directly to an image (Background) is destructive because actual image data is being thrown away in the process. Once that data is gone, it is no longer available to you for re-editing or tweaking the image at any future time. Adjustment layers, however, preserve the original image data like a negative by applying the editing adjustments above the original image.

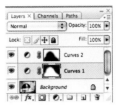

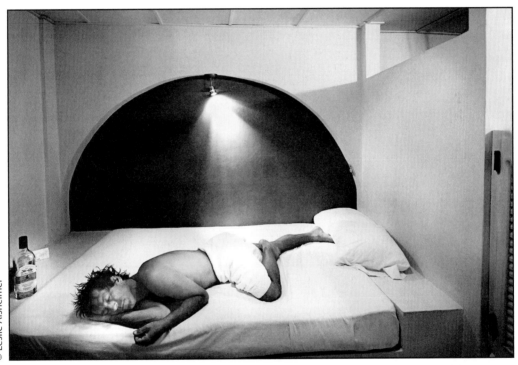

© Leslie Alsheimer

2. *Easily edited and reedited*

Adjustment Layers document, maintain and save the exact corrections applied, so the adjustment or edit can easily be accessed and readjusted by simply clicking on the adjustment layer icon in the layers palette.

3. *Reviewing changes*

Because the adjustment layer sits above the original image, reviewing image changes in a before and after state can be easily seen. Clicking the eyeball icons next to the adjustment layer allows you to turn the visibility of each adjustment on and off and make decisions accordingly.

4. *Layer options*

Adjustment Layers, as image layers, also provide layer options including opacity, blending options, masking, selective editing and the ability to transfer the adjustment layer to other documents.

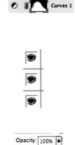

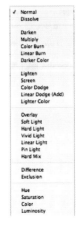

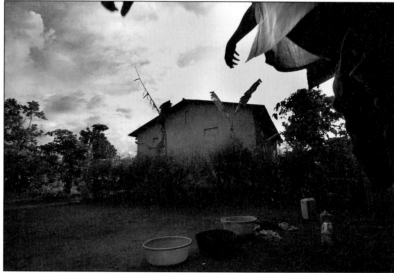

© Leslie Alsheimer

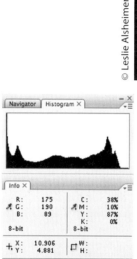

3. Monitoring Adjustments with the Histogram Palette

Open the Histogram and Info palettes. Choose Window Menu > Histogram.

The default configurations will bring up both the Histogram and the Info palette grouped together. In order to look at both palettes simultaneously as pictured to the left, click on the tab with the word Info and hold the mouse depressed and drag the two palettes apart.

The Histogram palette, introduced with Photoshop CS, allows the user to monitor the overall tonality and quality of an image dynamically as it is being adjusted. It is just as important to monitor loss of highlight or shadow information and detail as an image is being adjusted in the editing process, as it is in capture phase. Keep these palettes active and in view while editing and adjusting images in your digital darkroom practice. Slams to the right side of the histogram typically indicate loss of highlight detail, while slams to the left of the histogram exhibit loss of shadow detail. (See "Exposure Evaluation Tools", page 37 for a more in depth analysis of the histogram.)

The Info palette can also be useful in this process as one can mouse over the image and watch the Info palette dynamically measure image data in numerical values for each of the red, green and blue channels. To ensure that detail is not being lost, look at areas of concern and read the corresponding numbers as you mouse over the image, or shift click on specific areas to set target points to monitor. Equivalent values of 255 with each of the RGB channels is by definition pure white on the brightness scale, or white without detail. Equivalent values of 0 with each of the RGB channels is by definition pure black, or black without detail. Unless an image is aiming toward some creative interpretation, we typically want highlight and shadow detail within a photographic image.

Note:

If the Info palette is not grouped together with the Histogram palette, just go the Window Menu and check Info. Be aware, clicking on a palette toggles it either into view or out of view. If the menu is already in view, clicking on it in the Window Menu will actually turn it off.

4. Levels and Curves Overview: Tone and Contrast Corrections

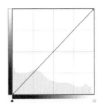

Levels and Curves are the fundamental digital darkroom tools in Photoshop for both global and selective tone and contrast adjustments. In Photoshop CS3, both Levels and Curves now offer a histogram feature providing important information on shadows and highlights as tonal values are mapped within an image during the corrective process.

4a. Levels

Input Sliders

The three colored triangles just below the histogram allow you to change the black point, white point and gamma of an image in real time. As you move one of the sliders, Photoshop starts remapping pixel brightness within the image. Create contrast by bringing the white and black sliders closer together.

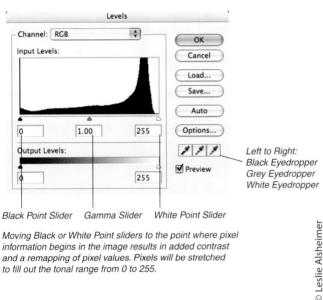

Black Point Slider   Gamma Slider   White Point Slider

Moving Black or White Point sliders to the point where pixel information begins in the image results in added contrast and a remapping of pixel values. Pixels will be stretched to fill out the tonal range from 0 to 255.

Left to Right:
Black Eyedropper
Grey Eyedropper
White Eyedropper

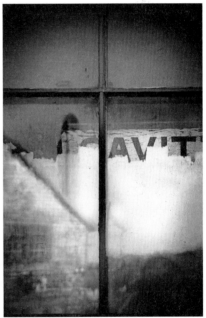

© Leslie Alsheimer

Moving the black point slider to the right, away from its default position at 0, will force any pixel information to the left of the slider to pure black. Moving the white point slider to the left will force any pixel information to its right to become pure white. Monitor the histogram as you pull the sliders to keep from inadvertently throwing out image data.

The Gamma slider, the middles slider, allows you to change the midtone values within the image without affecting the highlight or the shadow values. Moving the gamma slider maps where the middle gray or 128 tonal value will fall. Click OK, and Photoshop remaps the pixel data to your specifications.

Keep a close eye on the histogram as you make corrections in the digital darkroom to make sure that your editing is not creating significant gaps in the histogram. Too much pixel pushing can lead to posterization, which is the lack of smooth graduation between tones. (See "Exposure Evaluation Tools", page 37 for a more in depth analysis of the histogram.)

Output Levels

Output Levels also affect the brightness and contrast of the image. This control slider compresses the tonal range of an image. Moving the highlight output slider to the left decreases contrast and darkens the image. Moving the shadows output slider to the right also decreases contrast, but lightens the image. This slider is most often used for graphic design purposes in screening back an image, to overlay text, for example.

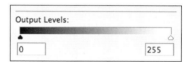

Preview

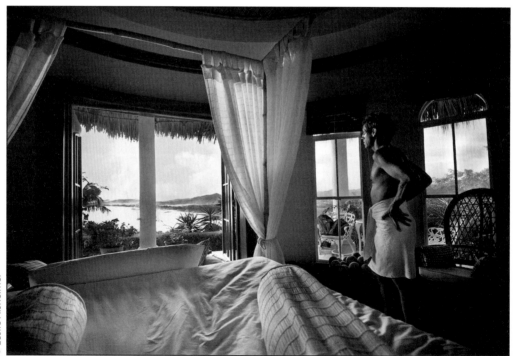

Turning on and off the preview check box allows you to view the changes you made to the image before you apply them.

© Leslie Alsheimer

4b. Curves

Curves is another tool providing the ability to affect tone and contrast correction within an image. Curves, however, is far more powerful. This is the digital darkroom power tool. Just as a hand held screwdriver and a power operated driver perform the same functionality, levels and curves, too, accomplish the same tasks. Levels is to the hand held driver with three points of adjustment as curves is to the power tool with 16 points of adjustment. The concepts are the same as in the Levels Dialog Box, the method however, is different. The Curves Box is also a graph that plots the relationship between input values along the bottom of the graph and the output values plotted vertically along the side.

Curves gives you far more control of the corrections you apply, due to the number of points that can be placed on the graph, but requires more skill in its application.

Levels and Curves have many similar controls. There are shadow, highlight and gray droppers that can be used to set white and black points, and a specific curve adjustment can be saved and/or loaded.

As with any power tool, the best way to work in curves is to make subtle gentle movements and adjustments with smooth flowing curves. Too aggressive or too many points haphazardly placed, and adjustments will be out of the photographic digital darkroom and into the way out art fast. Experiment with the new CS3 presets for medium contrast, linear contrast,

Auto Reset

Hold Down the Option Key and the Cancel button will become a Reset button in almost every dialogue box in Photoshop. Press Reset and the changes made will disappear.

Shadow Values, starting at 0.

Highlight Values, starting at 255.

Midtone Values, between 55 and 200.

Eyedroppers to set highlight, shadow and gray targets.

The Output Axis, or adjusted values.

strong contrast, lighter and darker image adjustments to get a feel for how to apply these corrections with a free hand – subtle, gentle, and smooth.

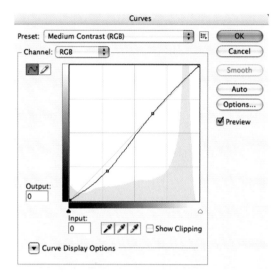

Medium Contrast Preset

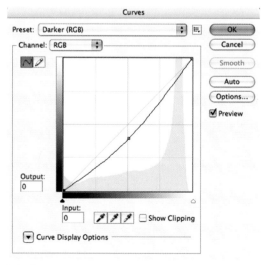

Strong Contrast Preset

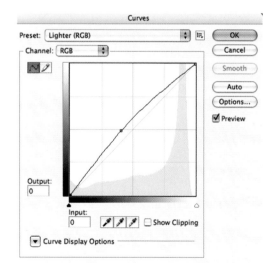

Lighter Preset

Darker Preset

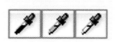

5. Setting Black and White Points

If true black and crisp whites are what you are after, then setting black and white points within an image is good place to begin your digital darkroom practice. This process will give you added tonal control, as well as eliminate unwanted color cast within an image. We will outline a few different ways to set black and white points.

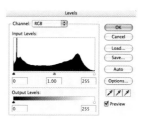

Before we begin, however, we need to reset the eyedroppers tools as Photoshop installs with values for the color correction eyedroppers set to default numbers that represent a pure black and a pure white. For photographic purposes, we need the settings to represent values for both a white and black with detail.

5a. Changing the Dropper Default Settings

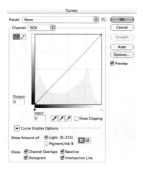

For photographic purposes it is necessary to first reset the black and white eyedroppers default target values

To maintain black and white with detail, first create a Levels or Curves Adjustment layer. As both levels and curves utilize the same eyedropper tool functions, changing the settings in either one corrects the tools universally.

Double click on the black and white eyedroppers within the dialogue box to bring up the color picker. Edit the RGB values to read as follows.

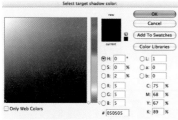
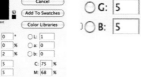
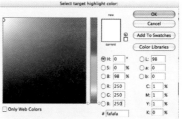

Black Point values:
RGB values: 5, 5, 5

White Point values:
RGB values: 250, 250, 250

There are a number of value settings on the market today. Those that we have outlined above are a typical Stock agency requirement. Although they vary among agencies, these numbers were recommended by the Corbis stock agency, who is currently one of the leading agencies setting standards for commercial digital imaging. Look under setting White Point in the Adobe Help Menu for additional number settings as recommended by Adobe. Save these as your defaults or talk to your agency or printer/service provider for their recommendations.

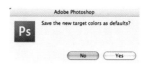

Save these as your target values!!!

Click OK to the Color Picker settings, click OK again to the levels box, and Yes to save the new values as the default settings.

5b. Setting Black and White Points Using Levels

We will outline two methods to determine black and white points within an image. Method 1 is a faster and easier approach, while Method 2 will prove distinctively more accurate but also a bit more complex. The process for setting black and white points for color and black and white images is exactly the same utilizing either method.

Method 1: This method is easier!

After the target values for black and white are set in the eyedropper tools. (See "5a Changing the Dropper Default settings", page 151.)

Create a Levels adjustment layer

Option Key Sliding

While holding down the option key (Alt key on the PC), click on the white point slider in the Levels display box (just under the histogram). The image will turn completely black. As you pull the slider, white will eventually begin to appear within the image indicating where to find the lightest area that contains detail within the image. This is very helpful when deciding where to click the eyedropper. You will be looking for the first place white presents itself

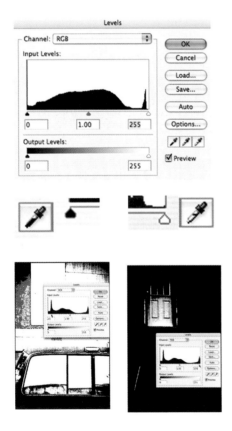

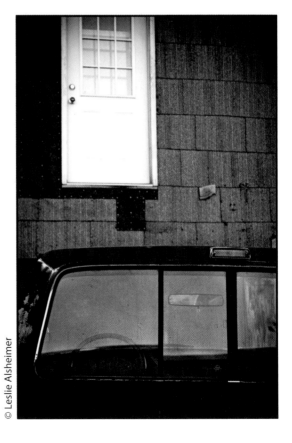

© Leslie Alsheimer

in an area with detail, (not a specular highlight). Choose the white dropper and click in exactly that spot on the image.

Step 3: Repeat the same process to find the black point, only this time use the black slider and the black eyedropper.

Use the middle dropper to set a neutral value, or something that should be neutral.

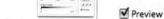

Note:
The slider method will not work for the gray dropper. It is a subjective placement. Try several different placements to see what looks to be the best to you.

☑ Preview

Tips:
Preview Turning on and off the preview check box allows you to view the changes you made to the image before you apply them.

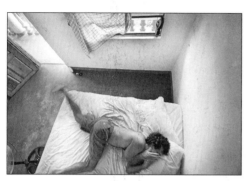

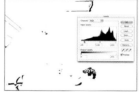

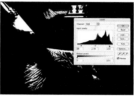

Before

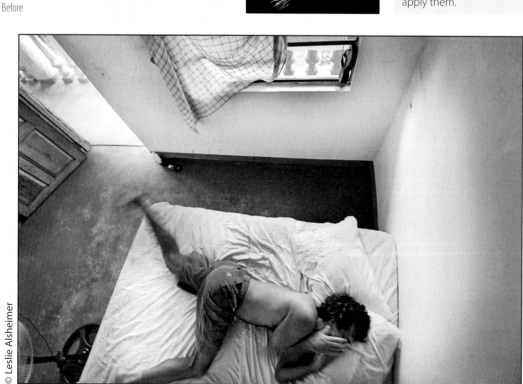

© Leslie Alsheimer

After

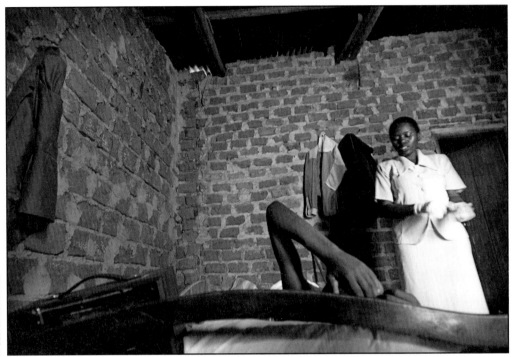

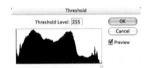

Method 2: Threshold; a more advanced and more accurate method.
Both Levels and Curves have the powerful eyedropper tools, and both are a great place to start preliminary tonal and contrast corrections with black and white point settings.

Step 1: Use Bridge to find an image that requires black and white point corrections File > Browse

Step 2: Find the White Point w/ Threshold. Create a new levels adjustment layer. Choose Layer > New Adjustment Layer > Threshold, or click the adjustment layer icon in the layers palette and choose Threshold to bring up the Threshold window.

Click on the white input triangle in the center below the histogram and drag it all the way toward the right to bring the image to all black. Slowly drag the slider back toward the right to reveal the first white pixels. Click OK.

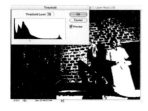

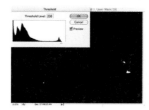

Step 3: Set the White Point Target

Zoom into the isolated white pixels. Click and hold the mouse on your eyedropper tool in the tool box to find the Color sampler tool nested underneath the eyedropper. Click in the white area created by the Threshold layer of the image to place a color sampler target point.

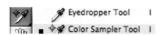

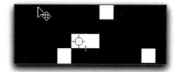

Step 4: Find the Black Point w/ Threshold

Double click on the threshold adjustment layer icon in the layers palette to bring back the threshold window. This time, pull the white slider all the way to the left to bring the image to all white. Then slowly drag the slider back to the right to reveal the first Black pixels. Click OK.

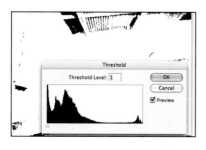

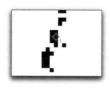

Step 5: Set a Black Point Target

Zoom into the isolated black pixels. Click and hold the mouse on your eyedropper tool in the tool box to find the Color sampler tool nested underneath the eyedropper. Click in the black area created by the threshold layer to place a color sampler target black point.

Step 6: Throw away the Threshold Adjustment Layer
Drag the threshold adjustment layer to the trash can at the bottom of the layers palette, or just turn the visibility off in the layers palette.

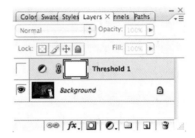

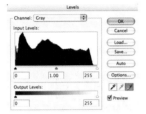

Step 7: Create a Levels Adjustment Layer
Go to the adjustment layer icon at the bottom of the layers palette and choose levels or curves.

Step 8: Set the White Point
 Single click on the white eye dropper to select the dropper, and click on your image in the center of the color sampler target you created for the white point.

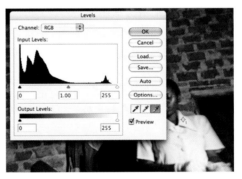

Step 9: Set the Black Point
With the Levels dialog box still open, single click on the black eye dropper to select the dropper, and click on your image in the center of the color sampler target you created for the black point.

Step 10: Set Neutral Point if there is one
Click on the gray dropper, and click on an area within the image that should be a neutral gray. It is ok to go "fishing", meaning just clicking around the image with the gray eyedropper to get different results if you do not know where a neutral exists.

Hint:
Finding a neutral point in an image for color corrective purposes is often a matter of "click fishing". Try clicking on gray hair on humans or animals, shadow areas, rocks and clouds are often places that contain a good neutral.

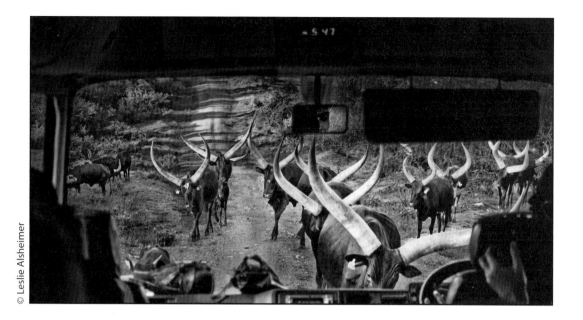

© Leslie Alsheimer

6. Photoshop: Dodging and Burning with "Soft Light"

While dodging and burning may be familiar terms to anyone brought up with traditional darkroom techniques, the ability to open shadows and burn highlights selectively and skillfully using a paintbrush tool is one of the most astounding tools Photoshop has to offer the black and white photographer. In fact, this is the technique that convinced me to move into the digital darkroom! With this method you can lighten and darken subtle detail work with the precision of a paintbrush. This is dodging and burning control and accuracy never dreamed possible!

Step 1: Create a New Blank Layer
At the bottom of the layers palette, click on the new layer icon or go to Layer Menu > New > Layer.

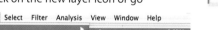

Step 2: Go to the Edit Menu > Fill.

Step 3: Select for the Contents, Use: 50% Gray. Make sure the other settings read 100% for Opacity and Normal for the blending mode.

Step 4: In the Layers Palette, set the Blending Mode to Soft Light or Overlay.

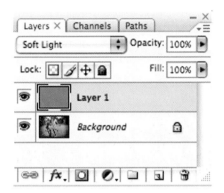

Step 5: Pick a paintbrush from the tool palette and reduce the brush opacity to 20%. Use a soft brush to blend and soften edges.

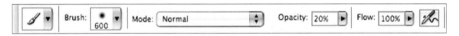

Step 6: Set your color picker to the default colors of black and white by clicking on the two little black and white square icon, or hit the "D" key on the keyboard.

Step 7: Paint with black in areas of the image you wish to burn, and paint with white to dodge. Be sure to zoom in so that you can really accentuate fine image detail.

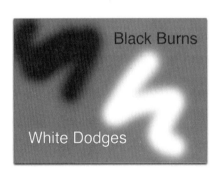

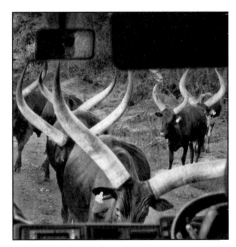

Step 8: Use the "X" key to toggle quickly between black and white.

7. Dodging and Burning with Adjustment Layers

Making separate adjustments to the highlights, midtones and shadow values is a digital technique that would be nearly impossible to reproduce in the traditional darkroom! Use this technique with the color range selection tool as outlined below, or with any selection tools that isolate an area for tonal adjustments.

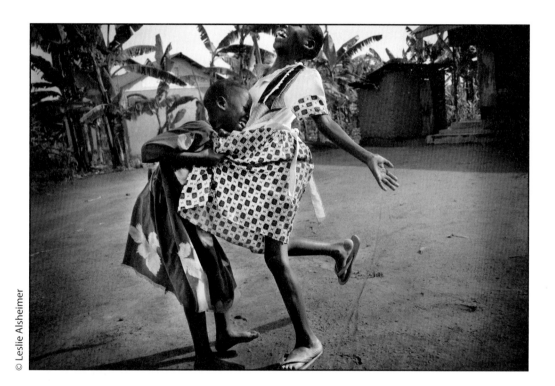

© Leslie Alsheimer

Step 1: Go to Select Menu > Color Range.

Step 2: In the Color Range dialog box dropdown menu next to Select: Sampled Colors and choose Highlights. Click OK.

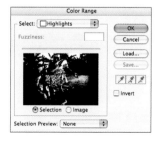

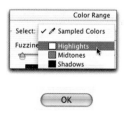

Step 3: Select Feather: Go to Select Menu > Modify > Feather. The amount of feather will vary depending on the file size and image data. I chose 15 Pixels for this image.

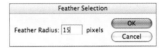

Step 4: Create an adjustment layer of levels or curves to modify the selected area. Go to Adjustment layer menu at the bottom of the layers palette and choose levels or curves. Pull up on the curve to dodge the selected highlight areas, pull down on the curve to burn them, or try one of the presets for increased contrast. The adjustment will only affect the selected highlight areas.

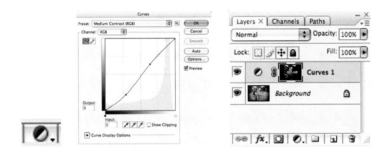

Step 5: Repeat steps 1–4 for the shadows and midtones creating two more adjustment layers if desired.

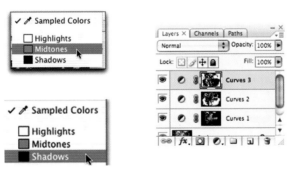

8. Creating a Neutral Density Filter

Most traditional photographers are familiar with the graduated and split neutral density filters. These filters reduce the exposure over part of the image in either a graduated or abruptly graduated manner. Often neutral density filters are used to equalize exposure when shooting a large amount of sky in the image. Used properly, metering and exposure can be adjusted for the foreground details, while preserving highlight detail in the sky and clouds.

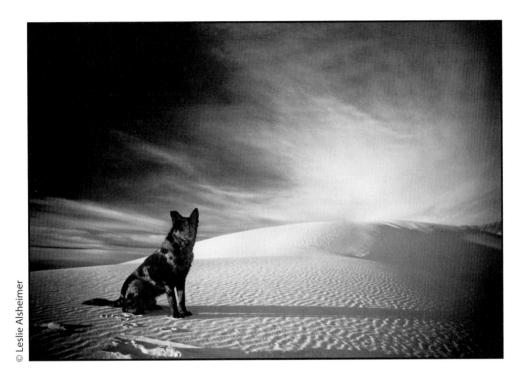

© Leslie Alsheimer

Step 1: Use Bridge to find and open an image that needs a graduated or neutral density exposure adjustment.

Step 2: Create a curves adjustment layer by clicking on the Adjustment Layer icon at the bottom of the layers palette, or go to the Layer Menu > New Adjustment Layer > Curves.

Create a curves adjustment layer that darkens the area desired to burn. This will actually darken the entire image…but do not worry, the filter we create will correct the exposure in the areas we do not wish to darken. In this example, we pulled a curve that darkened down the sky for a more dramatic effect.

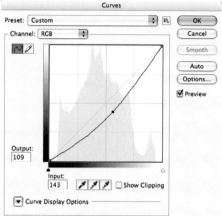

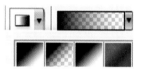

Step 3: Gradient tool

Click on the Gradient tool in the tool bar.

Hit the "D" key on your keyboard to return the Color Picker to the default settings of black as the foreground, and white as the background.

Step 4: Choose linear gradient

Look to your option bar from the gradient tool. Make sure that you have the first icon, the linear gradient selected.

Step 5: Draw a gradient

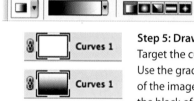

Target the curves layer mask by clicking on the mask icon in the layers palette. Use the gradient tool to draw a line from the top of the image to the bottom of the image area. Hold the Shift key to keep the line perfectly straight. Place the black of the gradient on the area you wish to protect from darkening and draw the white over the area of the image you wish to darken (black conceals the adjustment while white reveals the adjustment). The gray area in between will create the transition between the darkened area and the protected area. The longer the drag with the gradient tool, the greater the transition area will be. For a shorter and more abrupt transition, try a short quick drag with the gradient tool.

Step 6:

Apply a levels adjustment directly onto the neutral density mask filter to adjust the transition area visually. Go to the Image Menu > Adjustments > Levels or CMD "L" (Control "L" on the PC). Pull the midtone slider back and forth to suit the image. This will affect the transition edge of the gradient.

9. Vignetting

Burn Edges w/ Geometric Selection Tools

A classic fine art printing technique used by many masters was to burn the edges for a finishing touch on prints, or used more dramatically to create portrait vignettes. Photoshop's geometric selection tools allow us not only to do this quickly and easily, but also to soften the edges of an image by using the same technique coupled with a blur filter.

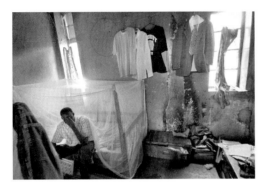

Before

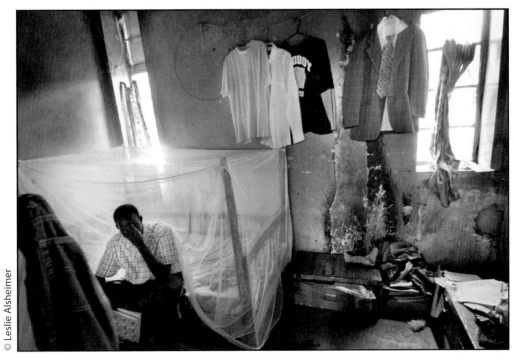

© Leslie Alsheimer

After

163

Choose document that needs edge burning

Step 1: Choose the rectangle or elliptical marquee and drag a rectangular selection a few inches from the image border.

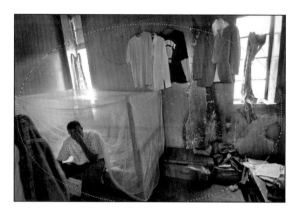

Step 2: Feather the Selection Select Menu > Modify > Feather. Choose a pixel radius depending on file size.

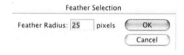

Step 3: Select the inverse. Select Menu > Inverse

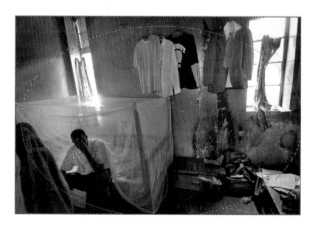

Step 4: Choose a Curves Adjustment Layer. Darken the select area by clicking once in the middle of the curve and slowly pulling the curve down. Click OK.

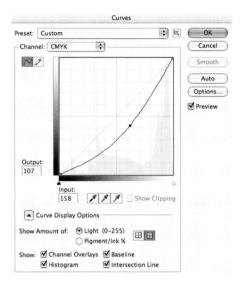

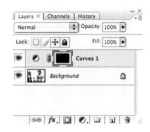

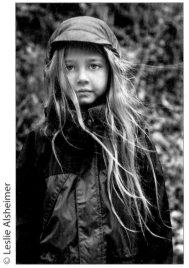
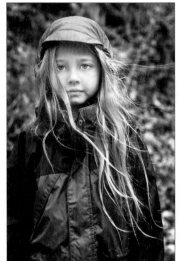
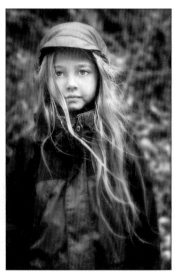

© Leslie Alsheimer

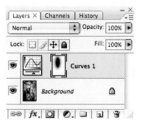

Try this technique with portraits!

To blur the background, repeat steps 1–3 then choose Filter menu > Blur > Gaussian Blur to soften the edges.

10. Correcting Exposure Issues with Adjustment Layers

If you have an image that is a little over or underexposed, then there is no need to worry – a quick and simple adjustment in Photoshop will have your image looking like it was correctly exposed in no time at all.

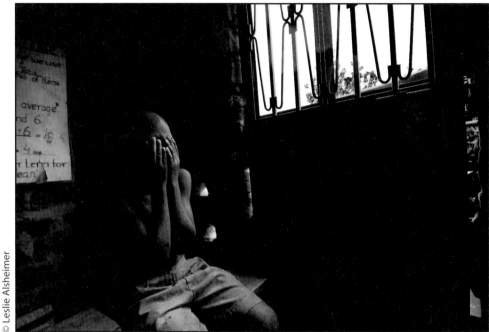

© Leslie Alsheimer

After

 Create an adjustment layer for levels or curves with the adjustment layer icon at the bottom of the layers palette. I usually choose curves. or, go to the Layer Menu > New Adjustment Layer > Curves.

Do not adjust … Simply click OK.

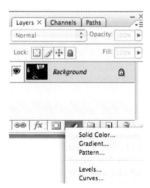

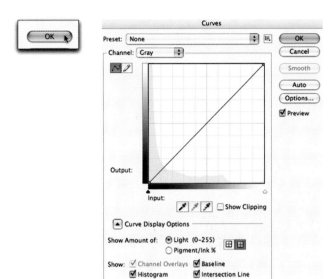

Set the blending mode in the layers palette to "Screen" to correct for underexposure (lighten an image), or set the blending mode to "Multiply" for overexposure (darken an image).

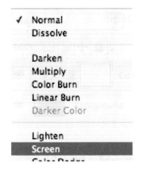

Decrease layer opacity 36% for 1 full stop adjustment.

36% = 1 stop

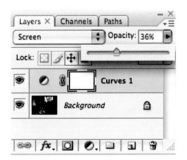

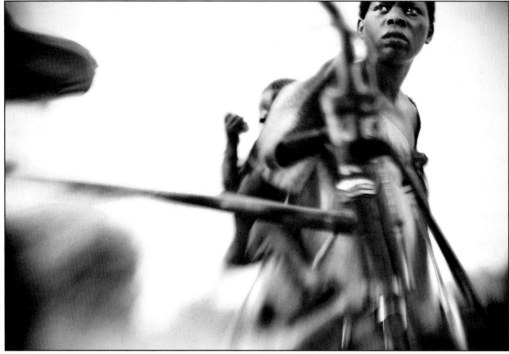

© Leslie Alsheimer

11. Creating Film Grain Effects

There are many ways to create this effect in Photoshop, with plugs-ins, as well as with third party software. Most all are created by doing one or more of the following steps.

Method 1

Take a piece of film with an empty frame from the ends of a roll and scan it! Copy and paste the scan into your image document and transform the size to fit your image. Set the Blend Mode to Multiply and reduce the opacity to taste.

Method 2

Step 1: Create a new empty layer on the top of your layers stack. Go to The Edit Menu > Fill > /and Choose 50% gray from the drop down menu.

Step 2: Go to the Filter Menu and choose Noise > Add Noise. Be sure to Check Monochrome and Gaussian and choose an amount to your liking. I choose 12 for this image. You can always reduce the opacity of the layer.

Step 3: Change the blend mode on the layer from normal to Softlight or Overlay (experiment with which looks to be the best to you!)

Step 4: Reduce the opacity if need be to suit your image preference.

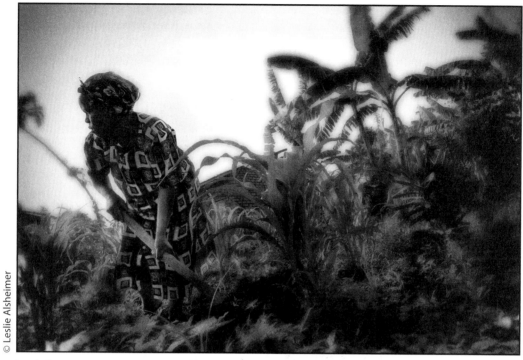

© Leslie Alsheimer

Digital Infrared

12. Digital Infrared

Infrared was one of my absolute favorite films to experiment with in undergraduate school. Although extremely difficult to expose well, the grainy and glowing quality of infrared gave it an ethereal feel I really loved. As the film responded to infrared radiation rather than to light, which is just outside the visible spectrum, learning to back off the focus just the right amount and expose infrared properly was quite an experimental process. The heat produced by green foliage and other living

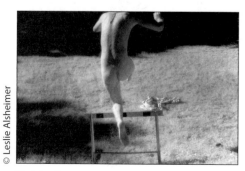

© Leslie Alsheimer

Film Infrared

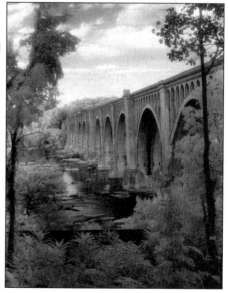

© Leslie Alsheimer

Film Infrared

things creates the glowing surreal quality we are not able to view with our eyes. The image of the Bridge and Hurdeler were exposed with Infrared film and printed in the silver process. In the following lesson, we will re-create this effect digitally, which, I have to concede, is far easier than it was the traditional way!

In order to simulate the infrared effect, there are two different methods I have found to work most effectively. The key to both methods is in accentuating the green foilage within an image.

Step 1: Convert to Monochrome and accentuate Green

Create a black and white conversion adjustment layer using either the Channel Mixer or the Black and White stand alone feature in CS3. Try both and see which one works best for your image!

With the black and white stand-alone, you need to increase the values of the green and yellow sliders so that the foliage in the image becomes very light, paying close attention not to blow out detail within the image.

With the Channel Mixer, increase the value of the green channel to close to 200%, and reduce it slowly paying close attention not to blow out detail in the image. Reduce the Blue and Red channels so that the sum of all three channels is roughly 100%. Totals can really be what looks best .. give or take a few! Start with Red −50 and Blue −50 and fudge the three until the image looks right to you.

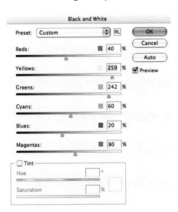
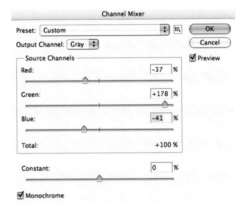

Step 2: Filter Diffuse Glow

The easy next step is to target the background layer (the image must be in 8 bit), or create a new merged layer on top, and go the Filter Menu and choose Distort > Diffuse Glow.

Choose a grain factor of about 5 to begin, a relatively small glow about a value of 2, and a clear amount of 10.

Note:
Make sure your background colors are set to the default of black and white before you initiate the filter

If you do not like the way the diffuse glow filter looks, or just want to experiment further, Undo the diffuse Glow and we will next create the effect manually.

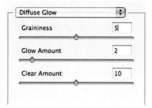

Step 3: Blur Green Channel

In order to do this, activate the channels palette, and click on the green channel. Go to the Filter Menu and choose > Blur > Gaussian Blur. We do not want to get too wild at first, so start with a radius of 5.

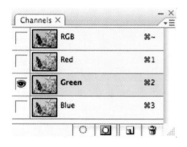

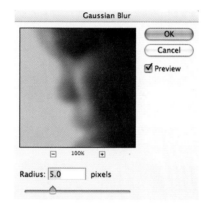

Step 4: Fade Blur

Go to the Edit Menu and Fade the Blur to Screen and reduce Opacity.

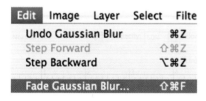

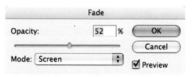

Step 5: Add Noise

Create a new empty layer with the new layer icon at the bottom of the layers palette. Next go to the Edit Menu and choose Fill. From the drop down menu choose 50% Gray. Go the Filter Menu and choose Noise > Add Noise. I usually choose an amount of 12 and make it Monochromatic and Gaussian. Next change the blend Mode to overlay in the layers palette, and reduce the opacity until it looks right to you.

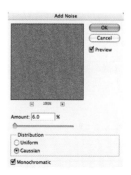

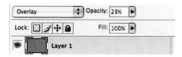

13. Reducing Noise with Photoshop CS3

The truth is that all digital cameras create noise. The more advanced and expensive cameras, at lower ISO's, will not produce much obvious detectable noise at first glance, however, as we raise the camera's ISO settings or underexpose an image, noise can become a serious problem. In most cases, the noise is predominantly more visible in the blue channel of an image. Some people feel the noise resembles film grain, and even like the look, while others find it unacceptable in their image files. While we cannot remove all noise altogether when it appears at extreme levels, there are some things we can do to reduce some of the effects at lower levels if the noise is not making us happy.

There are many available methods and techniques that produce excellent to moderate results depending on several factors, such as amount of noise, bit depth, file size and the type of noise. Just like the many different ways to convert an image to monochrome have advantages and disadvantages, so too are noise reduction techniques. Whichever method you choose to support, it is most important to be mindful that noise reduction does introduce a certain level of blur which is effectively sharpened back. Finding the right balance between technique, loss of image detail and acceptable noise is a tricky endeavor for even the most experienced digital users. The following Lab method is often a good starting point for a attacking an often very complex problem.

SMART FILTERS IN CS3

Using filter layers, reduce noise can be applied, changed or even turned off for previewing, web, saving, printing, etc. Working in layers also allows you to apply noise reduction using a myriad of blend modes and opacities.

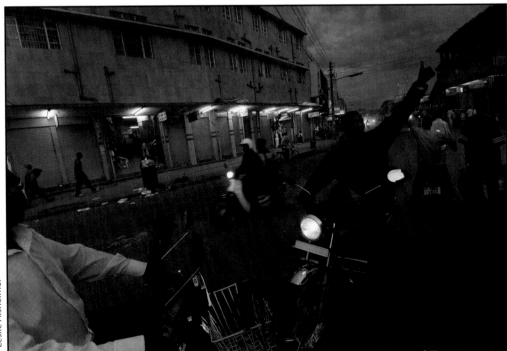

© Leslie Alsheimer

Blurring the Lab "B" Channel
The Method

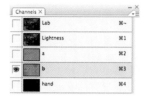

Step 1: Go to the Image Menu > Mode > Lab Color.

Step 2: Activate the Channels palette and click the "b" channel to make it active.

Step 3: Go to the Filter Menu > Noise > Dust and Scratches. Move the Radius until you blur the chunky look of the noise out of the image. Click OK. The "b" channel is where the majority of your noise will be.

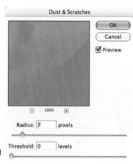

Step 4: Do the same to the "a" channel, but to a lesser degree.

Step 5: Click back to the Image Menu > Mode, and change the image back to RGB.

Or another quick method. Try converting your image to a smart filter. Filter Menu > Convert to Smart Filter. Then choose Filter > Noise > Reduce Noise. Fade and edit the filter to suit the image.

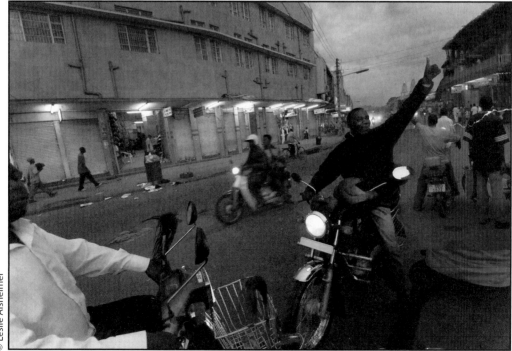

© Leslie Alsheimer

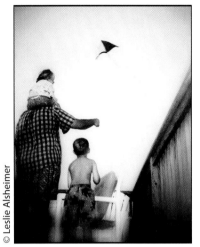

© Leslie Alsheimer

Before

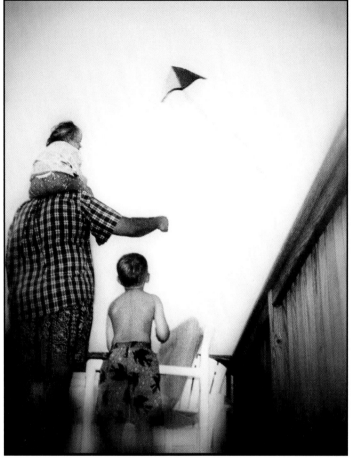

© Leslie Alsheimer

After

14. Hand Color Black and White

There are a number of techniques that can be used on black and white images to give them an interesting twist – and adding hand coloring is just one such method. By using the old fashioned Marshall Oil hand colored look you can give new life and vibrancy to a black and white image. In order to do this technique you will need to be relatively familiar with layers, selections, brushes and the color picker – although all of these tools are covered briefly here.

The Method

Step 1: Open
Open a black and white or toned image.

Step 2: Change the mode to RGB
Make sure that the Image Mode is RGB Image > Mode > RGB color in order for the document to be able to receive and display color values.

Step 3: Choose a color

At the bottom of the tool palette, you will see two square boxes filled with color. The default foreground color is black and the default background color is white. Foreground color is the color on the upper left of the display. In this example, my foreground is black and background is white.

To choose a new color, double click on the foreground square, and the Adobe Color Picker dialog box will open. You can choose a color by clicking anywhere inside the box and/or sliding the hue slider up and down to choose a different hue. You must click on the tone of color you want to actually pick a new color. Click to Pick! Click OK.

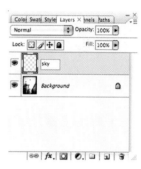

Step 4: Create a new Layer

In the layers palette, click on the new layer icon. It is a good idea to get in the habit of naming your layers, so go ahead and do it at this time. Just double click on the words Layer 1 and you can edit text.

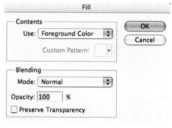

Step 5: Select an area and paint or fill with color

Choose an area you wish to color and select it with any of the selection tools, or just get a brush and start painting the area free hand.

If you have an active selection, you can choose to fill that selection with a color by choosing the Edit Menu > Fill. The Fill dialog box will appear. For contents, choose Foreground Color and Click OK.

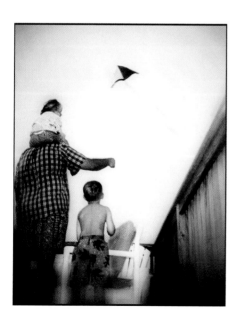

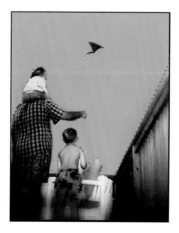

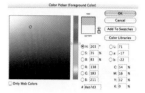

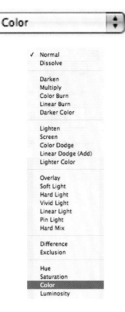

Step 6: Change the Blend Mode to Color

Change the blending mode to color. Normal is the default blend mode for the layers palette. This technique requires changing that to Color. Target the new color layer and choose Color for the blend mode.

Step 7: Reduce the Opacity

Reducing the opacity gives this method the appearance of the old time look. Type in a percentage value number or click the blue arrow next to the opacity value window to activate the slider. View in real-time how the outcome will look while sliding.

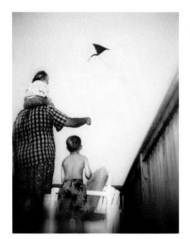

Step 8: Repeat steps 3–8

Create new layers, choose different colors and paint in different areas until you are satified with the image.

**Remember

Be sure to create a NEW LAYER for every different color pick. This way each color can be adjusted independently with more or less opacity.

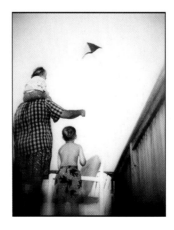

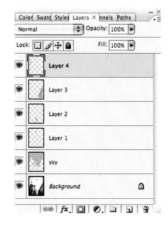

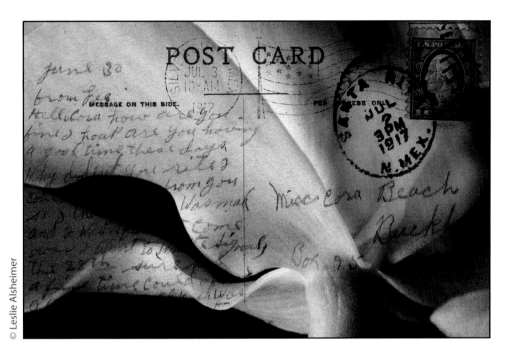

© Leslie Alsheimer

15. Sandwiching Negatives

Creative compositing with blend modes

This technique was originally created by combining two negatives or slides into the film carrier of the enlarger and printing them together onto one sheet of paper as a single image. This technique was often used to create a juxaposition of image elements within a single image. Utilizing blend modes with two digital images combined into one document, creative interpretation becomes almost limitless! Experiment further by combining techniques.

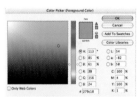

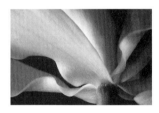

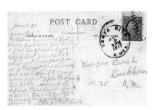

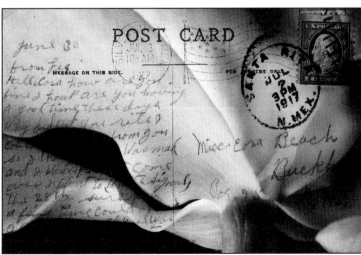

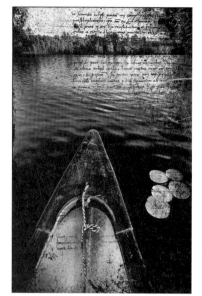

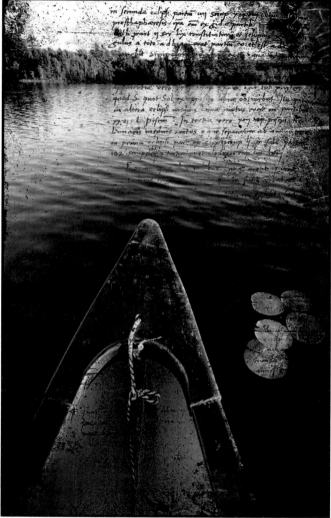

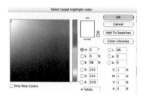

© Leslie Alsheimer

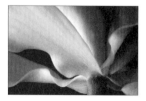

Step 1: Open two images you would like to combine together and resize both images so that they share the same width, height and resolution. Image Menu > Image Size.

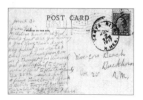

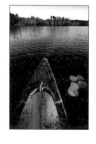

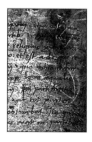

Step 2: Choose one image to select and go to the Select Menu > Select All.

Step 3: Edit Menu > Copy.

Step 4: Activate the destination document (or the second image) by clicking on the image.

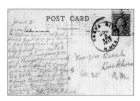

Select	Filter	Analysis
All		⌘A

Step 5: Edit Menu > Paste. The first image should appear in the layers palette completely covering the image below.

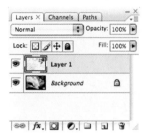

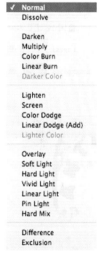

Step 6: Scroll through the different blend modes in the layers palette to find one that works with the images. Keep in mind that many blend modes may produce pleasing effects at all. The blend mode Darken worked best for my images.

Step 7: Experiment with reducing the opacity of the image in the top layer.

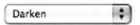

Step 8: Combine this technique with other techniques. I added color. (See "Hand Color Black and White", page 174.)

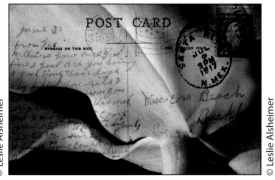

© Leslie Alsheimer

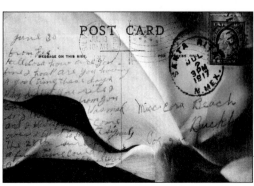

© Leslie Alsheimer

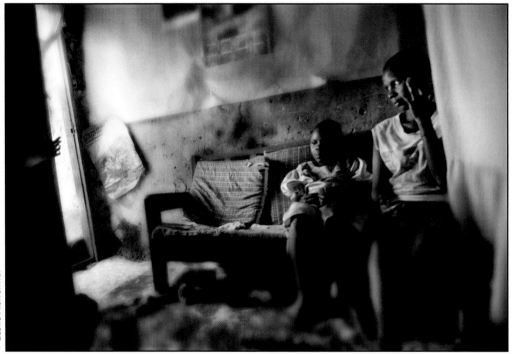

© Leslie Alsheimer

16. Toning Techniques with Photoshop

Most traditional photographers will be familiar with the range of aesthetically pleasing toners available in the wet darkroom, as well as their ability to infuse images with subtle, and more evocative moods. Traditional photographic prints have been toned since their beginnings for archival stability purposes and creative interpretation. Selenium, sepia, brown, copper, gold and blue toners are but a few of the time honored chemical processes for achieving tonal variations in prints. With the dawning of the digital age, we can now not only emulate the toning of traditional processes, but also utilize a whole new spectrum of toning possibilities never before possible; creating unique and wonderful new effects in the print-making process.

As with every process and tool in Photoshop, there are many different ways to add tone to an image. Let us start with some of the more simple methods and work our way into more complex ones. Keep in mind that these tutorials will create digital emulations that draw visual inspiration from their traditional sources, but can never fully recreate the truly distinctive look and feel of the actual processes. It is also important to note that the type of paper, tonality and brightness of the paper base will effect the results of these processes. Experiment with re-creating some of the old processes, and use these methods to create some new ones to your own!

16a. Sepia Tone 1: Photo Filter

Step 1: Convert the photo to black and white using your conversion method of choice.

Step 2: Create a new Photo Filter Adjustment Layer. Go to the Layer Menu > New Adjustment Layer > Photo Filter, or choose Photo Filter from the Adjustment layer icon at the bottom of the layers palette.

Solid Color...
Gradient...
Pattern...
Levels...
Curves...
Color Balance...
Brightness/Contrast...
Black & White...
Hue/Saturation...
Selective Color...
Channel Mixer...
Gradient Map...
Photo Filter...

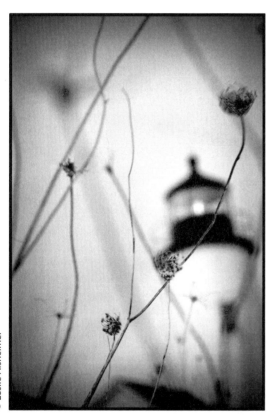

© Leslie Alsheimer

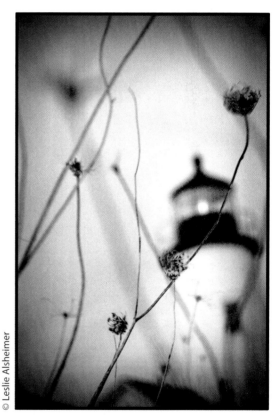

© Leslie Alsheimer

Step 3: Change the Filter to Sepia. Make sure Preserve Luminosity is selected and adjust the density to your liking, for this example I used 44%.

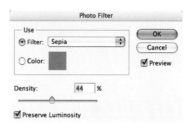

181

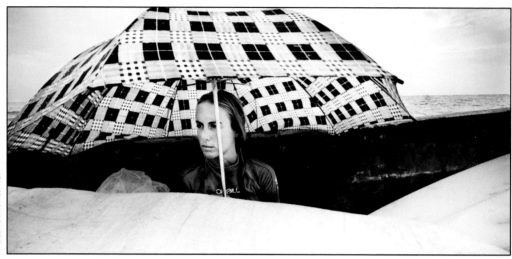

© Leslie Alsheimer

16b. Sepia Tone 2: Hue Saturation

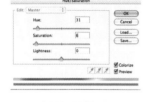

Step 1: Convert the photo to black and white using your conversion method of choice.

Step 2: Create a new Hue Saturation Adjustment Layer. Go to the Layer Menu > New Adjustment Layer > Hue Saturation, or choose Hue Saturation from the Adjustment Layer icon at the bottom of the layers palette.

Step 3: Click Colorize at the bottom of the dialogue box and choose a Hue that has a nice sepia feel. I chose a hue of 25 for this image and an opacity of 6. You should reduce the opacity, however, to something pleasing to you.

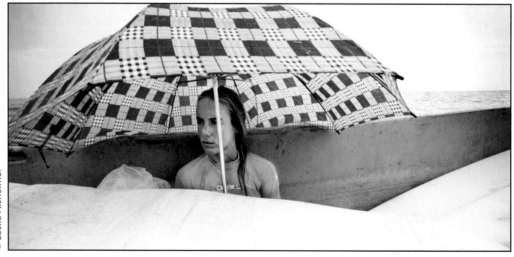

© Leslie Alsheimer

16c. Albumen Print: A Method for Split Toning

Albumen prints (1850–1890s) were made by coating ordinary paper with an emulsion composed of light-sensitive salts of silver suspended in albumen (egg white). Although these prints have been seen in many different color tones, the albumen print is most recognized by its very warm, creamy colored highlight areas and magenta to purple tone to the shadow values. With any color bias however, this process can be utilized as an easy method for split toning an image! See page 187 for more info on split toning.

Note:
You can choose any color interpretation you like.

Created with a Color Balance Adjustment Layer.

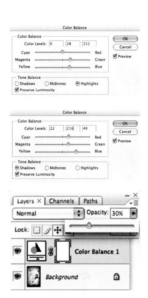

Step 1: Convert the photo to black and white using your conversion method of choice.

Step 2: Create a new Color Balance Adjustment Layer. Go to the Layer Menu > New Adjustment Layer > Color Balance, or choose Color Balance from the Adjustment layer icon at the bottom of the layers palette.

Step 3: For this image, I started with the highlight values and set the Color Levels input values to 0, −8, −52. For the shadow values I set the Color Levels input values to, −2, −16, 49.

Step 4: I found the results of these settings to be quite garish, so I next reduced the opacity of the adjustment layer to a pleasing interpretation. For this image I found about 30% to do the trick!

© Leslie Alsheimer

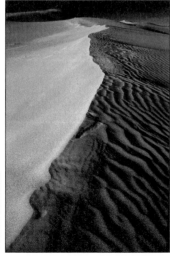

Gray

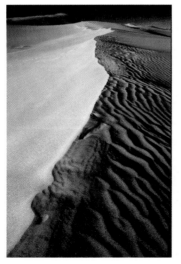

Split

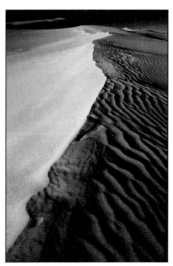

Albumen

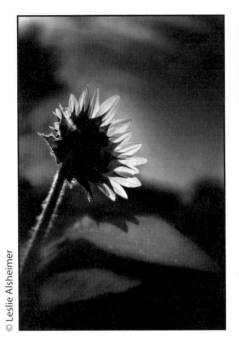

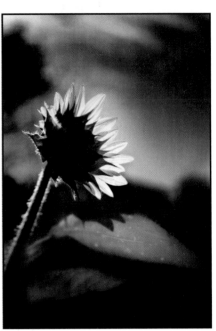

© Leslie Alsheimer

Also using a Color Balance Adjustment Layer, Try emulating the Van Dyke Brown tone, Sepia tone and Cyanotype Print.

The cyanotype print was created by an iron salt sensitizer which could be exposed in sunlight and developed in water. Cyanotype prints are characterized by a very moody dark, deep blue tonality. For this image of the car below, I set the midtone Color Levels input values to $-60, 0, 96$.

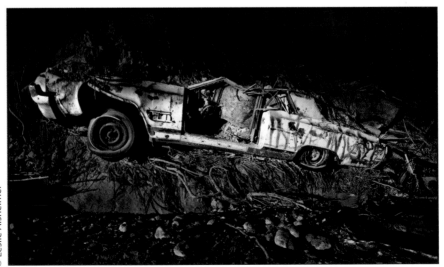

© Leslie Alsheimer

16d. Toning with Curves

Using an adjustment layer of curves is another powerful way to add tonality to a monochrome image. Any color imaginable can be achieved using curves simply by moving from the Master channel (RGB) into the individual channels of Red, Green and Blue. Placing a point in the midtone value, highlight, shadow, or any value on the curve and raising or lowering the curve will alter the tone of the image. Here are the steps:

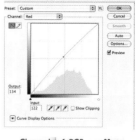

Step 1: Create an adjustment layer of Curves.

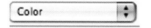

Step 2: Click on the Master channel (RGB) drop down menu and click into the individual channels of Red, Green and/ or Blue. Place a point in the midtone value of the curve to begin and raise or lower the curve to alter the tone of the image. For a browner sepia tone as in this example, you need to add red by raising the curve in the red channel, and simultaneously remove some of its complement color cyan by lowering the curve in the blue channel.

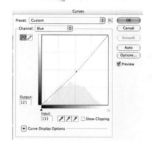

Step 3: Creating tonal adjustments with curves is a sophisticated method that requires a bit of control. Curves tend to shift the density of the overall image in the process of adding tonality. To compensate for this, change the blending mode of the adjustment at the top of the layers palette layer to Hue or Color.

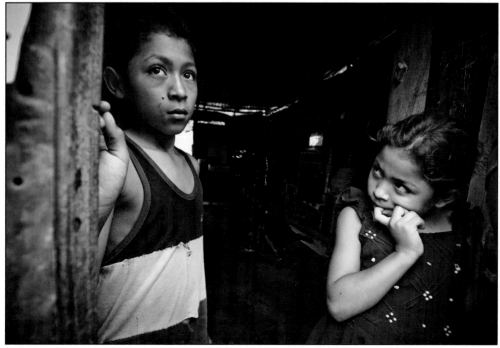

© Leslie Alsheimer

16e. Split Toning with Selections
Use this technique to create depth with still life, add energy to portraits, or mood to landscapes!

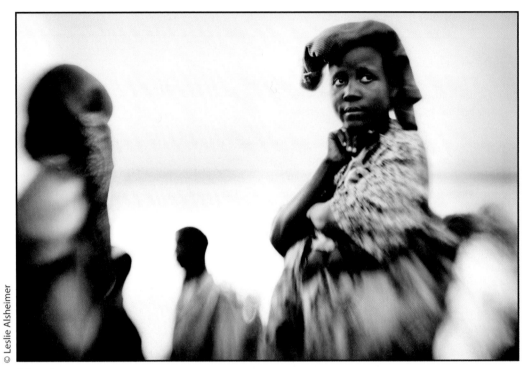

© Leslie Alsheimer

Split toned

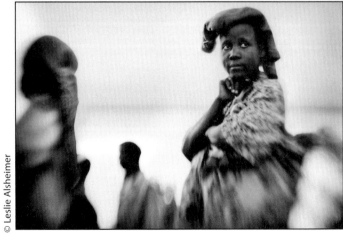

© Leslie Alsheimer

Black and White

Split toning is a traditional process that originated in the wet darkroom where the toners applied to an image would adhere to only certain areas of the print, like to the shadow values alone, for example, while leaving the remaining portions unchanged. One common technique with this method was to warm the highlights and cool the shadows. This technique would add more apparent depth to an image, as well as a greater amount of visual complexity.

Step 1: Apply your grayscale conversion of choice.

Step 2: Isolate the area you wish to tone. For this image, I chose to select the highlights. Go to the Select Menu > Color Range > Highlights.

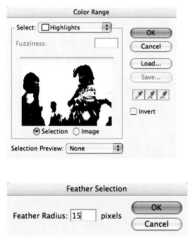

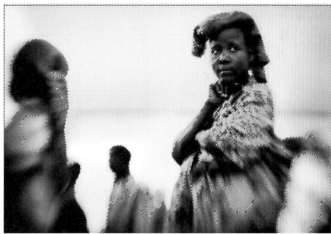

Step 3: Feather the selection to soften the transition edges. Go to Select Menu > Modify > Feather. Choose a value that works for the area selected relative to the image size dimensions. For this image I chose a value of 15.

Step 4: Create a new Hue Saturation Adjustment Layer. Go to the Layer Menu > New Adjustment Layer > Hue Saturation, or choose Hue Saturation from the Adjustment layer icon at the bottom of the layers palette.

Step 5: Click Colorize at the bottom of the dialog box and choose a Hue that has a nice sepia feel. I chose a hue of 45 for this image and an opacity of 10. You should choose the Hue and reduce the opacity, however, to something pleasing to you.

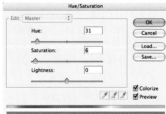

Step 6: Select the Shadows. Go to the Select Menu > Color Range > Shadows.

Step 7: Feather the selection to soften the transition edges. Go to Select Menu > Modify > Feather. Choose a value that works for the area selected relative to the image size dimensions. For this image I chose a value of 15.

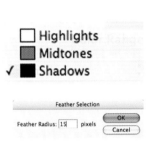

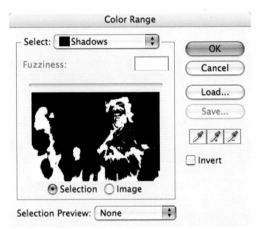

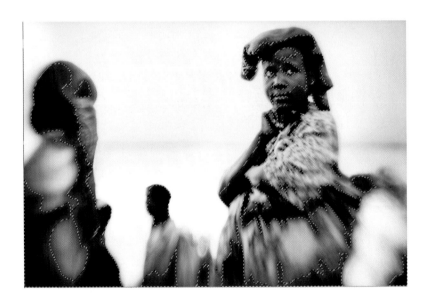

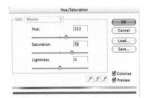

Step 8: Repeat Step 4 to create another Hue Saturation Adjustment Layer. Click Colorize at the bottom of the dialogue box and choose a Hue that has a cool selenium feel. I chose a hue of 45 for this image and an opacity of 10. You should choose a Hue and reduce the opacity, however, to something pleasing to you. For this image, I chose a Hue of 222 and a saturation of 72. Experiment with what looks to be the best to you for your images!

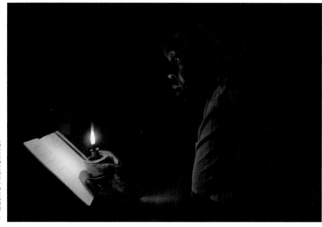

© Leslie Alsheimer

The advantage of working with selections is that changes can be edited and refined with precision and mastery via layer masks. With a selected area active, Photoshop automatically creates a layer mask for you as an adjustment layer is applied. Editing masks is easy. Activate the mask by clicking on it, and with a paint brush, paint with black in areas to conceal the adjustment, white to reveal, and with gray to reduce the intensity of the adjustment. Experiment with just how many different and compelling tonal variations you can create!

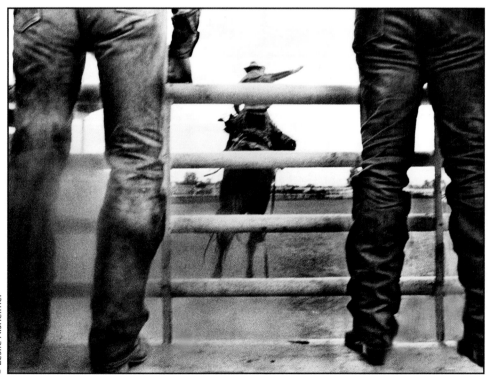

© Leslie Alsheimer

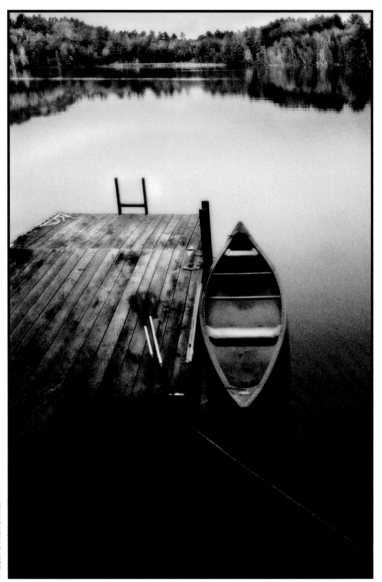

© Leslie Alsheimer

16f. Duotone, Tritones and Quadtones

Duotones, Tritones and Quadtones are yet another wonderful method to add tonality to a monochrome print, especially in the prepress world. A Duotone takes a monochrome grayscale image and typically uses a black ink color for the shadow information and a lighter tone of another color for the midtones and highlights. Tritones and Quadtones use a third or fourth color for finer gradations of control. As tritones and quadtones are the same basic concept as Duotones just with more colors in the mix, for the purposes of this text, we decided to discuss Duotones alone.

Duotones are created by printing a grayscale image in two different ink colors. Printing photographs by the duotone method produces a richer and far greater tonal scale than is possible using only one color. Like split toning, Duotones allow you to work within the tonal range of an image and specify a different color to any particular value within the image's tonal range.

Duotones require a color proofing system that can substitute PMS colors in place of the CYMK 4-color process, which, typically, most inkjet printers cannot accurately reproduce. Before taking on a duotone project, it is recommended that you consult your printer or service bureau.

Photoshop has some great preset duotone templates, as well as curves developed by my good friend Stephen Johnson, who also customized the duotone curves of my first book, *Reality from the Barrio*. Use these as a great starting point to create some pleasing effects. To access the curves, click the Load button in the Duotone options box and find the "Goodies" folder in the "Photoshop" folder for the duotone presets. These can be modified indefinitely or utilized as they were created.

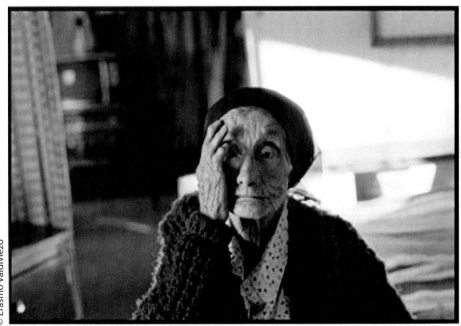

© Erasmo Valdiviezo

Taken from the book *Reality from the Barrio*, this image by photographer Erasmo Valdiviezo Age 15 was printed with the Duotone colors Pantone Warn Gray 7 CVC and Process Black U, with customized tonality curves created by Stephen Johnson specifically for this project. For more in-depth information on Duotones as well as everything else digital, check out *Stephen Johnson On Digital Photography, Perspectives & Techniques from a Digital Photography Pioneer Exploring the Intersection of Art & Technology*.

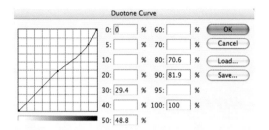

Pantone warm gray 7 CVC Curve

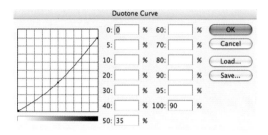

Pantone process Black U Curve

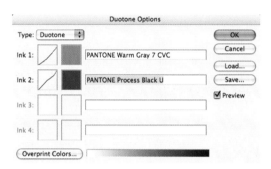

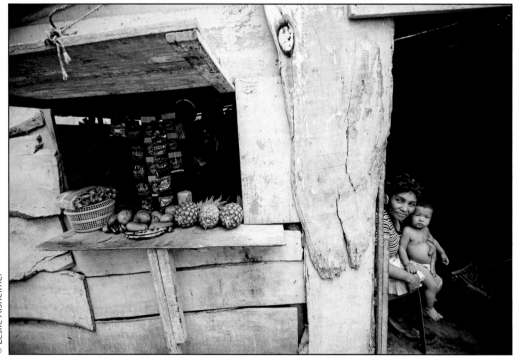

© Leslie Alsheimer

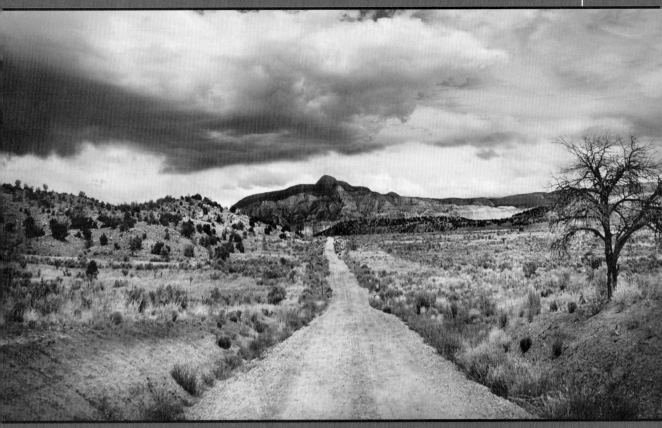

CHAPTER 6

© Leslie Alsheimer

Printing

With today's rapid technological advances in the quality of digital processes, many fine art black and white photographers are making the switch from darkroom enlarger printing to digital processes. For those that are doing so, this is truly an exciting time to make the move! The latest advances in digital printing technology have made it possible to create beautiful high-quality prints with relative ease and affordability. Although the passionate fine art photographer seeking the highest quality will find that the process still necessitates a fair amount of compromise, digital technology does offer many compelling new advantages to the printmaking process well worth exploring. It is, therefore, time for photographers to take the printing concept into a new era, not by replacing the old processes, but by integrating the methodology and tools into a new quiver for the craft. If we look at the digital process not as how we can merely recreate and mimic the silver process, nor at the strengths and weaknesses of each by comparison, but as a new and different format for translating our imagery onto fine art surfaces, then we may begin to realize that the possibilities have grown well beyond what was ever thought possible.

Traditional chemical processes utilize metals such as silver, platinum or palladium to create an image on surfaces coated with light sensitive materials. The unique aesthetic quality of the metallic print has long been a beautiful sight to behold. Inkjet, or giclee (French for fine spray) prints also have a unique look and feel because they are created by placing millions of tiny ink droplets onto the paper in order to simulate the continuous tone of emulsion prints. It is important to differentiate the unique beauty digital prints have on their own – as they cannot actually ever be the same as a chemically processed print – just as the movie version of a novel will never be the same as the book itself. My good friend and world renowned print maker, Jonathan Singer of Singer Editions in Boston, Mass. comments that he often has a difficult time working with photographers who want to reprint their favorite darkroom prints in a digital format. When their mindset is to copy what was, Singer feels that he must sometimes make an inferior print. As the technology allows for far greater precision – and with skill and mastery he can produce far more profound results – he often wonders why those who want to mimic do not just stay in the darkroom altogether.

While we still cannot mimic the silver gelatin look digitally, technology has refined the tools in ways that allow our digital darkroom to be far more refined than was ever possible in the traditional darkroom. Digital technology and software innovations have made it possible to apply controlled contrast and tonal adjustments to precisely selected areas with a degree of precision and control not possible using traditional methods. There have also been vast improvements with dynamic range capabilities that expand the shadow and highlight information to measurably more tonal latitude than conventional silver prints. Experienced fine art photographers who have switched to digital printmaking profess that they can make better prints than they ever could with an enlarger. This text will show you how to reproduce many traditional looks in digital format, and more importantly, it will help you realize that the scope of what is possible in the digital darkroom is far greater than ever before because of the commingling of the old and the new.

Silver Changing Form

For many of us who started in the chemical darkroom, the concept of loving the smell of fixer or hypo on our hands is a memory, or still a reality, that conveys a certain idea of tradition that is difficult to leave behind. It has been 25 years since my first venture into a darkroom; the alchemy, the magic, the smells, and the aesthetic quality of the results are all profound and powerful memories in my life. Not only was the darkroom a place to lose myself, a place where I was able to share photography with others as an educator, but it was also a process that – like many others – I fell in love with. With the rapid changes brought about by digital photography today, the reality is that fewer photographers are spending time in the traditional darkroom anymore. Many are even starting to put black and white silver printing on the veritable endangered species list of artistic processes. Eastman Kodak has announced that it will no longer manufacture black and white photographic papers, Agfa is no longer in the black and white photographic market, and there are rumors concerning the stability of the remaining companies who manufacture and distribute black and white silver materials. While many of the rumors are predominantly true, the black and white silver process is not necessarily dying, but changing form. All these disheartening gloom and doom scenarios do not necessarily have to equate to the death of black and white silver process however, if we recognize that we can still embrace them in the digital domain.

Since I found the digital darkroom, I do spend most of my time working digitally, but I know that I have not left the chemical darkroom for good. I strongly believe that the traditional darkroom still has a secure future in the photographic world. Just as platinum, cyanotype and gum printing have survived as "alternative processes", so will silver processes find their place among the beautiful and well-respected forms of artistic printing. It may be comforting to know that Ilford Photo is now leading the resurgence of black-and-white photography as the only manufacturer providing a full range of film, paper, photochemistry and ancillary products. Further, the process of "digital negatives"-created with digital darkroom processes and output onto clear acetate-can be printed onto fine art papers with various traditional chemical methods such as platinum, ziatype and silver. Digital negatives are but one of the new and exciting ways to integrate the benefits of both the traditional and digital worlds into a new medium altogether. This digital negative process, introduced to me by Dan Burkholder, was not only reminiscent of the processes of the chemical darkroom that made me fall in love with photography in the first place, but brought it all back to life! The combined strengths of the different technologies and processes are just one of the many benefits and creative innovations that the digital domain brings to the medium of photography. The savvy photographer who has both traditional and digital methods in their bag of tricks simply has more choices that can only serve to broaden the scope of creative possibility.

There are almost as many different types of photographic users, each with varying and disparate interests and levels of technical proficiency, as there are possibilities in the digital printmaking process. Although this text could neither cover the full gamut of makes, models, manufactures, brands, inks, etc. on the market today nor advocate any one particular printing method as "best" for all users, we can, however, give you a strong overview of what to look for in your output decision-making process.

Black and White Output Options
There are an overwhelming array of options available today for the black and white photographer to output digital files onto paper and other fine art surfaces. Here are a few to consider:

1. **Traditional photographic papers** such as the Fuji Crystal Archive or Ilfochrome. This process requires working with a service bureau that will

produce your prints for you. This is a wonderful way to output digital files onto traditional photographic archival materials. Having someone else do the work for you, is a great advantage however it does also take your hands and artistic interpretation out of the printmaking process. You will have to consult a service provider near you for information and pricing.

2. **Digital negatives,** digital images are inverted to negative form and output to film and printed in traditional chemical processes. The greatest advantage the digital negative provides is getting to work with traditional chemical processes and papers; a beautiful marriage of the strengths of the two mediums, and one of my personal favorites! For more in-depth information, check out Dan Burkholder's book *Making Digital Negatives*.

Digital negatives can be made in two ways. The first requires working with a service bureau that can output your files as negatives onto lithographic film with a halftone screen. These negatives print extremely consistently; however, some of the disadvantages include poor enlargement capacity, as one would be required to make new film for each enlargement to keep the dot structure intact. Although more expensive, a service bureau can also output using Light Value Technology, aka LVT, onto real film like T-Max or Plus-X with all the advantages that real film has to offer. The second method, much less expensive and time consuming, utilizes the inkjet printer to output the file as a negative onto a transparent substrate such as Pictorico. If you know your way around the traditional processes of silver, platinum, palladium, Ziatype, etc., this is an extraordinarily fun and fabulous way to make mind blowing prints with both mediums and produce consistent results everytime!

3. **Iris: digital print by Pro** As the first large format printer capable of producing a highly refined fine art print, the Iris printer is in a class all by itself. The Iris uses inkjet technology to produce fairly consistent, continuous-tone, photorealistic output on several varieties of paper, canvas, silk, linen and other low-fiber textiles. Iris prints are widely noted for their color accuracy and ability to match printing and proofing standards. They are also known for their superior dynamic range in reproduction of shadow information as well as for their low-cost inks compared to other technologies. The Iris printer is also typically a fairly expensive machine that is quite difficult to maintain and requires a rather specialized CMYK skill set. Today with more simplified technologies, more professionals are moving away from the Iris, giving the Iris the noteworthy status of the digital "alternative" process.

The Iris printer has the unique ability to print on natural surfaces, rather than papers with coating, which is one of its many selling points for the Fine Art printer. Desktop printers use glycols in their ink sets which are designed to keep the heads of the inkjets themselves from clogging up. The glycols, however, have a tendency to cause advanced dot gain, which basically causes the ink to spread more rapidly across the paper surfaces. The papers are therefore coated in a way that freezes the ink droplets in order for the paper to receive the ink and prevent it from spreading in a controlled manner. So inkjet surfaces are limited to papers whose surfaces have coating rather than a natural surface. In contrast, the Iris printer embeds the droplets of ink into the paper surfaces instead of floating them on top of the coatings, allowing for a much richer look and feel to the prints similar to traditional processes.

In side by side comparative tests, Jonathan Singer of Singer Editions in Boston, Mass. demonstrates the differences in shadow detail performance from the two types of printers. He shows how he is able to get a wider tonal range in the shadows in particular because he is able to build up different densities of black ink within the blacks. "I am attached to the print as an object", he says, "with the Iris I can print on natural surfaces and the materials themselves – the way ink is embedded into the papers, the natural surfaces, torn edges and texture – create a beautiful object in and of itself, image withstanding".

As these are large format very expensive printers, prints from these guns are typically made through a service provider who knows how to use them. The prints are exceptionally exquisite, and well worth trying one on to see for yourself. For more information, visit Jonathan at Singer Editions at www.singereditions.com.

4. **Inkjet: (or Giclee, French for fine spray)** As the most easily accessible and readily affordable option, many photographers are now choosing inkjet printers. Within the inkjet option, however, there is a significant variety of options and considerations for the black and white printer.

Ink

Types of Ink

Dye and Pigment
Color inks can be divided into two primary types: dye-based inks and pigment-based inks. Most non-photo specialized printers utilize dye based inks, while more specialized photo models tend to utilize the pigment inkjets. Most of today's longevity issues stem from the dye-based ink sets, which typically have a brighter color palette capacity, but tend to fade fairly quickly. Pigment inks, however, last much longer than dye-based inks but in the past have been plagued with difficulty for the black and white photographer.

In the color ink sets, the color pigments are made of various materials, and only the black ink is carbon-based. While all pigment based inks do typically last much longer than dyes, the color inks do not last as long as the blacks. There is some concern that over time the color inks will fade at different rates than the blacks. Depending on the purpose of the print, this may or may not be a concern for you.

Grayscale

Mostly known today as Quadtone and Piezography, these are gray ink sets designed to replace the color inks with various shades of gray in desktop printers. Most of these grayscale inks use carbon as the pigment for the black ink and create the lighter inks with various dilutions of the black inkjet. These grayscale ink sets can produce astounding results, maintaining neutrality throughout the entire tonal scale. As the carbon base is one of the oldest photographic materials, grayscale ink sets have marked longevity, considerably over 125 years. Although these ink sets can be purchased in warm or cool tones, one is limited to the single tonality of the ink sets as these inks are not easily toned in any other manner. Another consideration is that Quadtone and piezography inks are not yet distributed by major printer manufacturers and must be obtained from third party distributors, whereby typically voiding your warranty on the printers if utilized. These inks also require custom profiles. Some manufactures will provide them for certain printer and paper combinations, while others do not.

Issues with Ink

Neutrality and Metamerism

As inkjet printers use a mixture of the colored inks in an attempt to create the black and white tones, pigment inks historically tended to introduce slight color casts to the prints, giving the inks the reputation of having an incapacity for neutrality. Another issue for the black and white printer was the problem of metamerism. Viewed under different light sources of different temperatures, the effect of metamerism was to cause prints to dramatically shift color. For example, a print could have a greenish cast when viewed in daylight, a brownish cast under tungsten light on the market today and a magenta cast when viewed under fluorescent lighting. The latest generation of pigment inks on the market today, however, have improved tremendously. The days of metamersim are relatively behind us and the capacity for printing neutral tones from our desktop printers has arrived.

Image Permanence

Image permanence, also referred to as longevity and stability, has always been an important consideration in digital printmaking since the first fine art digital prints were created in 1989. Since then, there have been many significant advances in the development of more permanent inks, making the question of longevity less pertinent.

Today, the very best ink and paper combinations are rated at well over 100 years under normal display conditions and over 200 years in controlled storage environments with acid-free material.

Materials used for digital printmaking and traditional photography are independently tested by Wilhelm Imaging Research, Inc. considered the authority on the testing of image permanence. For comparison, Wilhelm reports on the number of years that display prints under framed glass will last until noticeable fading occurs. For traditional Chromogenic color prints such as the Fuji Crystal Archive paper, considered the most stable traditional silver halide color print, are rated at 60 years, Ilford Cibachrome are rated at 29 years and the Kodak Ektacolor at 22 years. For more extensive information on longevity visit Henry Wilhelm on line at http://www.wilhelm-research.com

Two alternatives of note have developed to overcome some of the black and white limitations to the inkjet approach.

Alternatives to Black and White Inkjet Limitations

Black Only Printing

One of the first solutions that comes to most people's minds in resolving the color bias issue is to turn off the color ink altogether and print with black ink only. Choosing the black ink only option in the printer driver options is certainly an easy solution to eliminating unwanted color casts. If made from a newer high-end printer, this approach will result in a fairly decent inkjet print and produce more of a grainy looking result with an older lower-end printer. This process is quick and easy and good enough for many users. Black only printing is a reliable, inexpensive and easy way to get started making beautiful prints with the highest possible archival longevity (using only a pure carbon black ink). It allows you to get started with the least expense and without committing to a particular system or software while you hone your skills and experiment with different papers. For the fine art printer, however, striving for better results, what we sacrifice for neutrality is dot structure. All the other colors in the CMYK or CMYKLBLMLC ink sets-in addition to the black-makes the dot structure and tonal range of the print dramatically smoother, as there are exceptionally more droplets of ink hitting the printed surface. Using only black ink will be notably less rich in tonality and density by comparison.

RIP Software (Raster Image Processing)

A RIP is really just software that replaces the printer driver that comes with your printer. It controls how ink flows to the print heads in a different way than the standard drivers, and gives the user more control over the tone and density of a print. The better quality RIPs produce beautiful results and offer a broad range of tones from neutral to sepia. Some RIPs are even capable of working with grayscale ink sets, allowing the photographer an even greater amount of control in the printmaking process. Sounds fabulous right? Before you get too excited, there are a few downfalls to note in the RIP process. First, RIPs are heavily technical, requiring the use of curves and profiles to control the inks. For the technically savvy, this is an approach well worth exploring; for the technically challenged, however, RIPs can be difficult to master. Also, RIPs can be very expensive, although there have been a few exceptions that work as GIMP printers. A little research can help you travel this path if you so choose. GIMP printers can cause significant headaches and operating system problems getting out of them if you choose not to use it for any reason, like making a color print if you wanted one day. Another issue to consider with all of this is that RIPs were developed when pigmented inks had an issue with color shifting. Most RIPs typically add small amounts of cyan and magenta and sometimes yellow to the print in order to control the tonality. Although invisible to most viewers, the well trained eye might find upon close inspection (like through a 6 × loupe) that the color ink dots can be seen.

Latest Developments

The result of all these choices has made digital printing quite confusing, as no clear single best path presents itself. In order to print from home using an inkjet printer and produce variable tonality, the reality is that color inks must be used. Whether the color inks are mixed on the paper as color dots or mixed in grayscale inks as toners, to date there is no other way.

Previous technology for the color inkjet required a RIP to optimize neutrality and was considered less lightfast than toned grayscale inks. The newest generation of pigment inks on the market today, however, have vastly improved in all of these previously problematic areas including stability for the color inks, longevity and neutrality. Although it is still recommended to research the latest results for any inks you want to use, today most of the latest developments in ink sets use carbon-based black ink and can achieve beautiful results right from your desktop.

Papers and Profiles

Matte vs. Glossy

Choosing a paper type is an aesthetic choice or preference much like chocolate is to vanilla, or fiberbase was to RC. Each paper type will carry with it inherent strengths and weaknesses in addition to its unique aesthetic. The latest glossy and semi-matte papers can produce a maximum density black (also called dmax) equal to or greater than silver papers. Matte papers however, typically do not match the dmax of silver papers. This creates a bit of a quandary for photographers who prefer the look and feel of the fine matte papers, and simultaneously want richer blacks. In addition, the choice of digital papers is complicated by the fact that many printers require different black ink sets for the different types of paper. Although some new printers carry both cartridges, eliminating the need to swap inks, the resulting headache and wasted ink in switching back and forth has caused many to choose one type and stick with it. There are now also many high-quality fine art papers on the market today. The 100% cotton, acid-free matte papers are predominantly considered to maintain the greatest longevity.

Profiles

Whatever paper choice you make, the greatest issue to keep in mind is its profile for the color management system. Hopefully, you would not have skipped over the chapter on color management and will, of course, remember that profiles are an essential piece of the digital printmaking process. Profiles are the translators that communicate the information in the image file from its source to its destination. Each type of inkjet, printer, paper type, paper surface and paper manufacturer combination will require a unique profile that translates the image information to its each unique destination accurately.

Printer manufactures typically provide free profiles within the print drivers. The catch, however, is that the profiles provided are only for the papers and inks made by the same manufacturer. For example, Epson will provide free profiles for Epson papers printed with Epson inks using Epson printers. Change any one variable and those profiles will no longer be accurate. The easiest way to deal with color management on the output end is, therefore, to stick to the papers and inks made by the same manufacturer of your printer. Of course, you must operate the driver properly and choose the correct profile, which is the next topic we will address in the printing workflow.

In order to work with papers not made by your printer manufacturer, you need to obtain profiles for each type. Hopefully, the paper manufacturer will provide free profiles, typically available for download from their website. If a paper manufacturer does not provide adequate profiles for their paper on your printer with the ink sets you have chosen, producing a decent print will be far from easy. You are then faced with creating your own custom profile, purchasing one, or experiential learning by tweaking and trial and error. This typically requires a fairly extensive amount of wasted time, paper and ink resources.

Custom profiles require you to print a target with all color management turned off using your printer and inks on the paper you wish to profile. You need to purchase a separate profile for each and every paper you wish to use. Custom profiles can be purchased online relatively inexpensively these days, and although quite a bit more extensive technically speaking, the results are well worth the effort. For more information on affordable custom profiles online, email Mac at Santa Fe Camera Center at www.santafecameracenter.com.

Workflow Phase 5: Printing Workflow

Whatever output path you choose, at some point in your editing process you will decide that you are ready to see the image in a printed format. Whether you have created extensive layers in Photoshop or choose to print straight from Lightroom, there is one essential concept to understand: your first print will not be your final award-winning portfolio piece. If you have ever printed in the traditional darkroom, you will remember that a final print was a celebration of many attempts toward your vision on paper. The digital process is exactly the same. Your first print will be for evaluative purposes. It may take several prints, over the course of many long work sessions to realize your aesthetic vision in its final portfolio piece format. As we learned with color management, the system is imperfect and the key to the inkjet output process is reducing the number of variables through a color managed system, and the rest is all in the tweaking! Just like in the darkroom we controlled the variables of temperature and dilution as consistently as possible, made a print, studied it, and made changes again and again until we were aesthetically pleased with the results; the digital darkroom is no different.

Monitor Tonal Detail from Monitor to Print: Creating a Step Wedge

If we have chosen an inkjet path – whether for prints or negatives – we need to be able to evaluate the first print effectively. Often times, we are able to see

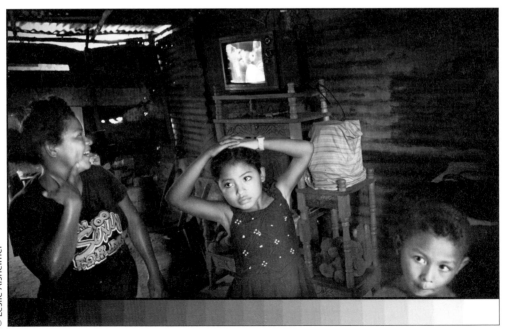

© Leslie Alsheimer

the shadow detail of an image on the monitor, but lose the tonal detail in the translation to the print. In order to easily monitor and evaluate what is happening, we are going to create a grayscale step wedge and print it out.

Step 1: Go to the File Menu > New.
Make the document 10 × 3.5 inches at 300 dpi.
Choose Color Mode Grayscale

Step 2: Select the gradient tool and set the default color to black and white by hitting the "D" key. Turn off Dither. Hold the shift key and click and drag a line from one end of the documents to the other making sure it starts and stops within the document itself.

Step 3: Go to Image Menu > Adjust > Posterize and type in 21 in the open text field. You should see 21 steps on screen.

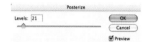

Print this out and check how consistent the step is on your monitor as compared to the print. Many fine art printers also like to add this file to their image test prints outside the image area to help evaluate each print as it comes out of the printer. Simply drag and drop the background layer of this file onto your image prior to printing, or select all, copy and paste.

Printing Workflow Overview

A. Printing From Photoshop

I: Set Image Size & Resolution
• Size the image for output with appropriate resolution and print size specifications.

II: Softproof
• Simulate how the image will look with various media and profile combinations.

III: Sharpen
• Choose a sharpening method and sharpen according to file size, image content and output specifications.

IV: Set Your Print Driver for Color Managed Output
• Select: Color Management strategy, rendering intent, profile and media type.

Method 1: Photoshop Managed Color
Method 2: Printer Managed Color
Method 3: No Color Management (Specific to newest Epson printers: Advanced Black and White Mode)

V: Tweaking
- Evaluate the Print under the correct lighting source.
- Return to Photoshop to make digital darkroom adjustments and corrections based on the printed results.
- Reprint and repeat until satisfied.

B. Print From Lightroom

Easy! Size, Sharpen, And More All In A Single Unified Interface

I: Print Job
- Select: Color Management strategy, rendering intent, profile and media type.
  Method 1: Photoshop Managed Color
  Method 2: Printer Managed Color

II: Tweaking (See V: Tweaking above)

Drydown
As many fiber based silver prints tended to drydown a bit darker, digital papers sometimes have a similar effect.

Try to give a print enough time to set before you do any major evaluations to be sure it has stabilized.

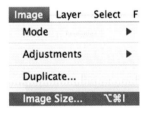

A. Photoshop Printing Workflow

I. Set Image Size and Resolution

Image size in Photoshop

Whether the final output destination of your image is to an inkjet printer, offset press, iris printer or even the web, understanding image size and output resolution is an extremely important lesson. A digital image, whether from a digital camera or from a film scanning device, has a finite number of pixels set in width and height dimensions. This number is determined by the camera or scanner capture settings. If you chose to shoot in Raw format with a digital camera, these numbers will be the maximum size your camera is capable of capturing at its native resolution. The top portion of the image size dialog box will illustrate what those pixel dimensions are. Be warned, however, these numbers can be easily and haphazardly changed having potentially detrimental effects on your image.

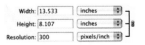

Resolution
For Printing purposes, the term "Resolution" in the image size dialogue box refers to the number of pixels per inch that would be required to produce a

final output print. Resolution can be presented with the formula: image size = physical dimension × (ppi or pixel per inch) resolution. This means that there is a reciprocal relationship between pixel size, the physical dimensions of the image and resolution.

Digital images are made up of pixels which are resolution-dependent. An image can be scaled up, but as the size of the image size is increased, the finite information and number of pixels available can only be stretched and diluted so much before the image begins to deteriorate, and the underlying pixel structure becomes increasingly visible.

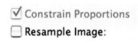

File Size
The file size of an image is measured in bytes, kilobytes, megabytes or gigabytes. This refers to the sum total of pixel information or simply the total number of pixels.

The Image Size Dialog Box
There are two important check boxes within the dialog box: constrain proportions and resample image. Unless you find a creative aesthetic for distorted images, constrain proportions should always remain checked. The resample image check box is where you take control of pixel allocation, resampling, interpolation and subtraction.

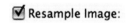

It is the best practice to always start with the resample image box unchecked, as this will protect your image from any potential haphazard up or down sampling. This will constrain the width, height and resolution of the image and merely redistributes the pixel allocation. The actual pixel count and total file size within the image will remain unchanged no matter what you type in each field. Type in the desired resolution for the image's output destination. Screen resolution is 72ppi, which is best for web work, while inkjet printers need between 180 and 360ppi for quality rendering, and offset printing (books, magazines, etc.) require 300ppi. Be sure to ask your service bureau for their recommendation.

Once you have set the resolution, check to see if the width and height dimensions of the image meet your specifications.

Downsampling & Upsampling (Danger!)
If the image is larger or smaller than that you need for print, you can check the resample image check box. Notice that the pixel dimension fields become editable, and type in the desired dimensions. The file size of the document will change and the size differences will be noted at the top of the box. It is recommended to use the "Bicubic sharper" algorithm for downsizing images and "Bicubic Smoother" for enlargement. While downsizing an image is not problematic to image data, extreme care should be taken in the enlargement

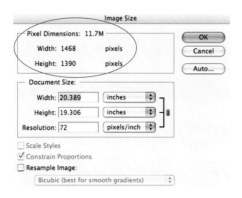 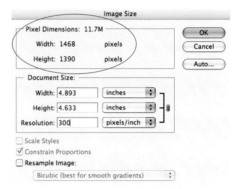

Note:
Always begin with "Resample Image" unchecked. This protects your image, and you can reallocate pixels within the width, height and resolution fields, without changing the actual image file size.

process as upsizing stretches and dilutes the pixel information. The finite information and number of pixels available can only be stretched and diluted so much before the image begins to deteriorate, and the underlying pixel structure becomes increasingly visible.

Notice these two size adjustments above. Resample is unchecked and both adjustments have different heights, widths and resolutions, but the total file size of each is the same (indicated at the top of the box next to "Pixel Dimensions").

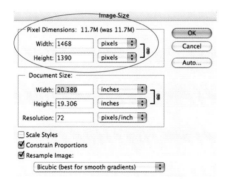 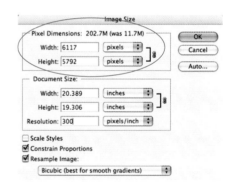

With the "Resample" box checked, you alter the number of pixels that make up the image. Notice the total File size change indicated next to Pixel Dimensions with the "Resampled" adjustment. 11.7 MB to 202.7 is a lot of diluting! For the highest quality reproduction it is best to output images at their native file size. If Upsizing is absolutely necessary, it is best to never exceed a 20–30% increase, and that is still pushing it!

Nearest Neighbor (preserve hard edges)
Bilinear
Bicubic (best for smooth gradients)
✓ Bicubic Smoother (best for enlargement)
Bicubic Sharper (best for reduction)

Image Size and Scanning
One of the most important factors in scanning an image or a negative is determining the final size you wish to achieve for output. If you plan on having multiple output versions for the web, inkjet print, film recorder, Iris,

etc., the image should be scanned at the largest optical resolution the scanner can produce, and then downsized with various version sizes to achieve the image size variance necessary for each output purpose.

Calculating the File Size with Photoshop

Photoshop has a built in calculation that can determine file size for you. In Photoshop, go to the File Menu > New. Next, type in the width and height dimensions of the image you would ultimately like to print and the resolution of your output device. Set the mode to RGB. The MB file size that is shown once these fields are entered is your approximate target file size for an 8-bit image. For maximum quality, we recommend doubling this number and scan in 16-bit. Also keep in mind the true aspect ratio of your image capture, and be mindful of the possibility of cropping the image when entering standard print dimensions such as 8×10, 11×14. (See "Highest Quality Capture Scanning Overview", page 34 for more details on scan sizing.)

DPI (dots per inch). Refers to the resolution of a printing device.

PPI (pixels per inch). Describes the digital, pixel resolution of an image.

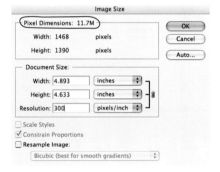

Output Devices and Resolution Requirements

Device	DPI
Inkjet Printers	180–480, 240 is a good average; best for prints 11 × 14 and larger 8 × 12 prints and smaller 360–480 optimal
Dye Sublimation Digital Printers IRIS, CMYK prepress, LightJet	300 5000
Film Recoders	2000
Web	72–96

II. Softproofing

Softproofing is a technique used to simulate on your monitor what your image will look like when it is printed, before actually printing the image. Softproofing will show you potential shifts in color contrast and tonality that will result from the printer, paper, ink and profile combinations chosen for

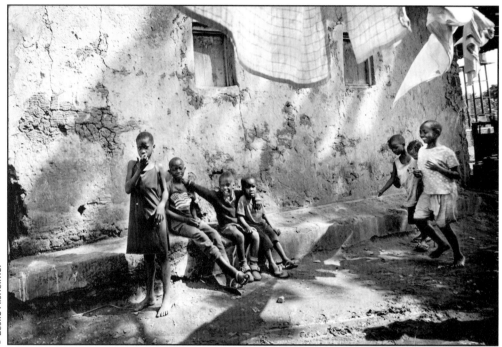

© Leslie Alsheimer

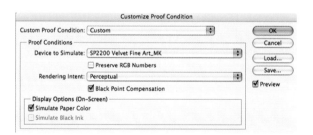

Note:
This feature necessitates an accurate ICC profile for both the monitor and for the output device.

output. In the translation, Photoshop CS3 now offers a softproofing feature in the Print dialog Window.

For full screen Softproofing in CS3

1. **Go to View > Proof Set Up > Custom**
2. **Specify the Correct Profile for the Desired Printer and Paper.** Turn the Preview button on and off to see the difference between what your monitor displays, and what you will actually see from the printer.
3. **Go to View > Gamut Warning** to see what colors in your image are or are not reproduceable with the paper, ink and printer selections chosen. The colors that are not printable or are "out of Gamut" will be represented with gray.

Preserve Color Numbers to simulate how the document will appear without converting colors from the document space to the proof profile space. This simulates the color shifts that may occur when the document's color values are interpreted using the proof profile instead of the document profile. Usually leave this deselected.

Simulate Paper Color
To preview, in the monitor space, the specific shade of white exhibited by the print medium described by the proof profile. Selecting this option automatically selects the Simulate Ink Black option.

Simulate Ink Black
To preview, in the monitor space the actual dynamic range defined by the proof profile.

If you are not Happy with the Results, Tweak the File Before Printing
1. Duplicate the file. Go to Image > Duplicate
2. Softproof the duplicate (not the original)
3. Create adjustment layers to compensate for unwanted results

Use these adjustment layers for printing the image to this printer/paper combination. Out only out of gamut colors cannot be further saturated to achieve intensity; however, adding contrast will make the image appear more luminous.

III. Sharpen

Sharpening Overview
Determining the correct sharpening technique for your images is always a difficult task. There are many advanced techniques for sharpening that include using the find edges filter, sharpening in channels, high pass sharpening, smart sharpen and many third-party plug-ins. Different output devices and print mediums require different amounts of sharpening, and that amount is based on image content and file size. Sharpening is the last thing you do before printing. Dodge and Burn, retouch, make image adjustments and corrections and size the image for output before you sharpen your image. You need to create a merged layer, or duplicate the image, flatten and sharpen on a duplicate layer.

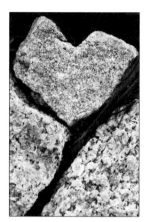

Unsharp Mask Overview

Using the Unsharp Mask Filter is the simplest way to sharpen up your pictures. It works by increasing the contrast along edge lines, thus giving the impression of a sharper image. Other methods include the High Pass Filter method and the Smart Sharpen Tool, which made its debut in CS3.

The Basic Method

1. Always zoom into 100%
2. Choose: Filter > Sharpen > Unsharp Mask
3. Choose an amount, radius and threshold

Amount: Controls the intensity of the sharpening applied to the image. The higher the amount the greater the sharpening effect will be. Be careful, too high a setting will create halos around high contrast areas. Different output devices and print mediums require different amounts of sharpening.

Radius: Affects the distribution of the sharpening effect. Determines how far out Photoshop looks to determine the width of edge contrast increase. The setting you choose will depend on the subject matter and the size of your output.

Threshold: Controls which pixels will be sharpened based on how much the pixels to sharpen deviate in brightness from their neighbors. A higher setting applies the filter only to neighboring pixels which are markedly different in tonal brightness, that is edge outlines. At a lower setting, more or all pixels are sharpened including smooth continuous tones. For example, a threshold of 5 will ignore all tones that are within 5 level values of each other. Using a setting between 3 and 6 will protect tonal similar areas from being sharpened.

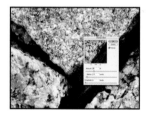

Tips:

1. Sharpen at 100%.
2. Try not to sharpen skies, skin, wrinkles or high speed film grain.
3. Use Fade USM to soften filter.
4. Experiment with selective sharpening by masking out image areas that do not need to be sharp.
5. Use the preview button in the USM dialog box.

Unsharp Mask Techniques (High Pass Filter Method)
The Method
1. Duplicate Layer to be Sharpened
2. Change the blend mode of the Duplicate Layer to Hard Light or Soft Light
3. Filter > Other > High Pass (Recommended Values of 1–10)
4. If Sharpened too much, reduce Duplicate Layer's Opacity (Globally or Locally)

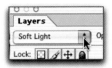

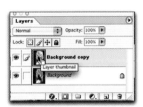

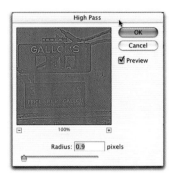

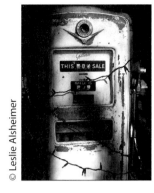

© Leslie Alsheimer

Smart Sharpen

Smart Sharpen was introduced in Photoshop CS2 to provide a modern tool for a common problem and to solve a number of issues with the aging and counterintuitive (to many) Unsharp Mask. Smart Sharpen's advantages over Unsharp Mask are numerous:

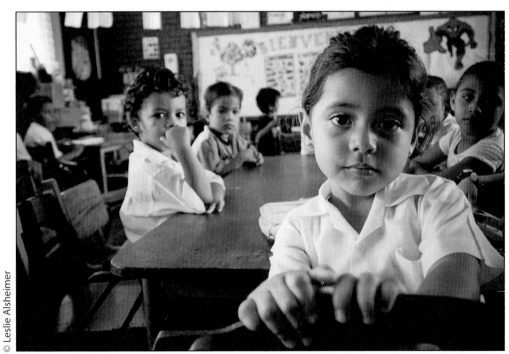

© Leslie Alsheimer

- Superior algorithms: While Unsharp Mask combats Gaussian Blurs, Smart Sharpen offers, too, the ability to sharpen Lens Blur and Motion Blur.
- Accuracy: Smart Sharpen has an option to apply multiple iterations, thus assuring more accurate results.

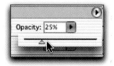

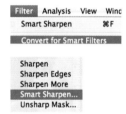

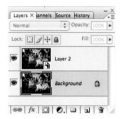

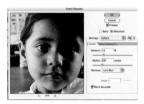

- Less Halos: Unsharp Mask shows ghosting or "halos" around contrasted edges when used with strong settings, whereas Smart Sharpen, on the other hand, allows for selective sharpening control in the shadows and highlights, virtually eliminating halos.
- A larger preview: Details are everything when sharpening, and with a larger preview comes more detail.
- The ability to save and load settings: Whether it means saving steps or sharing settings, this feature makes huge strides in workflow productivity.

Let us take a closer look at Smart Sharpen

*If you are in Photoshop CS3, sharpening can now be done non-destructively! First navigate to the Filter menu and select "Convert to Smart Filter" – now you have a filter layer and can change or turn off parameters at any time, no more saving various versions for preview, print and web!

1. Navigate to Filter/Sharpen/Smart Sharpen
2. For photographs, the Default target of Lens Blur removal is best
3. For superior results, always be certain to check "More Accurate"
4. While previewing at 100%, move amount slider to desired level
5. For Radius, I find that of ~1.0 for med-high resolution JPEG images, and 2.0–3.0 for high resolution files works well
6. By clicking Advanced, you can fade the highlight and shadow artifacts as needed
7. Settings can easily be saved and loaded from the dropdown at the top of the interface

For removing Motion Blur, the following steps are a bit different:

1. First use Photoshop's Measure tool to compute the angle of the blur and the distance (do so by measuring from common ends of the ghosted and actual images)
2. Then, in Smart Sharpen, select Lens Blur as the removal target and plug the angle and distance in. The result is better, but not perfect

IV. Set Your Print Driver for Color Managed Output

If you have chosen the inkjet route – regardless of inkjets, make, model and printer manufacturers – setting the print driver properly is the next most imminent order of business. Photoshop thankfully has made the process a fair bit easier than ever before by moving the interface into a single unified dialog box. Although the Photoshop interface has become easier, however, this still does not eliminate the need to address the operating system color interface.

Color Management

The printing dialog interface is the last phase of the color management system. This is where we apply profiles, choose rendering intents and control the output translation of our image from the monitor to the chosen printed surface. There are three methods of approaching the printing interface from Photoshop to managing color for output. We can allow color management to be controlled by Photoshop, necessitating an action to actually turn off the printer's color management system separately. Or, we can allow the printer to color manage, necessitating an action to turn off Photoshop's color management system. The third option, specific to the "Advanced Black and White" printing mode with the newest Epson printers, is to actually turn off all color management. This process is extremely important. If this is not done properly, we can inadvertently double color manage, or turn off color management all together. The results of either of these extremely common mistakes are prints that do not look like what we see on the monitor, often with color casts of magenta or green.

For many printers, the approach with the most accurate results for color images has been to have Photoshop control the color management system. However, with black and white processes, the best results have often been achieved with the printer driving the color management. You need to experiment with your printer to find out which works best for your system.

Rendering Intent

Rendering intents are also an important piece of the color management system when it comes to the print driver interface. The rendering intent you choose determines how the color management system will handle the color conversion from one color space to another. Each rendering intent utilizes different methods to determine how the source colors of an image are adjusted to the destination output in the translation process. For example, translation of colors native to the destination may be adjusted to preserve the original range of visual relationships between colors, or they can remain unchanged.

Choosing a rendering intent will produce varying results depending upon the content of the image and the chosen profiles. Some profiles will produce identical results for different rendering intents, while others produce distinctly different results. As there is no "best" rendering intent applicable to all images unilaterally, it is best to start with either Perceptual or Relative Colorimetric, which are the most applicable choices for photographic printing. Experiment with the differences as you refine your printmaking skills. The best rendering intent will be the one that looks the best to you. You can select a rendering intent when you set color conversion options for the color management system, softproof colors and in the print dialog interface.

Adobe Defines Rendering Intents as Follows

Perceptual: The goal of this intent is to preserve the visual relationship between colors, so it is perceived as natural to the human eye, even though the color values themselves may change. This intent is suitable for photographic images with lots of out-of-gamut colors. This is the standard rendering intent for the Japanese printing industry.

Saturation: Tries to produce vivid colors in an image at the expense of color accuracy. This rendering intent is suitable for business graphics like graphs or charts, where bright saturated colors are more important than the exact relationship between colors.

Relative colorimetric: Compares the extreme highlight of the source color space to that of the destination color space and shifts all colors accordingly. Out-of-gamut colors are shifted to the closest reproducible color in the destination color space. Relative colorimetric preserves more of the original colors in an image than Perceptual. This is the standard rendering intent for printing in North America and Europe.

Absolute colorimetric: Leaves colors that fall inside the destination gamut unchanged. Out-of-gamut colors are clipped. No scaling of colors to destination white point is performed. This intent aims to maintain color accuracy at the expense of preserving relationships between colors and is suitable for proofing to simulate the output of a particular device. This intent is particularly useful for previewing how paper color affects printed colors.

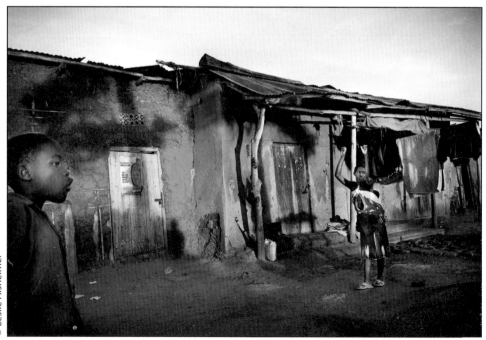

© Leslie Alsheimer

Method 1: Photoshop Managed Color

After you have sized and softproofed the image appropriately for output, go to the File Menu and choose > Print. Best practice is to follow the dialog box top down, left column first and then the right column.

Step 1: Choose your printer from the print drop down menu.

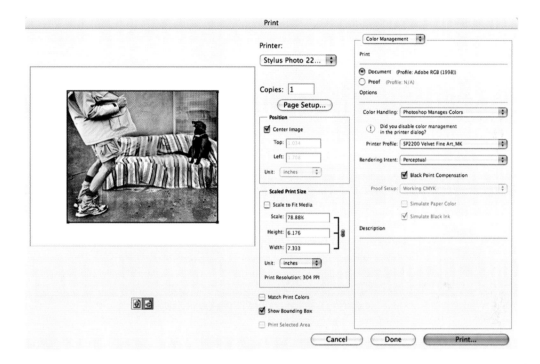

Step 2: Set Resolution and image size according to output preference. Center and scaling preferences can be set from the output settings drop down menu at the top right of the dialog box. (See "Set Image Size and Resolution", page 204 for more details).

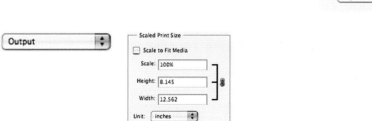

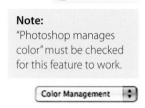

Note:
"Photoshop manages color" must be checked for this feature to work.

Step 3: Match Print colors can be toggled on or off by checking and unchecking the box. This is a softproofing feature built into the print dialog box in CS3 to simulate how the image will print on the chosen paper with the chosen profile. WAY COOL CS3! (See "Softproof", page 26 for more information).

Step 4: On the right side of the box at the top, you need to make sure that Color Management is active from the drop down menu. Fix your output settings separately and return to color management.

Step 5: Color Handling. With this method, we will choose Photoshop Manages Color. CS3 will give you a friendly reminder to disable the printer color management. Thanks Adobe!

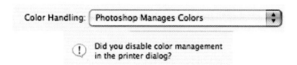

Step 6: Pick the Printer Profile. Specify the appropriate printer, paper surface and ink set. Your print driver should have installed profiles for the manufacturer's papers and inks. It is always best to stick with the same brand of printers, papers and inks in order to use the given profiles with best results. Custom profiles produce much greater results; however, they can be timely and expensive. (See "Papers and Profile", page 200.)

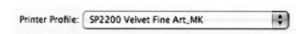

Step 7: Experiment with rendering intents. Relative Colorimetric and Perceptual will most likely produce the most pleasing results. The best choice will depend on the image and profile. (See "Rendering Intents", page 213 for more details.)

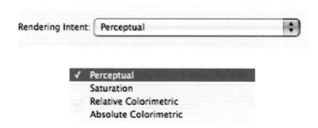

Step 8: Click Print. This should exit the Adobe print interface and launch the operating system print interface.

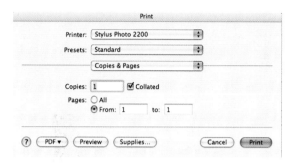

Step 9: Click on Copies and Pages and drop down to choose Print Settings.

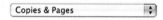

1. Choose media type.
2. Make sure the advanced mode is chosen.
   Choose Photo 1440 or Superphoto 2880 for larger final prints. (For proof prints it is not necessary to waste the ink with 2880 as the difference is not easily discernible.)
3. Choose Print Quality.

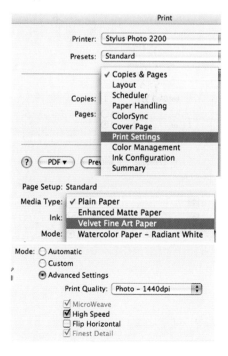

Step 10: Return to the Print Settings drop down menu and click it again. This time choose the next interface Color Management.

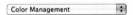

Since Photoshop will be handling color, we need to turn off the printers color management system here, by clicking No Color Adjustment.

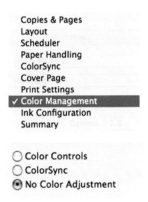

Step 11: Now you can click Print.

Method 2: Printer Managed Color

This approach typically produces more neutral results with older model Epson printers. Experiment with your printer to see which method does a better job!

Depending on your printer, printing neutral black and white images on a color printer can be a tricky task. Here are a few changes in the print driver options that sometimes achieve better results.

Step 1: Before you go to print, duplicate your image and convert to Grayscale mode:

Image > Mode > Grayscale

Document   (Profile: Gray Gamma 2.2)

Step 2: Choose File > Print

Make sure that the Print Document space is in Gray

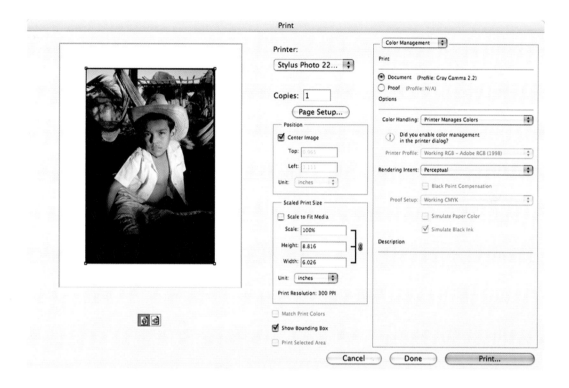

Step 3: Choose your printer from the print drop down menu.

Step 4: Set Resolution and image size according to output preference. Center and scaling preferences can be set from the output settings drop down menu at the top right of the dialog box. (See "Set Image Size and Resolution", page 204 for more details).

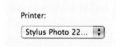

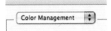

Step 5: On the right side of the box at the top, you need to make sure that Color Management is active from the drop down menu. Fix your output settings separately and return to color management.

Step 6: Color Handling; Set to Printer Manages Colors. CS3 offers a nice friendly reminder to be sure to enable color management in the printer dialog.

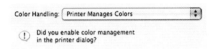

Step 7: Select your rendering intent. Remember to experiment with different choices.

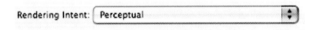

Step 8: Click on Copies and Pages and drop down to choose Print Settings.

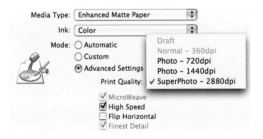

1. Choose media type.
2. Make sure the advanced mode is chosen.

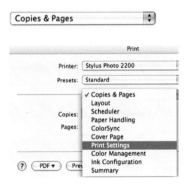

Choose Photo 1440 or Superphoto 2880 for larger final prints. (For proof prints if is not necessary to waste the ink with 2880 as the difference is not easily discernible.)

Step 9: Return to the Print Settings drop down menu and click it again. This time choose the next interface Color Management.

Step 10: Set to color controls: Photo Realistic

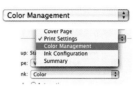

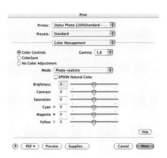

Step 11: Click Print.

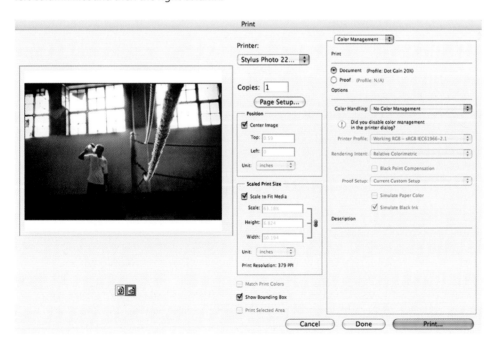

Method 3: Forget Color Management!
Among the latest technological advances in Black and White printing, Epson's Advanced Black and White Mode is worth mentioning. The Epson driver can now take color or grayscale files and use its three black inks predominantly mixed with small amounts of the remaining colors. The advantage is greater longevity, as the black inks are carbon based, greater dmax capabilities and a print more neutral than ever before!

After you have sized and softproofed the image appropriately for output, go to the File Menu > Print. Best practice is to follow the dialog box top down, left column first and then the right column.

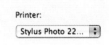

Step 1: Choose your printer from the print drop down menu.

Step 2: Set Resolution and image size according to output preference. Center and scaling preferences can be set from the output settings drop down menu at the top right of the dialog box. (See "Set Image Size and Resolution", page 204 for more details).

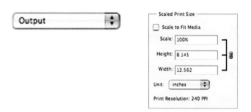

Step 3: On the right side of the box at the top, you need to make sure that Color Management is active from the drop down menu. Fix your output settings separately and return to color management.

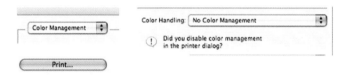

Step 4: Click Print.

This should exit the Adobe print interface and launch the operating system print interface.

Step 5: Click on Copies and Pages and drop down to choose Print Settings.

1. Choose Media Type: Advanced B&W Photo.

Choose Photo 1440 or Superfine 2880 for larger final prints. (For proof prints if is not necessary to waste the ink with 2880 as the difference is not easily discernible.)

2. Choose Print Quality: Check finest detail.

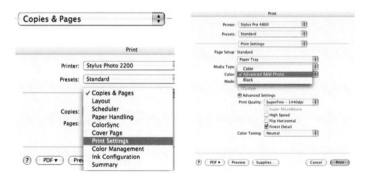

Step 6: Color Toning: You can select the default and continue to print, but to more fully control the black and white options available to you, select Printer Color Management from the drop down menu. Here, you will find a whole new set of print toning options.

The Tone Settings and Color Toning options will require some experimentation if you choose to tone using this method.

Under the tone settings, there are several options, listed as Darkest, Darker, Dark, Normal and Light. These are basically gamma adjustment settings. You will of course want to experiment with the choices to find the best settings for your images however, try starting with the Dark setting for a gray gamma of 2.2 and Darker for a gray gamma of 1.8.

Color Toning options in this interface are relatively limited, and the toning is applied uniformly over the entire image. The choices include Neutral, Cool, Warm and Sepia. The neutral setting may be more or less neutral depending on the media and profiles. The color wheel at the bottom of the dialog allows for fine tuning the color tint applied to the image.

Note:
Since we are now working with the operating system, you will not be able to see your image here in the dialog box.

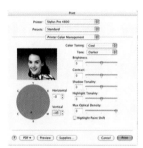

V. Tweaking

This is actually the heart and soul of the fine art printmaking process. The process of tweaking occurs after you have followed all of the previous steps and suggestions in the printing workflow with specific attention to color management, and you are still not completely happy with the results. If you have ever printed in the traditional darkroom, you will remember that a final print was a celebration of many attempts toward your vision on paper. The digital process is exactly the same. Your first print will be for evaluative purposes. It may take several prints, over the course of many long work sessions to realize your aesthetic vision in its final portfolio piece format. As we learned with color management, the system is imperfect and the key to the inkjet output process is reducing the number of variables through a color managed system, and the rest is all in the tweaking! Just as we controlled the variables of temperature and dilution as consistently as possible in the traditional darkroom, made a print, studied it and made changes again and again until we were aesthetically pleased with the results; the digital darkroom is no different.

You will need to go back to your working file and use your digital darkroom processes, tools and skills to make additional changes based on the look and feel of the print. Typically, prints translate darker than the monitor portrays the image, because monitors transmit light while ink on paper reflect light, and reflective light is darker than transmitted light. Make sure to evaluate the print under the correct lighting source in which the print is intended to be viewed, that is, not the kitchen fluorescent. Bring the image back into Photoshop to make digital darkroom adjustments and corrections, and repeat the entire process until you are satisfied with the results. Tweaking is really the art of the fine print, the extra attention that makes a print worthy of the portfolio or exhibition.

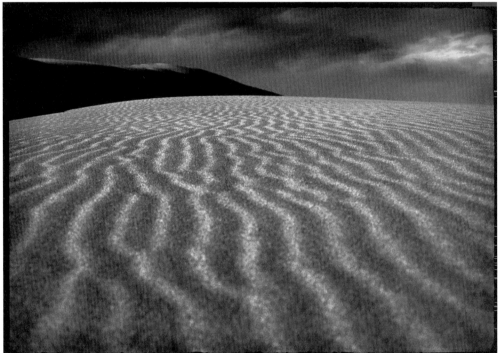

© Leslie Alsheimer

B. Printing from Lightroom

As with all of Lightroom, the print module offers walk-up simplicity and professional power. The interface allows for quick and easy prepackaged printing presets (and the ability to save your own), real-time re-factoring of the layout, movable image parameters, a variety of overlay information, borders and some color management.

While Lightroom has many quick easy features, there is only so much that the fine art printer can do in the Print module without needing to move over to its big brother, Photoshop. A few major drawbacks to printing from Lightroom include RGB only printing, lack of sharpening control and the inability to softproof your images prior to printing. Hopefully, these issues will soon be addressed, but until such time, our recommendation for highest quality output, with the greatest amount of control is to export and print from Photoshop as previously outlined.

Lightroom Print Module

Overview of Features

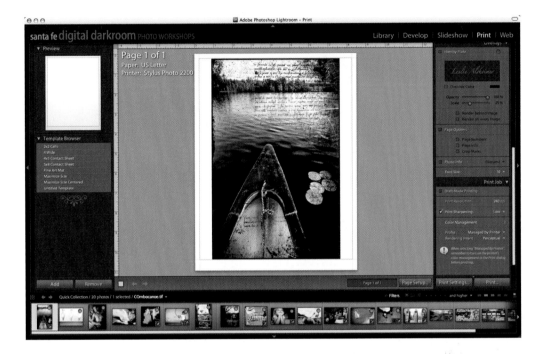

The main window previews your layout and interactively allows you to click inside the image grid lines and dynamically set the print layout upon the page visually.

The Template Browser: The Lightroom Print Module interface is fairly straightforward. The left panel contains the Preview window and Template Browser as well as the Add and Remove buttons for saving and removing printing templates. The default templates are very useful, including the three contact sheet templates. If you mouse over the templates, you will get to see a preview of the corresponding layout in the preview window above them. You can also create your own templates and arrangements. Play with different creative layouts by editing the columns, rows and cell spacing.

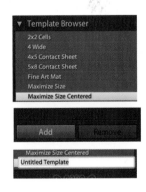

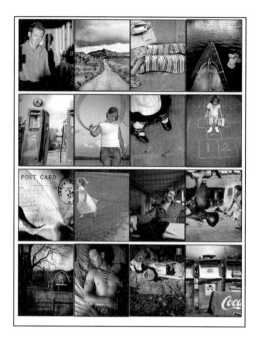

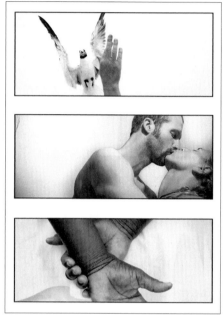

The Right side of the Print Module is laid out in four phases, containing the Image settings, Layout, Overlays and the Print Job interfaces.

Image Settings ◀

Image Settings

The Image Settings dialog is easy to follow. Work top down and play a little with each function and you will get the hang of it all in no time!

The Zoom to Fill Frame does exactly what it says and fills the frame of whatever template you have chosen.

Auto-Rotate to Fit function will rotate the image to fit the frame. Lightroom only displays paper in a vertical layout.

The Repeat One Photo per Page function allows you to print out the same image multiple times on one sheet of paper.

Stroke Border this feature allows you to add a simple border around your image. The Border width is easy to adjust with the slider.

Layout ◀

Layout

The Layout dialog addresses the Margins, Page Grid, Cell size, spacing and Guides.

There is a toggle arrow next to Ruler Units that allows you to choose centimeters, millimeters, points or picas instead of inches.

The Margins sliders are a nice addition to help setting up your pages. You can also work interactively in the image window and grab the guides with your mouse and move them dynamically, which will simultaneously move the margin sliders for you.

With the Page Grid sliders, you can adjust how many images fit on a page. This is a great feature for customizing contact sheets. Cell Spacing adjusts the spacing between the images in the grid, and the cell Size adjusts the size of each cell in the grid layout. You can also constrain them to a square cell by checking the Constrain to square box.

The Show Guides section toggles the guides on and off. It also allows you to turn on or off the Page Bleed, Margins and Gutters and Image Cells guides as well.

Overlays

The Overlays dialog includes options to add an identity plate, watermark, page options, photo information, font size, borders, page numbers, crop marks and much more.

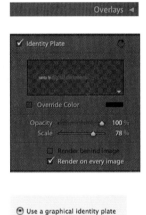

To create an Identity plate, click on the checkered box and the Custom plate fly out menu will appear. Click on the display name in the gray grid and choose Edit to choose font sizes and type whatever you want. You can also adjust the opacity and scale of the identity plate and select if they will be printed on every image or behind the images. Check Use graphical identity plate to add a logo or custom file.

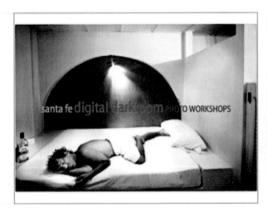
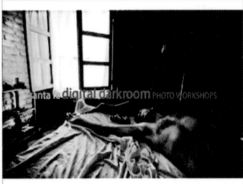

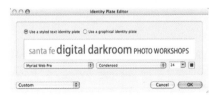

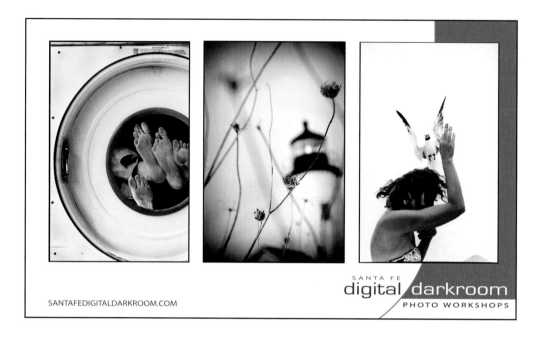

The Page Options dialog allows even more custom features. Here you can add page numbers, page info and crop marks to your image.

The Photo Info dialog allows the addition of any combination of metadata including filename, date, exposure, equipment, rating, title, caption, copyright or keywords. Just below these check boxes, you can also adjust the font size for this information as well.

Print Job

The Print Job dialog is where we deal with the printing mode, resolution, sharpening and color management.

Draft Mode printing is as easy as checking the box.

Print Resolution is changed just by clicking on the dpi box and typing in a new resolution.

The Print Sharpening allows you to add rudimentary sharpening to your image with little control. The options are low, medium and high. Our best recommendation is to use the low setting only. You will not be able to see how much sharpening the low setting applies, nor the effects until you print the image. This is certainly one of the larger downsides of printing with Lightroom.

Lightroom: Set Your Print Driver for Color Managed Output Color Management

Print Settings...

Method 1: Color Managed by Printer: Profile

In this section, you choose your printer and paper profile as well as the Rendering Intent – either relative or perceptual. Most of Lightroom's Print module features are fairly self evident. Our greatest concern here is in the color management portion at the bottom of the interface.

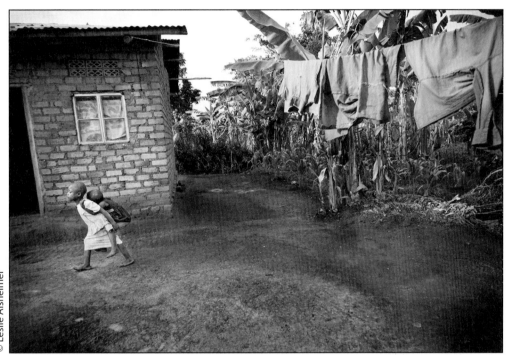

© Leslie Alsheimer

Move to the bottom of the interface to the Color management box. Click on the drop down next to profile and choose Other.

✓ Managed by Printer
Other...

Another box will appear asking you to choose the profile for your specific printer, paper and ink combinations. I am choosing Epson Velvet Fine Art with MK inks for a 2200.

Lightroom offers a nice reminder to remember to turn off color management in the Print Dialog before printing. It also comments that black point compensation will be used for this print.

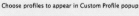

Choose profiles to appear in Custom Profile popup:

- SP2200 Enhanced Matte_MK
- SP2200 Standard_MK
- ☑ SP2200 Velvet Fine Art_MK
- SP2200 Watercolor – RW_MK

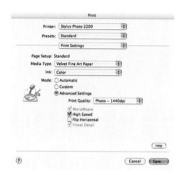

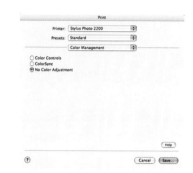

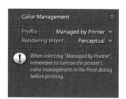

Next choose a rendering intent. There are only two choices in Lightroom Perceptual and Relative Colormetric. Experiment with both. (See "Rendering intents", page 213 for more information.)

Move down to the print settings in the drop down menu.

Choose your media type, ink and quality.

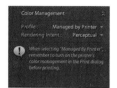

Next move into Color management and choose No Color adjustment to turn off printer management.

Choosing a printer, paper size and the overall page set up is done by clicking the Page Setup button in the toolbar. This is the normal Page Set up dialog box that comes with your printer. To print, just click the Print button next to the Print Settings button.

Lightroom Method 2: Color Managed by Printer (Without Profile)

Just as with the Photoshop techniques previously illustrated. We can also approach the print using the Printer color management by simply not choosing a profile.

Remember to go next directly to the Print settings and choose the appropriate ink, paper type and quality and next choose the color management box.

Turn on the color management with color controls, and choose Photo Realistic.

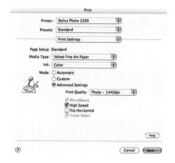

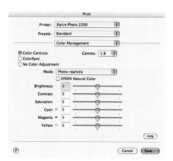

AFTERWORD

Since its inception, the photographic medium has been in an almost constant state of change and development. In 1839 when photography was first introduced, many artists of the time were fearful and even prophesized that photography would signal the end of painting as an art form altogether. The evolution of color photography further introduced a challenge to the integrity of the medium in the early 20th century – placing the traditional monochromatic image in direct conflict with the newly introduced polychromatic image. Of course, as history has shown, photography never replaced painting, and color was eventually accepted and valued for the new and exciting dimension it added to the artistic photograph. Over 150 years later, color, black and white, daguerreotype, wet plate collodian, calotype, and the many other photographic processes that have come since, have survived the scrutiny and have found their place, separately, as valid and accepted forms- all within the singular medium of photography.

Change is inevitable and photography does not stand outside of that axiom; so today, whether the contemporary photographer maintains a traditional "film is better" stance, rides the digital wave, or assimilates the strengths of either to any varying degree; recognizing the history and understanding the growing pains in photography will serve us all well as the medium continues to evolve and transform for the better.

It is our hope that this text will have illustrated that both film and digital have many rich and disparate characteristics – each with its own set of strengths and weaknesses – and yet can still compliment one another quite well in the photographic process. Utilizing their combined strengths, the contemporary black and white photographer now has a quiver of tools that serve to broaden the artistic options at his or her disposal

During the civil war era John Moran debated whether photography itself could be considered an art form. He proposed that the essence of art is the stimulation of an emotional response by the viewer. Moran suggested that standards of art by which photography could be tested were "its ability to imitate present truth and communicate beauty." This broad definition of art does not exclude on the basis of technique, but rather values the end product and its ability to stimulate response. Both traditional photography and its digital form most certainly fall within this definition. So, with that, put down the book, pick up your camera and go out shooting. After all, isn't it the images that really matter?

Happy Image making!

Bryan and Leslie

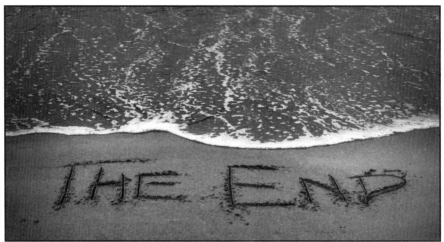

© Leslie Alsheimer

ABOUT THE AUTHORS

LESLIE ALSHEIMER

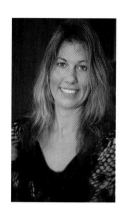

Leslie Alsheimer is a freelance photographer, creative imaging consultant and digital photography workshop educator based in Santa Fe, New Mexico. She has worked extensively with many of the foremost image makers in the country, and integrates a hybrid of experience, teaching styles and technical knowledge into her unique educational approach. As the director of the Santa Fe Digital Darkroom Photography Workshops, Leslie organizes and hosts volunteer vacation and photography workshops around the globe, designed to inspire photographers with the creative possibilities of digital processes. Leslie also travels to work with clients as a creative imaging consultant, private instructor and trainer. She specializes in helping photographers and artists transition into digital technology and processes with ease, using collaborative image processing and printing techniques in a calibrated workflow. As a professional freelance photographer, a member of the Adobe Photoshop Beta Testing Team and an instructor with Nikon and American Photo Mentor Series, Leslie's knowledge and expertise of both traditional and digital photographic darkroom techniques allows her to bring significant passion, experience and enthusiasm to all she does in this field.

Leslie believes in using photography to help empower others to find their own creative voice and vision. She was the creative director of the published book, *Reality from the Barrio*, a social documentary honored in the PDN Photography Annual 2003 as The Best Photos of the Year. Inspired by a traditional wet darkroom teen photography program that Leslie developed, and directed for a nonprofit organization's gang diversion program, the book became a thesis project for Leslie's master's degree in social work.

Combining her love for photography and background in social services, Leslie developed Community Photography Outreach, a project based nonprofit collecting and disseminating donated cameras to organizations and programs in need. Additionally, she directs Forward Focus: Workshops with Creative Purpose, a pioneering series of nonprofit educational journeys for experienced and emerging photographers who want to cover developmental, environmental and relief efforts worldwide. Combining adventure with philanthropy while learning digital photography techniques in the field, the Forward Focus Workshops utilize the power of visual imagery and the written word to support and encourage grassroots nonprofit and NGO initiatives dedicated to fostering social and environmental change. The Workshops provide a collaborative forum that combines education, adventure and creative purpose to celebrate what people are doing to create a better world, supporting and encouraging acts of connection, compassion and contribution, that is creating works that matter.

Note: All images in this text from Uganda, Africa, Nicaragua, and Santa Fe, New Mexico were created in partnership with grassroots NGO organizations providing relief work and humanitarian aide in the regions. Organizations included Soft Power Health, Empowerment International, Uganda Youth Development Link, Connect Africa Foundation, Reach Out, Rotary Club of Kampala, Action for Youth Development and the Santa Fe Boys & Girls Club. All images were donated to these organizations in support of their efforts.

Leslie's web address is www.santafedigitaldarkroom.com

BRYAN O'NEIL HUGHES

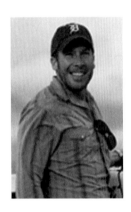

Bryan O'Neil Hughes fell in love with photography when he was only seven years old. He began collecting cameras and experimenting with the medium anywhere he found himself; from his mother's office parties to the sprawling Carmel Valley ranch he grew up on. Bryan was a teacher's assistant in his photography courses throughout high school, and could always be found working in the darkroom.

After school, Bryan began a lifelong passion for world travel, and he would venture overseas with little more than a camera, film and backpack. Upon returning to the states, he worked in the high-end photo retail environment: From custom prints, to framing, to sorting, to sales and even repair, Bryan has always had an insatiable appetite for anything related to photography. Hoping to combine a passion for racing cars with his love for photography, Bryan shot professionally for a brief time. When he began to notice that both passions were waning, he looked to the future. In 1996, upon seeing Photoshop 4.0 demonstrated at Seybold, Bryan knew what he wanted to do with his life.

Bryan O'Neil Hughes has been with Adobe since 1999, helping to test, develop, drive and demonstrate Adobe's digital imaging applications. Bryan is Product Manager for the Photoshop Team and Product Evangelist for the Lightroom Team. Bryan's name, energy and even photos can be found within Photoshop 6.0 forward, PhotoDeluxe 4.0, Photoshop Elements 1.0, Photoshop Lightroom 1.0 and beyond.

Beyond Adobe, Bryan is a published photographer, editor and author. He still loves his time spent driving race-tracks, traveling the world over and taking photos. Bryan lives in the Santa Cruz Mountains with his fiancée, Alex, and their two "boys", Cassius and Irving.

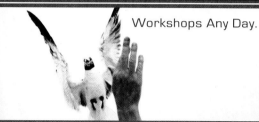
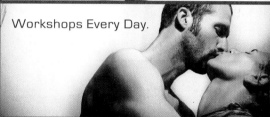
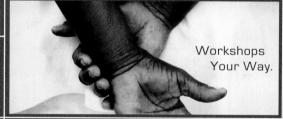
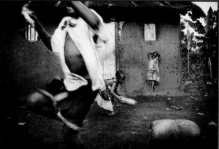

INDEX